Passive Investing, 25 papers explaining why

Will y Fog

20/10/2024

Dedicated to the heroic retail investors,
who have to learn enough
to be able to compete in the markets
at the same level as the professionals.

Table of Contents

1. Introduction 5
   1.1. What Does This Book Contain? 5
   1.2. Why Is This Book Necessary? 5
   1.3. Could I Have Obtained This Information Another Way? 6
   1.4. Indexed vs. Passive 7
   1.5. About Science 7
   1.6. Summarizing 9
2. Papers 11
   2.1. Speculation Theory 12
   2.2. Portfolio Theory 22
   2.3. Asymmetry in Returns 35
   2.4. Fat Tails 41
   2.5. Asset Valuation 50
   2.6. Efficient Market Hypothesis 59
   2.7. The Flap of a Butterfly 73
   2.8. Challenge to Judgment 81
   2.9. Determinants of Portfolio Performance 87
   2.10. Fama-French Three Factor Model 95
   2.11. Withdrawal Rates 101
   2.12. Irrational Exuberance 111
   2.13. Impact of Size and Skewness 121
   2.14. A Multifractal Walk Down Wall Street 129
   2.15. Trading Is Hazardous To Your Wealth 136
   2.16. An Index Funds Fundamentalist 141
   2.17. Disagreement, Tastes, and Asset Prices 149
   2.18. No Person Can Serve Two Masters 154
   2.19. False Discoveries in Mutual Fund Performance .. 158
   2.20. Is Alpha Just Beta Waiting to Be Discovered? .. 162
   2.21. Passive Investing Is Worse Than Marxism 169
   2.22. Shooting the Messenger 177
   2.23. SPIVA: S&P Indices vs Active 187

2.24. Morningstar Active/Passive Barometer 201
2.25. Mind the Gap 208
3. Conclusions 221
3.1. Summary of Papers 221
3.2. Passive Investing is Counterintuitive 226
3.3. Passive Investing vs. Other Forms of Investing 227
3.4. Final Remarks 228
Acknowledgements 231
Alphabetical Index 233

Chapter 1. Introduction

1.1. What Does This Book Contain?

This book shows a representative group of papers on finance.

Most of them are peer-reviewed scientific papers, which have the highest credibility. Others are articles in the press by famous researchers, or periodic studies of the industry.

Everything is designed to be read by investment enthusiasts, explaining the ideas simply, without mathematics, and without the need to be an expert.

1.2. Why Is This Book Necessary?

In the public debate among retail investors, we frequently hear that "this works for me". People who have tried this or that strategy, it has worked for them, and they support it. And defending what has worked for oneself makes sense, but it also has several limitations.

On the one hand, it is a subjective opinion. In order to have a strong opinion, the tools of science, statistics, comparing and benchmarking, etc. must be used. This person recounting his experience could be an exceptional, infrequent case, a fluke.

We also have the "Survivorship Bias", because the successful person tells us his case, but those who failed are ignored. This would lead us to be excessively optimistic. To have a complete understanding, we must know all the failed cases and explain why they happened.

> **With enough luck almost anything is possible**
>
> 1024 people could participate in a game of flipping a coin. Those who get "face" win and those who get "cross" lose.
>
> In doing so, it is expected that half of them, 512, get "face". Those, they win and stay in the game. And the 512 participants who got "cross" leave the game.

Then, these 512 people who got "face" can flip the coin a second time. Half of them, 256 people, get "face" again. The 256 who got "cross" are eliminated.

We could go on like this until there were only 2 people left, and the coin is flipped a tenth time. Then, we can assume that one person will have gotten "face" and the other "cross".

That is, there is one person who will have gotten "face" ten times in a row. Is this amazing?

That person could argue that he has great capabilities, power of concentration, ability to repeat the movement of the fingers with accuracy, perhaps hidden powers, but we all know that it was really luck.

In summary: It is normal that when many experiments are done, and chance is a fundamental part, apparently surprising results can be obtained. Which are not so surprising when statistics are taken into account.

1.3. Could I Have Obtained This Information Another Way?

The short answer to this question is that it is difficult for a retail investor to know the papers and studies discussed in this book.

Since index fund managers compete on price (because they are aware that price is the main parameter to distinguish them), they do not spend on advertising. It is difficult to find index funds' staff members publicizing their positive aspects.

This means that we, retail investors, are bombarded by information on active investment (managers who want to sell us their products, journalists who charge for advertising products, brokers who want a lot of trade to earn more on commission fees...).

And besides, investment professionals, as a general rule, cannot speak well of passive investment. Because if they did, they would be frowned upon in their environment, and in the long run they would lose their jobs as active managers.

Despite all this, a revolution in finance is currently happening. Because transferring funds between investments is easy, in recent years there is a flow from expensive active investing to cheap indexed investing.

Those who publicly support passive investing are usually outsiders, a few people who are not paid directly by the financial sector, who can speak out without fear of retaliation.

1.4. Indexed vs. Passive

In this book we usually refer to "passive investing", generally as opposed to "active investing".

However this is not accurate, because passive portfolios are usually composed of different assets, such as stocks and bonds (a good example are the Bogleheads© portfolios[1]). These different assets have to be rebalanced to keep their percentages in the portfolio constant, by buying the asset that has devalued and/or selling the asset that has appreciated. And therefore, as it requires investor intervention, deciding when to rebalance and to what extent, it is no longer "passive" in a strict sense.

But on the other hand, "passive portfolios" encourage going on "autopilot", minimizing the decisions taken by the investor, reducing costs and simplifying the portfolio. These are all positive characteristics, as we will see throughout the book.

Perhaps we should say "index investment", but this may give the impression that you are only buying an index mutual fund. This would be a very limited portfolio. The index fund would rather be the instrument with which passive portfolios are implemented.

Therefore, even at the risk of stretching the definition too far, we will generally refer to "passive investing".

1.5. About Science

Science is not just an accumulation of knowledge. It is a way of understanding the world, an ongoing process of discovery, testing and revision.

Investment banks and hedge funds are usually very secretive, so new ideas developed by such firms are rarely aired or discussed publicly, unlike science.

When a researcher discovers something new, he attempts to publish a paper describing it in a professional journal, where it is scrutinized by other experts, a process by which new scientific ideas are reviewed by other scientists. And important: reviewed before appearing in print.

If the paper passes this first filter, it is then submitted to the analysis of the scientific community at large. Many ideas do not survive this process: either they are never published or they fall into oblivion. Even the ideas that are accepted by the community, those that prove to be most useful, are not accepted as sacrosanct. But they serve as a starting point for the next generation of theories and models.

Do not confuse a good model with the "truth" about financial markets. Markets evolve in response to changing economic realities, new regulations, and also in response to innovation.

We will never be able to predict everything that may happen, and for this reason it makes sense to be cautious in our statements and decisions. However, this should not make us think that we can do nothing. Our models explain a reality of the world around us, and each new model implies an improvement over the previous ones. Models, despite their limitations, have brought us a long way forward.

Mathematics are necessary. A full criticism of mathematics and models, for example as the one made by Nassim Taleb in The Black Swan, is inappropriate. It can always occur that we are walking down the street and a meteorite falls on our head. It is possible that it will happen, but this does not change our behavior because we are aware of how unlikely it is. We go out on the street accepting the possibility of this Black Swan.

And this is similar to the application of mathematics and models to finance. A Black Swan, a catastrophe beyond forecasts, can happen. But it is unreasonable to over-prepare for something bad that we may never live through.

1.6. Summarizing

The rationale for passive investment is well known in academia, but that information is not passed on to retail investors. In part this is because those who should inform have incentives not to do so, or to do it badly (managers who sell their financial products, journalists who advertise products, brokers who want to earn more commissions, etc.). And individual retail investors who tell their success story may not take into account financial science and survivorship bias.

This book helps to spread these ideas. To raise the level of the retail investor debate.

Finally, the papers shown here are not perfect knowledge, but they are our best knowledge. And being science, it applies equally to retail investors in Europe, Africa, Asia, or the USA; liberal or conservative, independent of their religion or lack of religion; etc.

[1] For information on passive portfolios, nothing better than https://bogleheads.org

Chapter 2. Papers

The following sections show the papers that we have found interesting. Other topics could have been listed, but then we would have deviated from the subject of passive investing. And more papers could have been included, but it would have become too long. Also the new papers would have been less relevant.

They are arranged in chronological order, as they were published.

For each paper, the author is mentioned, the content of the paper is described, and some conclusions are given that may be useful to retail investors.

The authors are renowned, exceptional people who have accumulated a multitude of distinctions and honors. Let this serve to make us realize that the current generation has the privilege of living "on the shoulders of giants", being able to learn what others discovered, and being able to use what others invented.

These papers are accessible on the Internet, because transparency is, of course, a fundamental part of scientific knowledge.[1]

2.1. Speculation Theory

2.1.1. Paper

Title   *Théorie de la Spéculation*

Author   Louis Bachelier

Publication   *Annales Scientifiques de l'École Normale Supérieure.* series 3, volume 17, year 1900, pages 21-86.[2]

THÉORIE

DE

LA SPÉCULATION,

Par M. L. BACHELIER.

INTRODUCTION.

Les influences qui déterminent les mouvements de la Bourse sont innombrables, des événements passés, actuels ou même escomptables, ne présentant souvent aucun rapport apparent avec ses variations, se répercutent sur son cours.

Figure 1. First lines of the paper by Louis Bachelier.

2.1.2. Author

Louis Bachelier (1870-1946) was a French mathematician. He was the first person to apply mathematics of random processes to stock market prices, which today is known as the Brownian motion or Random Walk.

The paper discussed here was his doctoral thesis, which was originally published in the *Annales Scientifiques de l'École Normale Supérieure*.

The paper is written in French, which is his mother tongue, reminding us of the importance of this language in science and technology from the 17th century until the beginning of the 20th century, when English took over.

Paris was at its peak at the end of the 19th century. The Eiffel Tower was built between 1887 and 1889, on the occasion of the Paris Universal Exposition of 1889, which commemorates the centenary of the Storming of the Bastille, the symbolic start event of the French Revolution.

His father was a wine merchant, amateur scientist, and vice-consul of Venezuela in Le Havre. He graduated in Paris, at the Sorbonne, and worked for many years as a professor at the University of Besançon.

His thesis supervisor was Henri Poincaré (1854-1912), physicist and mathematician with many contributions in science. Henri Poincaré was also Tobias Dantzig's thesis supervisor, of whom we will speak later on.

2.1.3. Content

Bachelier's paper was exceptional applying advanced mathematics to the behavior of stock market assets.

As Bachelier explains in his paper:[3]

> [...] it is possible to study mathematically the static state of the market at a given moment, i.e. to establish the law of probability of the price variations that the market accepts at that moment.
>
> The search for a formula to express this probability does not seem to have been published to date; it will be the subject of this work.
>
> — Louis Bachelier, "Théorie de la Spéculation"

As a curiosity, his paper predated by a few years another paper by Albert Einstein, who wrote in 1905 about the Brownian motion in a paper with a title that we could translate as "On the movement of particles suspended in liquids at rest as required by the molecular kinetic theory of heat" (see Figure 2). [4]

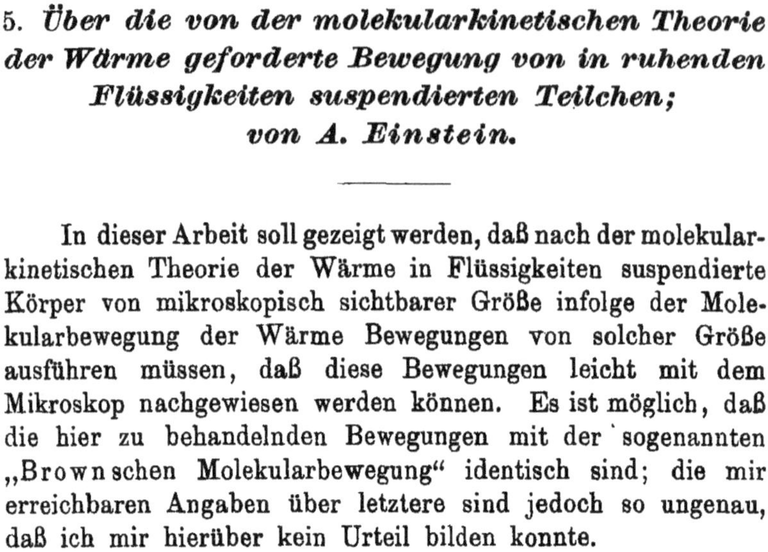

5. Über die von der molekularkinetischen Theorie der Wärme geforderte Bewegung von in ruhenden Flüssigkeiten suspendierten Teilchen; von A. Einstein.

In dieser Arbeit soll gezeigt werden, daß nach der molekularkinetischen Theorie der Wärme in Flüssigkeiten suspendierte Körper von mikroskopisch sichtbarer Größe infolge der Molekularbewegung der Wärme Bewegungen von solcher Größe ausführen müssen, daß diese Bewegungen leicht mit dem Mikroskop nachgewiesen werden können. Es ist möglich, daß die hier zu behandelnden Bewegungen mit der sogenannten „Brownschen Molekularbewegung" identisch sind; die mir erreichbaren Angaben über letztere sind jedoch so ungenau, daß ich mir hierüber kein Urteil bilden konnte.

Figure 2. First lines of the paper "Über die von der molekularkinetischen Theorie der Wärme geforderte Bewegung von in ruhenden Flüssigkeiten suspendierten Teilchen", by Albert Einstein, published in "Annalen der Physik" in 1905.

The Brownian motion is named after the Scotsman Robert Brown, who discovered it in the 19th century. In 1827 he observed that pollen particles suspended in water moved randomly. In general, Brownian motion consists of the random motion observed in particles in a fluid medium (liquid or gas) as a result of collisions with the molecules of that fluid.

Usually the credit for the mathematical explanation of Brownian motion goes to Einstein, for his 1905 paper (see Figure 2). But curiously Einstein was five years late, Bachelier had already described the mathematics of random walks in his thesis in 1900.

Both Albert Einstein and Louis Bachelier used the same mathematical apparatus, but they applied it to two different physical processes:

1. Einstein was thinking of the motion of tiny particles due to collision with atoms.
2. Bachelier thought about variations in the price of shares in the stock market.

As they worked on two different fields of knowledge, this made Einstein unaware of Bachelier's previous work.

A graphic way to describe a Brownian motion, or Random walk, is to think of a drunk person taking out the garbage from home. This person is holding a garbage bag that is dripping with grease. In principle he has a direction, towards the garbage can, but he is not able to follow it properly. What happens is that he moves forward a few steps, stumbles, stops, changes direction, moves forward again. The direction he follows after each stumble is random, unrelated to his supposed destination.

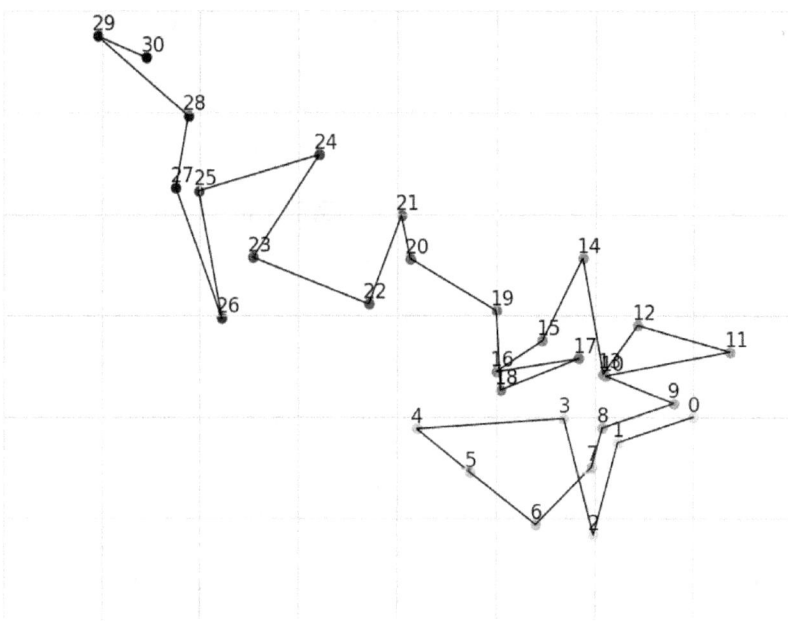

Figure 3. Example of Brownian motion in 2 dimensions. Starting from the initial point "0", in the lower right area, in each step it goes forward and backward in a random way, until ending at the point "30" in the upper left area.

If we were to observe him from above, at each instant the drunk person has a 50% chance of moving to the left and a 50% chance of moving to the right. And likewise, he is 50% likely to move in an upward direction, and 50% likely to move in a downward direction.

Following the drops of grease on the ground, we find that the route followed by the drunkard is similar to those shown in the Figure 3.

But the Brownian motion of the Figure 3 is in two dimensions (left-right, up-down), and the stock price has only one dimension (it can either go up or down).

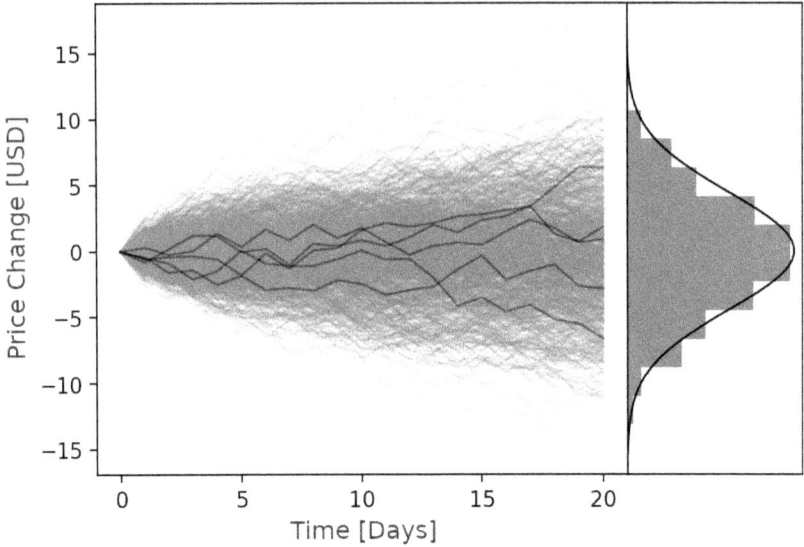

Figure 4. Let us take the price of a stock in the short term. If we could repeat the experiment hundreds of times, we would see that the price of that stock after 20 days is concentrated in the central area. Each curve is a random walk, almost unpredictable, but the result of all possible cases is a normal distribution and this gives us a lot of information. Five curves are highlighted in black just for convenience.

Bachelier showed that, if the price of a stock describes a random walk, the probability of it getting a certain value after some time is given by a curve known as a "normal distribution". See the simulation in Figure 4.

The price distribution follows a Gaussian Curve, or bell distribution (see Figure 5). As the name suggests, it is a bell-shaped curve, rounded at the top and widening at the base.

The peak of the curve is centered on the initial price. This means that the most likely scenario is that the future price will be at some value close to where it started.

If we move away from this central peak, the curve drops rapidly, which indicates that it is less likely to find the share price there.

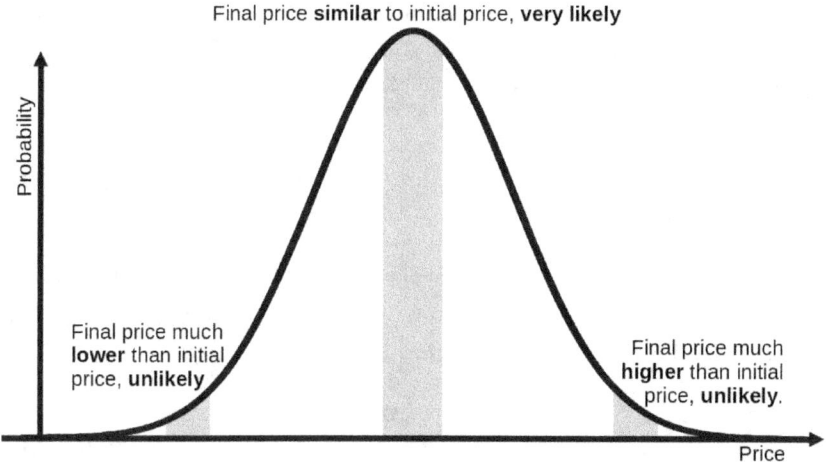

Figure 5. The normal distribution allows us to estimate what prices are possible in the long run. The final price is most likely to be similar to the initial price. It is less likely that the price will go down a lot, or up a lot.

As time increases, price uncertainty increases as well. The Figure 6 shows the expected distribution of a stock price as time progresses. It can be seen how over time the central area decreases and the wings widen.

In the Figure 7 the same idea is clearly seen: as time goes by the stock price is less likely to stay at the initial value, and is expected to move away, either toward higher or lower prices.

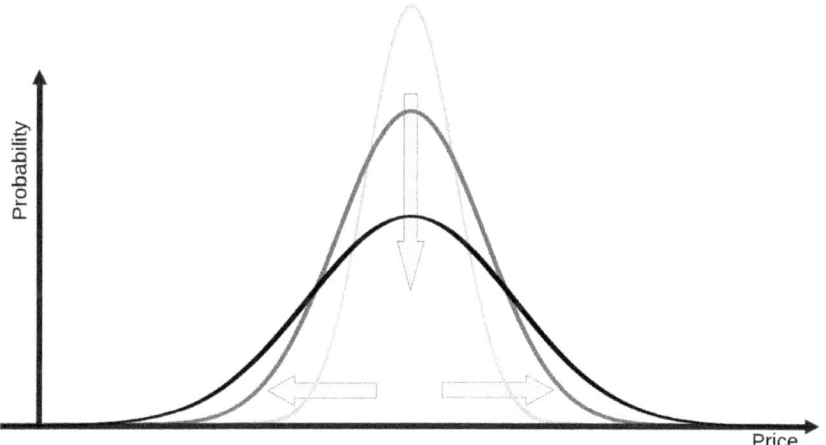

Figure 6. As time goes by, the distribution changes. It is still bell-shaped, but the central part is getting lower, and the wings are getting higher.

This view of stock prices as Random Walks was a huge breakthrough. It allowed abstraction, looking beyond prices, and thus being able to apply complex mathematics to prices.

But why should we take for granted that markets fluctuate randomly? Prices go up on good news, and down on bad news. There is nothing random about that.

Bachelier knew this. He had experience in the Paris Stock Exchange, and was aware of the effect that information could have on stock prices, that it was more complicated than just chance.

In retrospect, it is easy to point to good or bad news to explain stock market movements. That is what we are used to when reading the business press.

But Bachelier aspired to understand the probabilities of prices in the future, without knowing what the news was going to be.

Bachelier argued that any predictable event would already be reflected in the current price of a stock or bond.

That is, if you suspected that there might be positive news regarding a particular company in the future (a revolutionary new product, etc.), surely you would be willing to pay more for that company's stock than someone else who did not know about that good news.

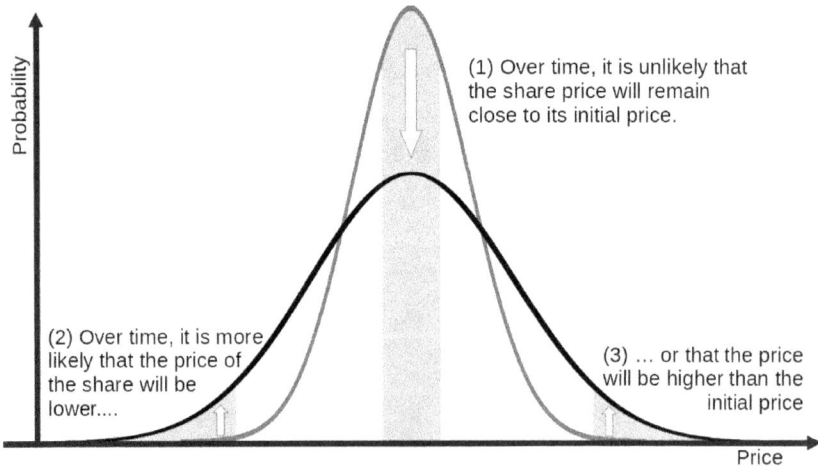

Figure 7. As time goes by, expected prices change.

Information that makes positive future events more likely, leads to price increases now. While information that portends a negative future, leads to price decreases now.

However, if this reasoning is correct, then stock prices must necessarily be random. What happens when a trade is executed at a given price? Then it is the moment of truth. A transaction implies that two investors, a buyer and a seller, have agreed on a price. Both the buyer and the seller have analyzed the available information, they have decided what value they place on the stock, but with one important difference:

- The buyer, buys the share at that price because he believes it is likely that the price will increase in the future.
- The seller, on the other hand, sells at that price because he believes it is more likely that the price will fall in the future.

And looking at the market as a whole, from a bird's eye view, if we have a market composed of multiple informed investors who constantly agree on the prices at which transactions should occur, the current price of a stock can be interpreted as the price that takes into account all possible information. It is the price at which there are as many investors willing to bet that the stock will go up as there are investors willing to bet that it will go down. In other words, at any point in time, the current price is the price at which all available information suggests an equilibrium, that the probability of the stock going up is 50%, and the probability of it going down is also 50%. If markets work as Bachelier advocated, then the random walk hypothesis is reasonable. We will read more about this in the Section 2.6 about the Efficient Market Hypothesis, by Eugene Francis Fama.

Bachelier's paper studies in detail the pricing of financial derivatives, like futures and options. An option is a derivative that involves a contract to buy or sell an underlying asset (e.g. a stock). This contract gives the buyer of the option the right to buy or sell the agreed underlying asset at a future date. The term "option" refers precisely to the fact that the buyer of such a financial derivative has the right (has the "option") to execute the provisions of the contract, if he so wishes.

In general, to determine whether a bet is fair, it is necessary to know the probability of each possible outcome and how much would be won or lost if such an outcome were to occur. To do this, you have to study the profit or loss of each case, and the probability of it happening.

It is easy to establish how much will be gained or lost, because it is the difference between the strike price of the option and the market price of the underlying tradable security.

And thanks to the random walk model, you can calculate the probabilities that a given asset will exceed (or not exceed) the stock's strike price at some future time.

Combining these two elements, Bachelier was able to calculate the fair price of a financial option.

This paper by Bachelier that we are discussing was recovered after decades forgotten and published along with others in the 1967 book "The Random Character of Stock Market Prices", edited by the economist Paul Harold Cootner, by MIT Press.[5] In the following sections we will look at more papers that were also published in it.

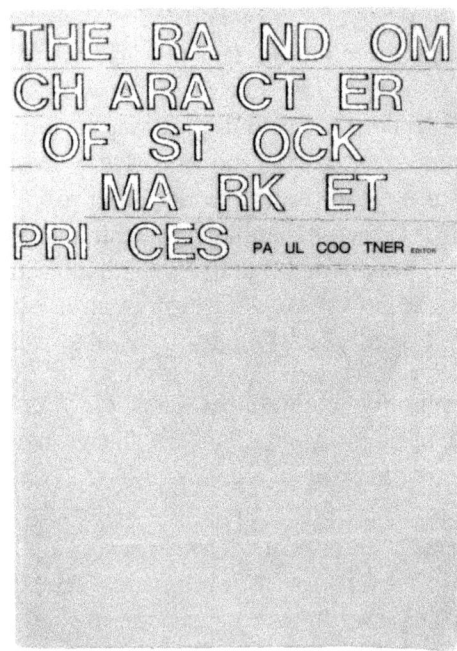

Figure 8. This book marked a turning point in the understanding of financial markets and their relationship with random walks and chance.

2.1.4. Conclusions

Bacheler's work opened new routes to the understanding of financial markets.

- On the one hand it advanced in the direction of the Efficient Markets Hypothesis, which will be further developed by Eugene Fama (see the Section 2.6).
- On the other hand, it gave way to models for pricing financial options such as that of Black-Scholes-Merton.

Finally, arguing that financial markets are random does not conflict with being at the same time predictable. Some aspects of prices are still foreseeable. And paradoxically, it is the fact that markets are random that allows us to use probabilities to understand it.

Whenever you trade the stock market, think of your counterparty as a professional, an insider with non-public knowledge, or a faster algorithm. If it is not clear to you who is winning the trade, then it is the other side that is winning.

2.2. Portfolio Theory

2.2.1. Paper

Title *Portfolio Selection*

Author Harry Max Markowitz

Publication *The Journal of Finance*, published by *The American Finance Association*, volume 7, number 1, pages 77-91, March 1952.[6]

> **PORTFOLIO SELECTION***
>
> HARRY MARKOWITZ
> *The Rand Corporation*
>
> THE PROCESS OF SELECTING a portfolio may be divided into two stages. The first stage starts with observation and experience and ends with beliefs about the future performances of available securities. The second stage starts with the relevant beliefs about future performances and ends with the choice of portfolio. This paper is concerned with the second stage. We first consider the rule that the investor does (or should) maximize discounted expected, or anticipated, returns. This rule is rejected both as a hypothesis to explain, and as a maximum to guide investment behavior. We next consider the rule that the investor does (or should) consider expected return a desirable thing *and* variance of return an undesirable thing. This rule has many sound points, both as a maxim for, and hypothesis about, investment behavior. We illustrate geometrically relations between beliefs and choice of portfolio according to the "expected returns—variance of returns" rule.

Figure 9. First lines of Harry Markowitz's paper "Portfolio Selection" (1952).

2.2.2. Author

Harry Markowitz (1927-2023) was a Jewish American economist.

Markowitz studied liberal arts at the University of Chicago. He then went on to study economics, with professors such as Tjalling Koopmans (Nobel Prize in economics 1975[7]) and Milton Friedman (Nobel Prize in economics 1976[8]).

In 1952 Harry Markowitz went to work at the RAND Corporation, where he met George Dantzig (1914-2005).

George Dantzig was a mathematician, son of Tobias Dantzig (1884-1956), also a mathematician. Tobias was born in Shavli (at that time Russian Empire, now Lithuania), lived in France, and moved to USA in 1910. Interestingly Tobias Dantzing had been a student of Henri Poincaré in Paris, and as we have already discussed in Section 2.1 on the paper *Théorie de la Spéculation*, Henri Poincaré was also the thesis supervisor of Louis Bachelier.

With the help of George Dantzig, Markowitz researched optimization techniques, developing the Efficient Frontier algorithm for the identification of optimal portfolios.

In 1954 he received his PhD in Economics from the University of Chicago with a thesis on portfolio theory. As an anecdote, he mentions that the topic of his thesis was so novel that, while Markowitz was defending his thesis, Milton Friedman argued that "portfolio theory was not Economics, and that they could not award a PhD degree in Economics for a dissertation which was not Economics".[9]

During 1955-1956, Markowitz spent a year at the Cowles Foundation, which had moved to Yale University, at the invitation of James Tobin (1918-2002) (Nobel Prize in Economics 1981[10], and known for the "Tobin Tax", a tax on currency exchanges intended to reduce speculation).

Subsequently Markowitz divided his time between teaching at the School of Business at the University of California, San Diego (UCSD), and consulting work.

In 1968 he worked with Paul Samuelson (Nobel Prize in economics in 1970[11]) and Robert Merton (1944-) (Nobel Prize in economics in 1997[12], and known for the Black-Scholes-Merton model) at the company Arbitrage Management, where they created a hedge fund that is considered the first known attempt at computerized arbitrage. There he became chief executive.

He received the John von Neumann Prize in 1989 (this prize is awarded annually for outstanding contributions in the field of applied mathematics, and for communication of these ideas to society), and the Nobel Prize in economics in 1990.[13]

23

2.2.3. Content

2.2.3.1. Introduction

During his doctorate at the University of Chicago, Markowitz chose as his dissertation topic the application of mathematics to stock market analysis.

His thesis supervisor was Jacob Marschak (1898-1977), a Jew born in Kiev (at that time Russian Empire, now Ukraine), who was such an exceptional person that he is said to have spoken a dozen languages.

While researching the theory of stock prices at that time, Markowitz realized that the theory lacked an analysis of the impact of risk. This insight led him to develop his fundamental theory of portfolio allocation under uncertainty, published in the paper discussed here.

Harry Markowitz describes how he came up with the idea[1-4]:

> The basic concepts of portfolio theory came to me one afternoon in the library while reading John Burr Williams' "Theory of Investment Value". Williams proposed that the value of a stock should equal the present value of its future dividends. Since future dividends are uncertain, I interpreted Williams's proposal to be to value a stock by its expected future dividends.
>
> But if the investor were only interested in expected values of securities, he or she would only be interested in the expected value of the portfolio; and to maximize the expected value of a portfolio one need invest only in a single security [whichever is best].
>
> This, I knew, was not the way investors did or should act. Investors diversify because they are concerned with risk as well as return. Variance came to mind as a measure of risk. [...] Since there were two criteria, risk and return, it was natural to assume that investors selected from the set of Pareto optimal risk-return combinations.
>
> — Harry Markowitz, autobiography submitted to the Nobel Prize committee

Considering investors' risk aversion in addition to their interest in profitability makes a lot of sense. By the way, an example of risk aversion in everyday life is to note that people typically take out multiple insurances: life, car, health, travel, etc.

A good description of Markowitz's theory is the following, in his own words:

> A good portfolio is more than a long list of good stocks and bonds. It is a balanced set, which provides the investor with protections and opportunities with respect to a wide range of contingencies. To reduce risk, it is necessary to avoid a portfolio whose stocks are all highly correlated with each other. A hundred stocks whose returns rise and fall in near unison offer as little protection as the uncertain returns of a single stock.
>
> — Harry Markowitz

A Markowitz efficient portfolio is one in which, for a given expected return, more diversification cannot further reduce portfolio risk. Or in other words, additional expected return cannot be obtained without increasing portfolio risk.

A key component of the theory is diversification. Until then, investments were assumed to be either "high risk/high return" or "low risk/low return". But thanks to Markowitz investors can get the best results by choosing an optimal combination of the two, based on an assessment of their personal risk tolerance.

The Markowitz's Efficient Frontier is the set of all portfolios that offer the highest expected return for each given level of risk.

These concepts of efficiency were essential for the development of the Capital Asset Pricing Model (CAPM, as we will see in Section 2.5).

The Modern Portfolio Theory (as this theory is called) assumes that investors are risk averse, which means that, given two portfolios that offer the same expected return, investors will prefer the less risky one. Thus, an investor will only take a higher risk if he is rewarded by a higher expected return. Conversely, an investor who wants a higher expected return will have to accept a higher risk.

The exact payoff will not be the same for all investors. Different investors will evaluate compensation differently based on their individual risk aversion characteristics.

2.2.3.2. Description

The model requires the following parameters for each asset:

- Expected returns of each asset,
- Expected volatility of each asset,
- Correlation between pairs of assets.

We assume that, given some assets in the portfolio, their proportions are kept constant, rebalancing them periodically.

Always thinking in the long term. Like a gardener who plants the seeds, waters them, and takes care of them so that they grow, and after a long time they become flowers. In the same way, the investor chooses the assets, rebalances them, keeps them for the long term, so that in the end they provide the expected return and volatility.

The theory explains that by combining different assets in a portfolio:

- The aggregate portfolio return is simply the proportional combination of the asset returns.
- The volatility of the aggregate portfolio is also the combination of the volatilities, but in this case the correlation between the assets must be taken into account.

All the magic consists in the correlations between assets, making up a combined portfolio with better risk/return properties than any of the assets separately.

The Figure 10 shows an example with two types of assets: companies in the S&P 500, and international companies (from the perspective of a US investor). Using historical data, the portfolio return would have been the average return of the assets, but the volatility would have been lower than any of both asset volatilities (this is the key point).

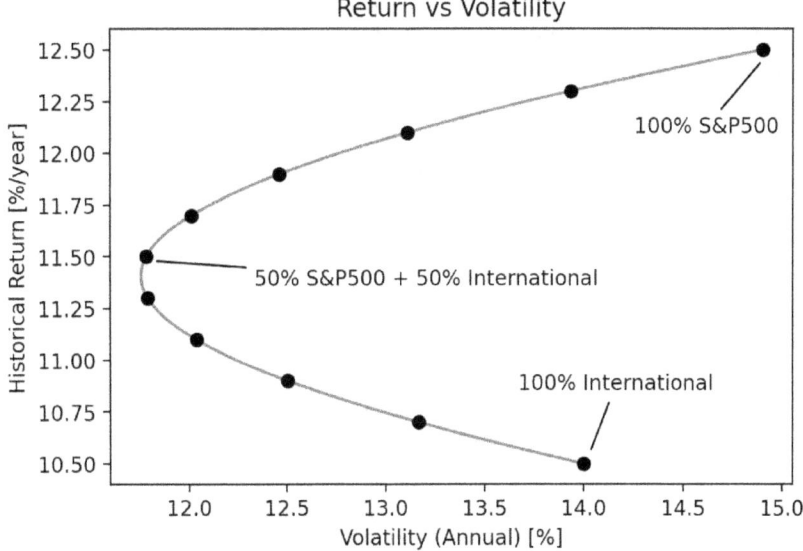

Figure 10. Example of the effect of correlations between two different assets. Taken from the textbook "Modern Portfolio Theory and Investment", by E. J. Elton et al.

Throughout this section, plots of expected return vs volatility are shown, such as the Figure 11.

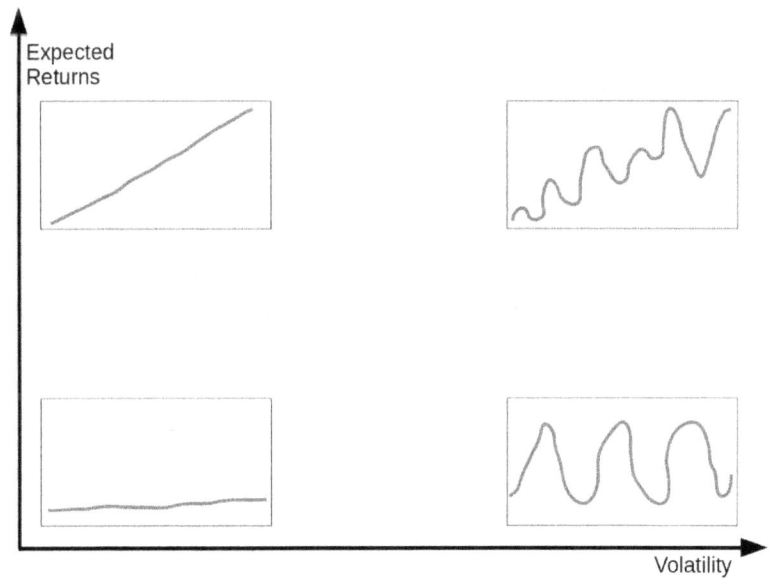

Figure 11. Expected return vs volatility for four different assets.

In the upper area the assets and portfolios with the highest expected return are shown, and in the lower area those with the lowest expected return.

In the left zone the assets and portfolios with the lowest volatility are shown, and in the right zone those with the highest volatility.

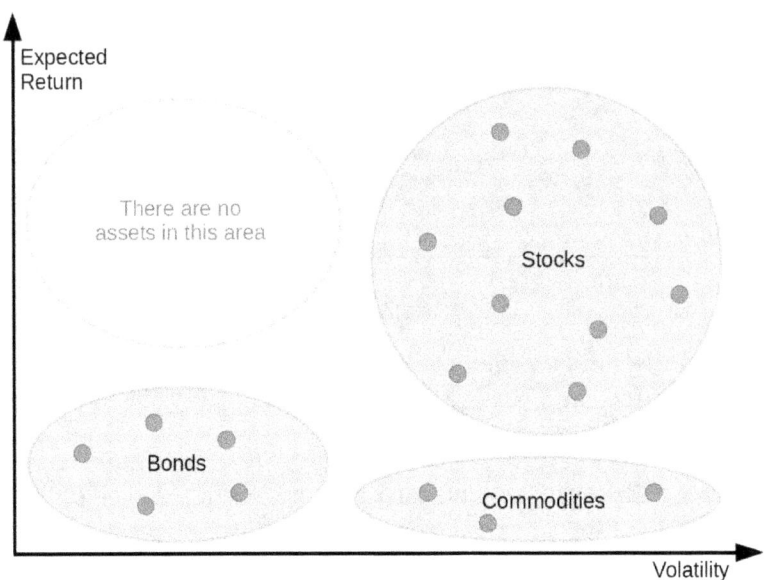

Figure 12. Asset classes to build portfolios.

The assets to be combined in the portfolios are show in the Figure 12:

- In the lower left area there are the lower yielding, lower volatility assets. These are government bonds, from stable countries with strong currencies, with good credit quality.
- In the lower right zone there are assets with lower yields but high volatility. A good example is gold. It does not provide profitability (it does not give dividends or coupons, at most it may grow with inflation), and in addition it suffers from high volatility.
- In the upper right zone there is the star asset: stocks. They provide great profitability, at the cost of suffering great volatility.
- Finally, the upper left zone is empty. There are no assets that provide high returns and low volatility. Could a portfolio in this zone be possible combining the above assets?

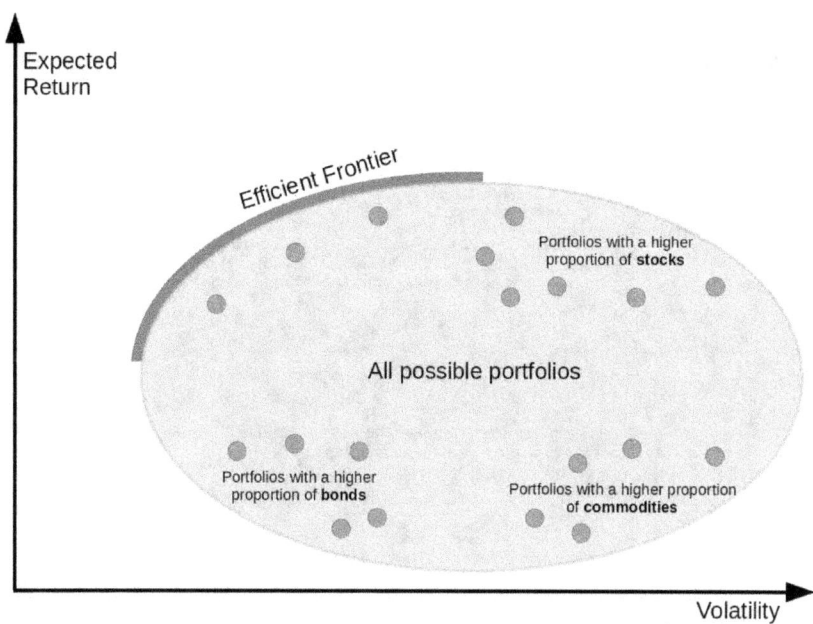

Figure 13. All possible portfolios, depending on their composition, along with the Efficient Frontier.

In the Figure 13 all possible portfolios are shown, which are obtained by combining the assets of the Figure 12.

Within the area of possible portfolios (shaded area) all possible combinations are shown. The exact shape of the area of the possible portfolios, and their exact return/volatility values, are not important. The relevant information is:

- in the lower left area the portfolios are predominantly composed of government bonds,
- in the lower right zone by commodities, and
- in the upper right zone by equities.

Note that there are no portfolios in the upper left zone. The closest portfolios to that area are located in the Efficient Frontier.

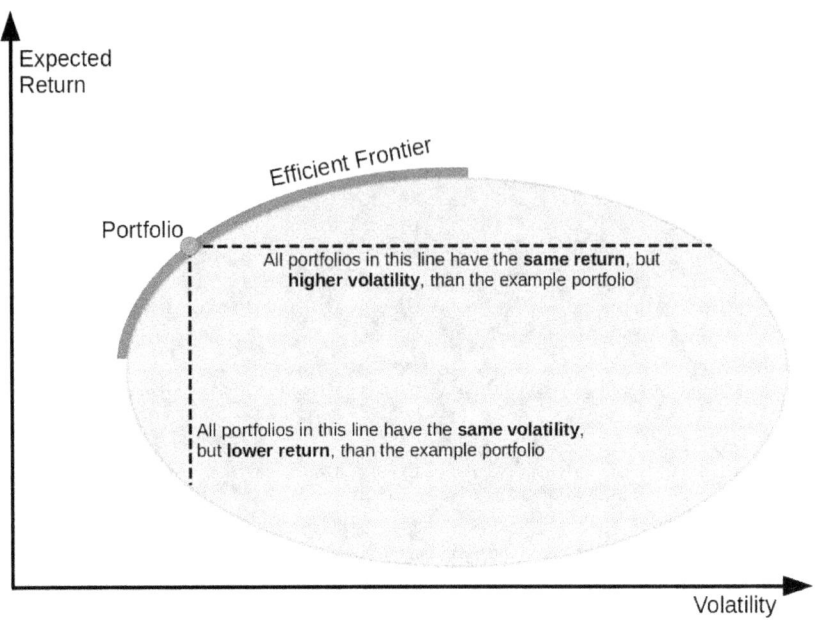

Figure 14. The Efficient Frontier portfolios are the only ones worthwhile.

How important is the Efficient Frontier?

Well, it turns out that only portfolios that are part of the Efficient Frontier are worth investing in, and we can ignore all other portfolios.

The reasons are (see the Figure 14):

- Given the **same return**, all other portfolios have **higher volatility**, and therefore we are not interested in them.
- Given the **same volatility**, all other portfolios have **lower profitability**, and therefore we are not interested.

Notice that no portfolio in the Efficient Frontier is better than another portfolio in the Efficient Frontier. They simply have different expected returns and different levels of risk.

Moreover, the slope of the Efficient Frontier curve decreases with increasing risk. That is, increasing risk results in proportionally smaller and smaller increases in expected return. This tells us that the most reasonable segment of the curve is the intermediate zone.

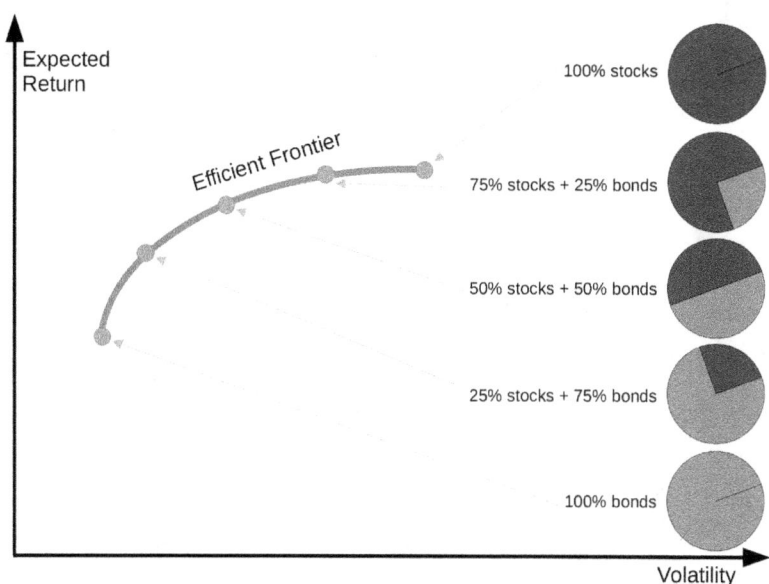

Figure 15. The portfolios that are part of the Efficient Frontier are only composed of stocks and bonds.

And what is the asset composition of the portfolios that are part of the Efficient Frontier? Well here is the magic, see the Figure 15. The Efficient Frontier is made up of the most anti-correlated assets, which are government bonds and stocks.

The anti-correlation between bonds and stocks was clear in the past, but during the last years it has been weaker. This anti-correlation is not perfect, not even constant over time, but still a reasonable approximation. Any other portfolio composition (100% stocks, stocks & gold, etc.) is worse (implies higher correlation between assets). In fact, according to the formula that calculates the total portfolio return based on the return of the assets and their correlation matrix, bonds do not need to be perfectly "anti-correlated" to stocks. Bonds just need to be the "least correlated" asset to stocks. Thus, both together form the portfolios of the Efficient Frontier.

The anti-correlation that has been observed can be justified theoretically. According to historical data, in bad economic times, stock prices normally fall, and governments go into debt to maintain economic activity, generating more public debt, bonds with lower and lower yields, which are equivalent to higher prices. And vice versa when the economy is doing well.

Going back to the Figure 15, at the lower left boundary of the Efficient Frontier, the portfolio is composed of 100% bonds.

As you move up the line, an increasing component of stocks appears, and bonds decrease.

At the upper right boundary, the portfolio is composed of 100% stocks.

The Efficient Frontier greatly simplifies the portfolio choice. We no longer have to choose two parameters (return and volatility), to know our position in the area of all possible portfolios (see Figure 13). The Efficient Frontier is a simple line, and to know the position in a line only one parameter is needed (either return or volatility). The other parameter is calculated via the Efficient Frontier.

If we want to accept the highest risk, we will choose a portfolio composed 100% of stocks. If we want to fully minimize the risk (volatility), we will choose a portfolio composed 100% of bonds. And in between, all possible combinations of stocks and bonds.

This is why the 60% stocks and 40% bonds portfolio is so common, because it is somewhere in between, a good combination.

Look at the top of the Efficient Frontier. Compare the position of a 100% stock portfolio with another portfolio of 90% stocks and 10% bonds. Both have about the same expected return, but the portfolio with bonds has clearly lower volatility. For this reason, financial service providers[15] usually avoid providing 100% stocks portfolios, because a 90%/10% is just better.

The Efficient Frontier concept is a conceptual framework that allows the investor to make better, more informed decisions by selecting the desired combination of return and volatility within the possible ranges. The exact values of expected return and volatility do not matter, only the conceptual framework matters.

2.2.3.3. Criticism

Several criticisms can be made to the Modern Portfolio Theory.

On the one hand Modern Portfolio Theory evaluates portfolios on the basis of their volatility. But it seems more reasonable to do so on the basis of potential loss (using parameters such as Value-at-Risk, VaR). This criticism is being resolved with new developments, such as the Post-Modern Portfolio Theory. Once again, we are faced with the dilemma of choosing a relatively simple but inaccurate mathematical model over another model that is more perfect but also more complicated to use.

Another criticism is that managers must rebalance portfolios when the percentages deviate from what has been decided according to the risk accepted by the investor. In practice, however, rebalancing is relatively infrequent.

There are several reasons for not rebalancing. On the one hand because it involves paying transaction costs and perhaps capital gains taxes. And also because rebalancing implies having a "contrarian" attitude, selling when others buy, and buying when others sell, in the hope of selling high and buying low. But this is easier said than done.

Moreover, managers who follow Modern Portfolio Theory cannot be a majority in the market, otherwise when they want to sell there will be no one willing to buy, they will not find a counterpart.

And that counterpart will typically be given by active Technical Analysis managers (managers who try to predict future asset prices based on their past prices).

This is because if the value of an asset increases more than others, by Portfolio Theory you have to sell to rebalance, but a Technical Analysis manager can assume that the trend will continue and therefore you have to buy. And vice versa, when the price of an asset is falling, the Modern Portfolio Theory manager will want to buy, and will buy the asset from a Technical Analysis manager who will want to sell because he may think that it is in a downward price trend.

On the other hand, a Fundamental Analysis or value style manager has incentives to buy and sell similar to those proposed by Portfolio Theory (sell the overvalued, buy the undervalued), and therefore contrary to Technical Analysis.

In short, for Harry Markowitz's ideas to work there has to be a certain symmetry, for every Modern Portfolio Theory managed dollar there has to be another managed dollar that follows price trends.

2.2.4. Conclusions

The Modern Portfolio Theory requires applying returns, volatilities, and correlations. But all these parameters are only known *a posteriori*. Therefore we must remember once again that "past performance does not guarantee future results".

When choosing a portfolio to invest in, it is better to choose one that is in the Efficient Frontier. For the same expected return, those are the lowest volatility portfolios. It is not rational to choose others.

The portfolios that are part of the Efficient Frontier are composed of government bonds and diversified stocks. According to the model, all other asset classes are irrelevant. In fact, adding other asset classes takes us away from the Efficient Frontier.

The objective is not to "get the highest possible return", but to choose the proportion between stocks and bonds so that the resulting portfolio has the combination of return and volatility that best suits our needs.

Investing in a portfolio composed only of individual stocks implies high volatility. What if you get 3 years in a row with losses? Is it worth it? Because this is statistically possible, are you sure you won't need the money at the worst time? Or if you need it, will you accept to sell at a loss?

Finally, Portfolio Theory represents the orthodoxy in finance, the most common recommendation. If you decide to move away from it and invest with different assets, it is not necessarily wrong, but it would be good to think about it and be able to justify your reasons.

2.3. Asymmetry in Returns

2.3.1. Paper

Title   Brownian Motion in the Stock Market

Author   Matthew Fontaine Maury Osborne

Publication   Operations Research, year 1959, volume 7, issue 2, pages 145-173.[16]

Operations Research

March–April 1959

BROWNIAN MOTION IN THE STOCK MARKET†

M. F. M. Osborne

U S Naval Research Laboratory, Washington 25, D C

(Received February 6, 1958)

It is shown that common-stock prices, and the value of money can be regarded as an ensemble of decisions in statistical equilibrium, with properties quite analogous to an ensemble of particles in statistical mechanics

Figure 16. First lines of the paper by M.F.M. Osborne.

2.3.2. Author

M.F.M. Osborne (1916-2003) was an American who worked for 30 years as a researcher at the US Navy Research Laboratory (NRL). Doctor in biology from the University of Maryland in 1952. He worked in fields like physics, astronomy, entomology, oceanography, and, in what concerns us, also in finance. Osborne published his work without knowing the one previously done by Louis Bachelier (see Section 2.1).

He was the grandson of Matthew Fontaine Maury (1806-1873), American naval officer, and one of the founders of modern oceanography.

2.3.3. Content

As Osborne writes in his paper:

> It is the purpose of this paper to show that the logarithms of common-stock prices can be regarded as an ensemble of decisions in a statistical steady state, and that this ensemble of logarithms of prices, each varying with the time, has a close analogy with the ensemble of coordinates of a large number of molecules. We wish to show that the methods of statistical mechanics, normally applied to the latter problem, may also be applied to the former.
>
> — M.F.M. Osborne, "Brownian Motion in the Stock Market"

In many respects, the work of Osborne synthesizes the work done by Louis Bachelier. But there is an important improvement. Bachelier explained that, from one moment to the next, stock prices could both rise and fall by "a given amount". On that assumption, stock prices have a normal distribution (i.e., bell curve). This was a reasonable approximation, given the rudimentary techniques of the time.

However, when one looks at the data in detail, one finds that the best distribution is not the normal distribution, but a logarithmic one. Osborne assumed a logarithmic distribution, because the change from one day to the next is not "an amount" (example: measured in dollars), but "a percentage" (example: +1.5%). These changes are not added, they are multiplied. This approach is more realistic.

Therefore, the normal distribution does not apply to the "prices", but to the "returns". And then these returns are applied to prices.

The Osborne price distribution is a kind of deformed bell curve, where the right tail is very long and the left tail is practically non-existent.

The idea of using logarithms comes from the property of converting "the logarithm of multiplying quantities" (in this case: the return of the first day, multiplied by the return of the second day, multiplied by the return of the third day...) into "the sum of the logarithms of each day" (going from multiplication to addition). This transformation is what, applied to the price, makes the normal distribution of returns visible.

Moreover, in a practical way, investors know that what concerns us are changes in percentage, not in absolute values.

Let us imagine a stock priced at 20 euros (or dollars, pounds, etc.) that increases by 5 euros (25%). Let us now consider that we have a second stock with a price of 200 euros. If this second stock increases its price by 50 euros (25%), we will be happy as with the first stock. But if it goes up only 5 euros (2.5%), it is fine, but it does not generate in us the enthusiasm of the first stock.

Therefore, logarithms express investors' feelings better. Osborne formally justifies this through two 19th century psychologists who described this effect, the Weber-Fechner law:

> The stimulus of price in dollars, and the subjective sensation of value in the mind of the trader or investor, are related in accordance with the Weber-Fechner law. [...] The Weber-Fechner law states that equal ratios of physical stimulus, for example, of sound frequency in vibrations/second, or of light, or sound intensity in watts per unit area, correspond to equal intervals of subjective sensation.
>
> — M.F.M. Osborne, "Brownian Motion in the Stock Market"

This logarithmic Osborne distribution solves a problem that the Bachelier normal distribution has: over a long-time frame, the mathematical model of the normal distribution may result in the stock price being negative. But we know that this does not make sense; stocks always have positive prices, or at the very least are worthless.

However, with Osborne's logarithmic model, the stock price may tend to zero, but it will never be negative.

Moreover, as prices multiply higher and higher, the right wing of the distribution (higher prices) shows more cases than the left wing (lower prices). There is no symmetry.

The Figure 17 shows four images of the same example. Suppose all the possible prices of a stock after 100 days.

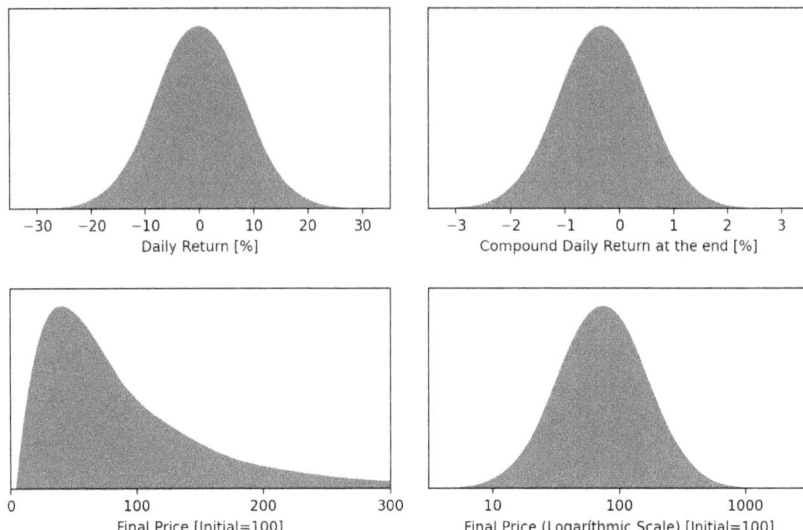

Figure 17. These four panels show 100-day simulations of the price of a stock. Its daily volatility is 8%. See explanation in the text.

1. The first panel (upper left) shows the daily returns. In this example we assume that the average is 0% and that the daily volatility is 8%. We see, following Osborne's approximation, that we have a normal distribution in the daily returns.

2. The second panel (upper right) shows that after 100 days of simulation the daily compound returns (i.e., the return that if held constant over the 100 days would have produced an equivalent return) also follow a normal distribution. In fact, it is narrowed by a factor of 10, because in this statistical case the volatility decreases with the square root of the number of days (100 days).

3. The third panel (bottom left) shows that the final prices after 100 days **do not** follow a normal distribution. This is the distribution Osborne was referring to. The peak can be mistaken for a normal distribution, but the left tail is almost non-existent, and the right tail much larger.

4. The fourth panel (lower right) shows the same data as the third panel, but with the horizontal scale logarithmic, not linear. Visually this "expands" the left tail, and "contracts" the right tail. It is exactly the same data as the third panel, but displayed differently. This panel is what Osborne meant, that the price distribution is "Log-Normal".

The Figure 18 is a more practical way of looking at it. In the long run prices follow a distribution that is not symmetric. Compare with the Figure 4, which is a similar plot but in the short term, where the effect of time stretching the distribution towards higher prices is not yet apparent.

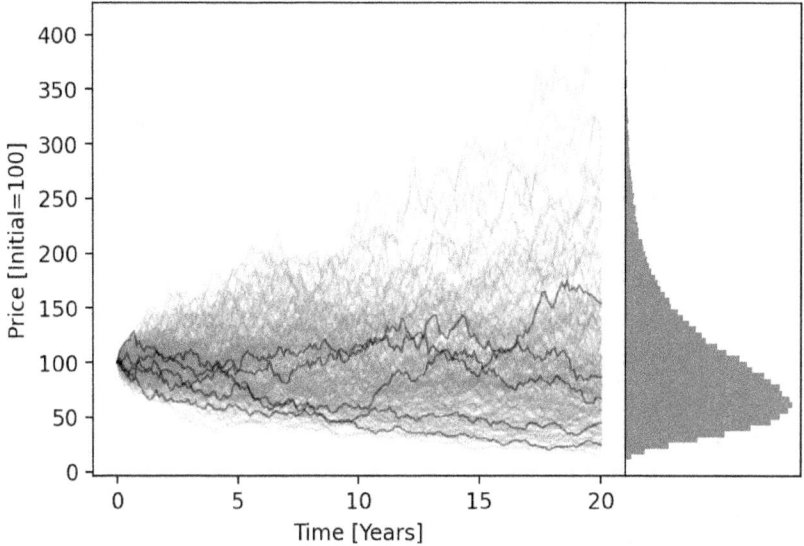

Figure 18. Prices follow a log-normal distribution. It is simply a simulation where daily returns follow a normal distribution. This figure is like the Figure 4 from Section 2.1, but that one is short-term and symmetric, and this one is long-term and asymmetry is already observed. For convenience, 5 curves are shown in black.

The Figure 19 shows Osborne's data, as presented in his paper. The distribution of stock prices on the New York Stock Exchange follows a log-normal distribution, remarkably similar to that in the fourth (lower right) panel of the Figure 17. That is, when the horizontal axis follows a logarithmic scale, the distribution is similar to a normal one.

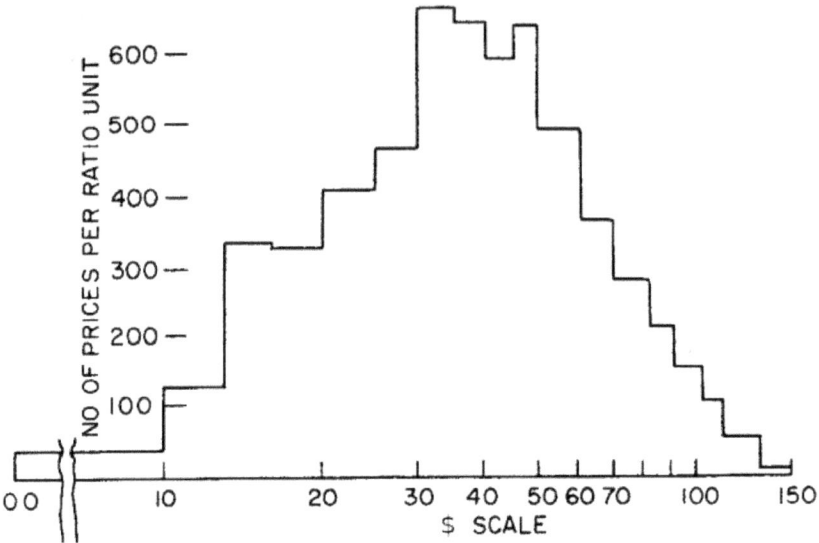

Figure 19. Distribution of stock prices on the NYSE as of 31/July/1956. Source: Figure 4 from the paper "Brownian Motion in the Stock Market", by Osborne.

2.3.4. Conclusions

M.F.M. Osborne rediscovered the application of the Brownian Motion to stock prices.

In addition, he emphasized the importance of the log-normal distribution, rather than a simple normal distribution. The log-normal distribution of returns is not symmetric, and there are stocks that earn exceptionally high returns. This has implications for the likelihood of active managers underperforming their benchmarks, as we will see in the Section 2.13.

2.4. Fat Tails

2.4.1. Paper

Title   The Variation of Certain Speculative Prices

Author   Benoît Mandelbrot

Publication The Journal of Business, volume 36, number 4 (October, 1963), pages 394-419.[17]

> THE VARIATION OF CERTAIN SPECULATIVE PRICES*
>
> BENOIT MANDELBROT†
>
> I. INTRODUCTION
>
> THE name of Louis Bachelier is often mentioned in books on diffusion process. Until very recently, how- modity, at the end of time period t. Then it is assumed that successive differences of the form $Z(t+T) - Z(t)$ are independent, Gaussian or normally distrib-

Figure 20. First lines of the paper by Benoît Mandelbrot.

2.4.2. Author

Benoît Mandelbrot (1924-2010) was born in Poland, the son of Lithuanian parents.

As a Polish Jew, he suffered the disaster of Europe during the 20th century. His family emigrated as a young man from Warsaw to Paris. When World War II broke out, they emigrated again to Tulle, a small town in the South of France, in the area controlled by the Vichy government.

He studied in Lyon, obtained his doctorate in Paris, and then went to the USA where he worked during 35 years for IBM.

Thanks to his work at IBM he was able to use one of the first computers in existence. He could apply numerical analysis to areas of science that until that moment were unattainable. He was a pioneer thanks to having that unique tool, the computer.

Eventually he returned to France to work at the CNRS (*Centre National de la Recherche Scientifique*).

He received countless decorations and honors, including the Barnard Medal (1985), the Franklin Medal (1986), and he became Officer of the French *Légion d'honneur* (2006).

2.4.3. Content

So far we have assumed normal distributions, also called Gaussian distributions, after Carl Friedrich Gauss (1777-1855) who studied them in the 19th century. Regarding changes in asset prices, Louis Bachelier (Section 2.1) considered absolute changes, and M.F.M. Osborne (Section 2.3) considered relative changes (percentages).

All this is reasonable. Normal distributions are common in normal life, like the weight of newborn babies, height of people, measurement errors, etc.

In addition, when a large amount of randomness is combined, such as rolling six-sided dice a thousand times, adding their values, and repeating the experiment a thousand times; the distribution of the sums approaches a normal distribution. This is the so-called Central Limit Theorem, developed by the mathematician Pierre-Simon Laplace (1749-1827).

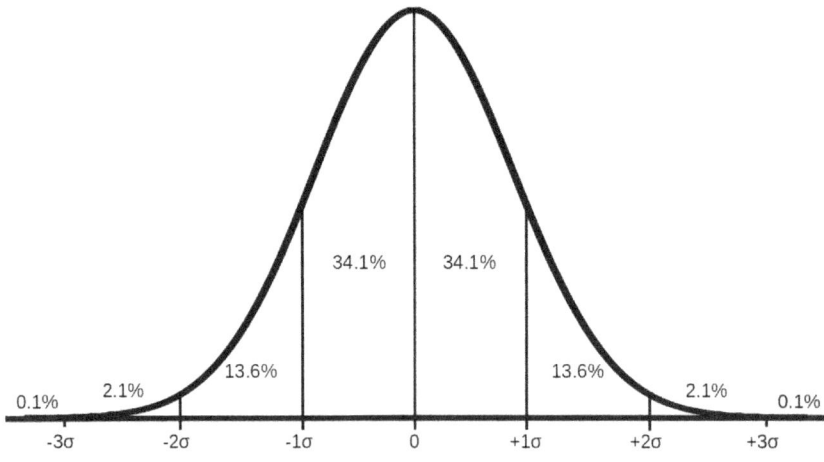

Figure 21. The probability in a normal distribution. Each band has one standard deviation (σ) width, and the labels indicate the proportion of the corresponding area. Source: M.W. Toews via Wikipedia.[18]

Normal distributions have the important property that knowing their mean value and their standard deviation (σ, the Greek letter "sigma"), one can estimate the number of cases in various intervals. Let us see, following the Figure 21:

- Between -1σ and +1σ we have about 68% of the cases (approximately 2 out of 3 cases).
- Between -2σ and +2σ we have about 95% of the cases (approx. 19 out of 20 cases).
- Between -3σ and +3σ we have about 99.7% of the cases (approx. 332 out of 333 cases).

However, not all probability distributions are normal distributions. It could for example be a "Cauchy distribution" (studied by Augustin-Louis Cauchy (1789-1857), French mathematician). A Cauchy distribution is given for example by transforming a normal distribution with respect to an angle, to with respect to a linear distance to the axis[19] (see the Figure 22).

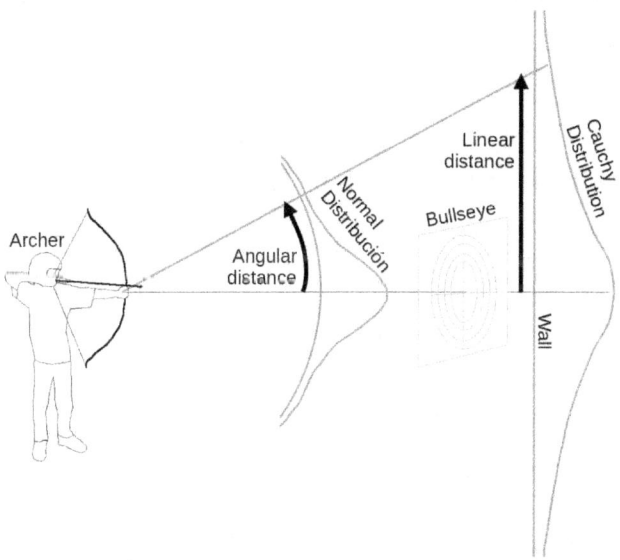

Figure 22. Let us suppose an archer shooting arrows at a target, which is located on a wall up and down the figure. If we assume that the "angle" of error follows a normal distribution, then the "distance" to the center of the target follows a Cauchy distribution.

In an extreme case, assuming an archer with Parkinson's Syndrome, the archer could shoot his arrows in almost any direction. Suppose he launches an arrow toward the top of the Figure 22. In this case, the arrow would travel parallel to the wall.

Notice that the arrow has been shot at a relatively extreme angle, at 90 degrees from the direction to the bullseye. However, the distance on the wall would be infinite, it would never touch the wall. This is why the two distributions differ.

Importantly, the Cauchy distribution is also often called a "fat tailed". If we compare a normal distribution with a Cauchy distribution (see the Figure 23) it is apparent that the Cauchy one is more extreme:

- On the one hand because it is sharper. This means that central events are more likely than in a normal distribution. If we think about stock market returns, most of the returns are close to the average.
- On the other hand, because of having fat tails, events far to the left or far to the right abound. In the context of stock market returns, it is more likely to observe in a Cauchy distribution either incredibly positive or terribly negative returns.

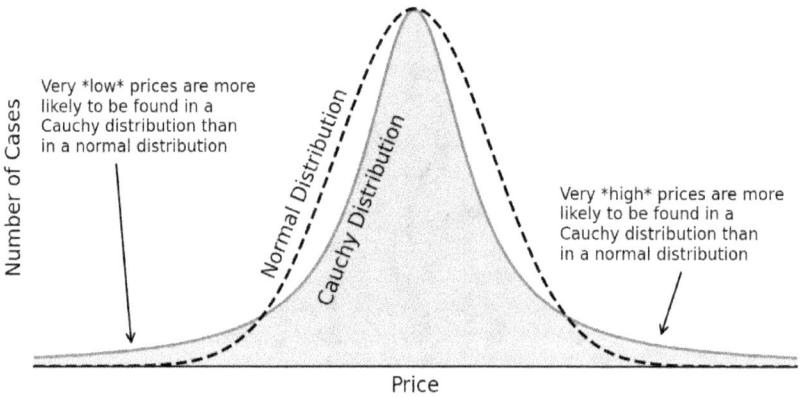

Figure 23. Example comparison between Cauchy distribution and normal (Gaussian) distribution. For the same area under the curves, and fixing the point of maximum likelihood, the Cauchy distribution is more extreme, it has fatter tails.

This problem of modeling nature using normal distributions when they are not really the best choice is not something that applies only to finance. It is a general problem in physics and mathematics.

As it is explained in the Wolfram MathWorld mathematical encyclopedia:[20]

Because they occur so frequently, there is an unfortunate tendency to invoke normal distributions in situations where they may not be applicable.

— Eric W. Weisstein, article "Normal Distribution" in the Wolfram MathWorld mathematical encyclopedia

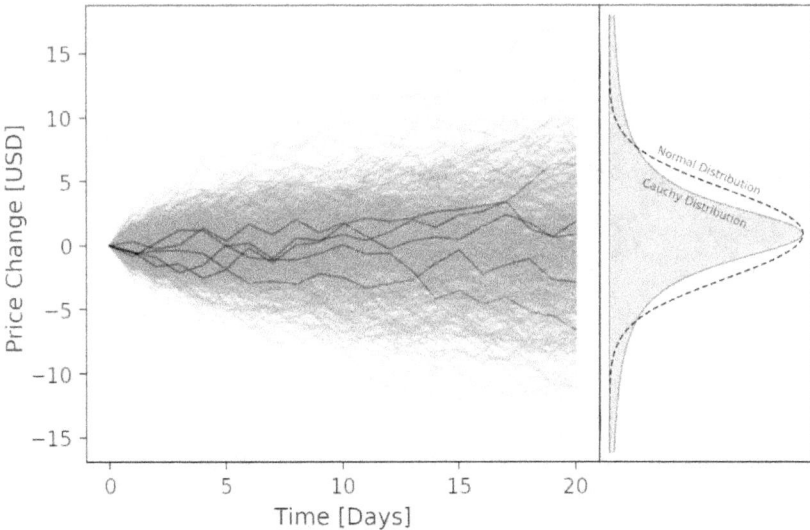

Figure 24. When we assume that prices behave according to a distribution which is inaccurate, for example according to a normal distribution instead of a Cauchy distribution, we may find that extreme cases (prices that are either very high or very low) are more frequent than expected. These extreme cases would be few compared to all possible cases, but even if they are few, they may be many times more frequent than would be expected according to a normal distribution.

The mathematician Paul Lévy (1886-1971) also studied random processes. He generalized these ideas about probability, defining "stable distributions", of which both the normal distribution and the Cauchy distribution are particular cases.

These are stable distributions because they have a particular characteristic: a combination of stable distributions is itself another stable distribution.

The family of stable distributions can be explained by a parameter α ("alpha", which is not related to alpha defined as "return above market"). This alpha parameter can be a value between 0 and 2. The lower the alpha parameter, the more extreme the randomness, the fatter the tails.

These distributions have an important behavior with respect to basic statistical parameters, as can be seen in the Table 1.

Table 1. Stable Distributions may not have well defined values for their mean value and/or their standard deviation. These are the differences as a function of their parameter α (alpha).

Alpha (α) of the distribution	Is its mean value well defined?	Is its standard deviation well defined?	Comment
α=2	☑ Yes	☑ Yes	Normal Distribution
1<α<2	☑ Yes	☐ No	Typical values found by Mandelbrot (see text)
α=1	☐ No	☐ No	Cauchy distribution
0<α<1	☐ No	☐ No	

Note the Cauchy distribution (shown in the Figure 23), which although it does not appear to be special, has neither defined mean value nor standard deviation.

The key detail is that Mandelbrot claimed that observed prices behave like a stable distribution with α between 1 and 2. In particular, his data shows that cotton prices have a parameter α of about 1.7. That is, that the mean value can be calculated, but that it has no well defined standard deviation. And in the context of investments, that its volatility is meaningless.

The Figure 25 shows data for the price of wool (not cotton as we have discussed in other paragraphs), and how the distribution of these prices is quite different from the normal distribution. Therefore, in this case the normal distribution is a poor approximation.

The fact that the mean value or volatility may not be defined is quite tricky.

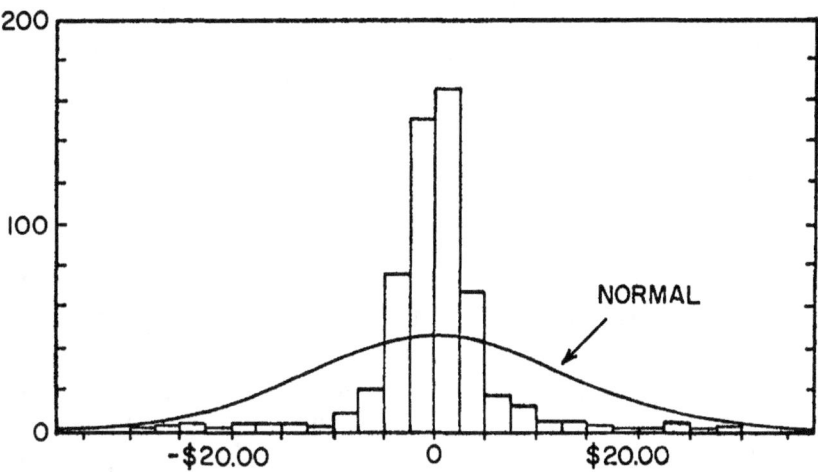

Figure 25. Probability of the wool price distribution (differences between monthly prices, during 1890-1937). The normal distribution shown is the one that would correspond to the same standard deviation. Source: Figure 1 from the paper by Benoît Mandelbrot.

In an analogous way, we could ask ourselves about climate and where it rains on Earth. Where on the surface of the Earth is the center of the rainfall (average value)? Where does it rain "in average"? And we all know that this is meaningless, the "surface" (in 2 dimensions, ignoring the 3rd dimension) of the Earth has no center, there is no mean value.

There is no area where rainfall is concentrated. Something like: "Z kilometers around point XY on the surface of the Earth" (which is equivalent to volatility with respect to the average value of the price), does not make sense.

Another way to look at it, in an extreme case, is to imagine a price distribution between zero and infinity in which any price is equally possible. In that case the mean value is not defined (what value is halfway between zero and infinity? Half infinite? This is absurd). And it also makes no sense to calculate the volatility of such a price distribution.

In practice what happens is that, if prices follow a normal distribution, when taking into account the price of a new day, the mean value and volatility converge to the representative values of the distribution.

However, if prices follow other distributions, when taking into account the price of a new day, the average value and/or volatility can make huge jumps. They may not converge to any representative value.

Cotton prices are quite random, it is true, but much more wildly random than Bachelier or Osborne had imagined.

The cotton market was the first place where Mandelbrot found evidence of stable Lévy distributions. But if cotton prices varied wildly, why would other markets be any different? Mandelbrot studied other commodities, stocks, bonds.... And in all cases he found the same pattern: The alphas associated with these markets were less than 2. That meant that the random walk theories and the normal distributions of Bachelier and Osborne were poor approximations to reality.

From a practical point of view, this forces a decision. We can continue to use the normal distributions of Bachelier and Osborne, because their mathematics is well known and relatively simple, and although it is a poor approximation, depending on the case it may be acceptable. Or we can use Mandelbrot's fat-tailed distributions, which are much more realistic, but devilishly complex.

These ideas of fat tails and "wild randomness" processes prompted Nassim Taleb to write his book The Black Swan, as he understood that the global financial sector chose to describe reality using the "affordable but inaccurate" model (Bachelier, Osborne) instead of using the "realistic but difficult" model (Mandelbrot). And that led to mispricing of financial assets, a fundamental part of the Great Financial Crisis of 2008-2009 (see for example CDOs — Collateralized Debt Obligations —, and its subset of MBS — Mortgage-Backed Securities —).

It is now generally accepted that stock asset returns exhibit distributions that are fat tailed, but also that they are tractable. Usually we do not find mathematical extremes such as infinite variability, and therefore relatively "simple" models of normal distributions are generally acceptable approximations.

2.4.4. Conclusions

These studies confirmed Mandelbrot's basic thesis, namely that log-normal distributions are insufficient to condense the statistical properties of markets. The rates of return exhibit fat tails.

We could use normal distributions for simplicity, as a first approximation. But the reality is more complex. This applies directly to Modern Portfolio Theory (as we saw in Section 2.2), which was developed assuming normal distributions.

Investors should be careful with the prices of options and other financial derivatives. In principle, their prices are calculated using the Black-Scholes-Merton model[21], which implicitly assumes normal distributions. Thus, it is possible to earn for a long time a little every day, until a wild random event comes along in which everything is lost.

Certainly, the best thing that retail investors can do is to avoid being in a situation where "wild randomness" can negatively affect them.

2.5. Asset Valuation

2.5.1. Paper

Title   Capital Asset Prices: A Theory of Market Equilibrium Under Conditions of Risk

Author   William Forsyth Sharpe

Publication   The Journal of Finance, edited by The American Finance Association, Volume 19, Number 3, pages 425-442, September 1964.[22]

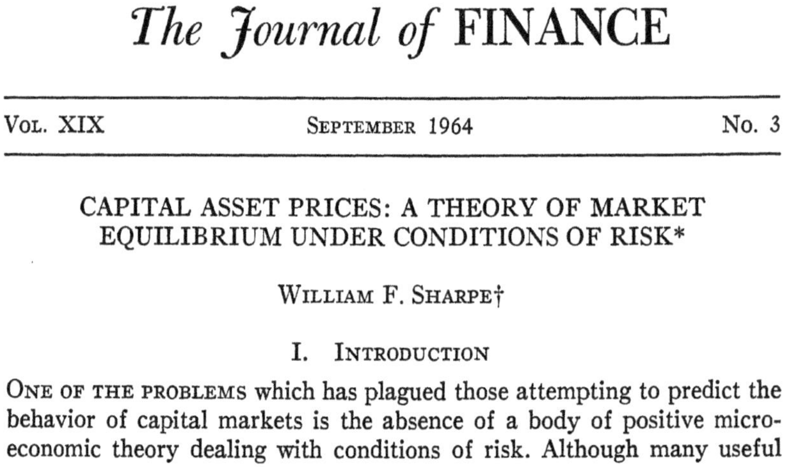

The Journal of FINANCE

Vol. XIX   September 1964   No. 3

CAPITAL ASSET PRICES: A THEORY OF MARKET EQUILIBRIUM UNDER CONDITIONS OF RISK*

WILLIAM F. SHARPE†

I. INTRODUCTION

ONE OF THE PROBLEMS which has plagued those attempting to predict the behavior of capital markets is the absence of a body of positive microeconomic theory dealing with conditions of risk. Although many useful

Figure 26. First lines of William F. Sharpe's paper "Capital Asset Prices: A Theory of Market Equilibrium Under Conditions of Risk" (1964).

2.5.2. Author

William Forsyth Sharpe (1934-) is an American economist.

He began his studies at the University of California, Berkeley, in medicine. But after the first year he switched to business administration at the University of California, Los Angeles (UCLA).

After college he went to work as a researcher at the RAND Corporation. There he started his PhD, supervised by Armen Alchian, an American economist of Armenian origin.

At the RAND Corporation he met Harry Markowitz, the creator of Portfolio Theory (see Section 2.2), with whom he had long conversations on the subject, and from that mutual relationship many ideas emerged.

In 1961 he completed his PhD on asset pricing.

After completing his PhD he went to work to the University of Washington, afterwards to the University of California, Irvine campus, and finally to Stanford University.

In addition to teaching at the university, he provided consulting services to financial firms such as Merrill Lynch and Wells Fargo. And in collaboration with the Frank Russell Company (a financial firm known among other things for its Russell indexes) he founded Sharpe-Russell Research, a firm that provided portfolio asset allocation advice to pension funds and university endowments.

He also co-founded Financial Engines, which now has more than 200 employees.

He was awarded the Nobel Prize in Economics in 1990 for his work on the Capital Asset Pricing Model (CAPM), although he also made many other developments in finance, such as the creation of the "Sharpe Ratio".

William F. Sharpe is president of the American Finance Association. And he is also Doctor Honoris Causa from several universities.

2.5.3. Content

At the RAND Corporation he authored the paper, in 1962, and sent it to the Journal of Finance. But surprisingly it was rejected as an irrelevant topic. Fortunately he persisted, sent it again, and it was finally accepted and published in 1964.

William Sharpe was not the only person who discovered the CAPM. There were also other people who came to similar conclusions during those same years, such as Jack Treynor and John Lintner.[23]

The research of William Sharpe gave rise to the Capital Asset Pricing Model (CAPM). The theory of the CAPM is based on the earlier work of Harry Markowitz. The model allows the performance of a portfolio to be judged by the amount of risk inherent in those investments, and helps managers decide when the potential return is worth the investment risks.

The basic idea of the model focuses on assigning a price to risk. In this context, risk refers to uncertainty or price volatility. There are certain types of assets, for example US Treasury bonds, that are considered "risk free" (because there is reasonable certainty that the debt will be repaid, and its price is not volatile). And despite being risk free, they do generate some return.

However, most investments involve risk (uncertainty, price volatility).

The CAPM model shows that it does not make sense to invest in a risky asset unless a higher return can be expected as a reward.

This extra return that risky assets have, over and above the return on the Risk Free Asset, is the so-called "risk premium".

The CAPM is a model that allows to relate risk and return, through a cost-benefit analysis of the risk premium.

2.5.3.1. Two Assets to Master Them All

The CAPM model justifies that stock market investments have two fundamental characteristics:

- the "expected return" (which may not be met in reality), and
- the "risk" (usually indicated by the Greek letter "beta").

According to the CAPM, every investment can be decomposed into only two assets (see Figure 27):

1. The "Risk Free Asset" (short-term government debt), which provides a small return in exchange for having no risk (beta=0).
2. The "market", with its "expected return" and with the "market risk" (also called "non-diversifiable risk", beta=1).

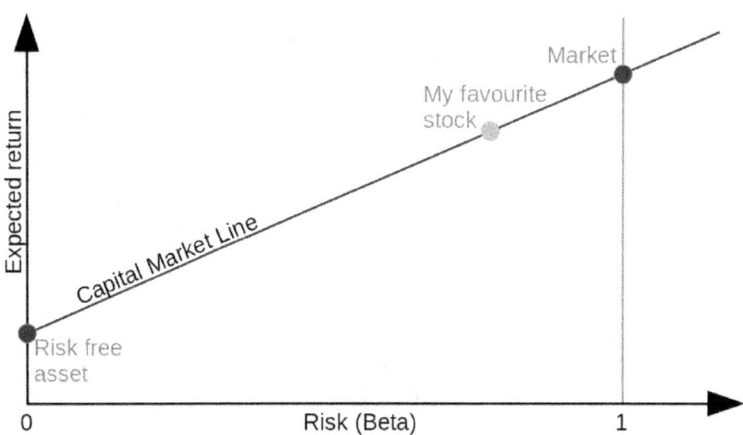

Figure 27. Investment in any individual company can be made synthetically by investing in a combination of two assets: The Risk Free Asset and the market aggregate. This way, we get the same expected return and market volatility, but without the specific risk of that stock.

According to the Figure 27, individual stocks are not worth investing in, because their expected return and their risk/volatility are related. Applying the laws of proportionality, we can argue that the return and volatility of "my favorite company" can be obtained (for example) by investing 75% in the market and 25% in the Risk Free Asset.

An investor, when investing in riskier assets wants to receive a higher return. This proportionality is indicated by the "Capital Market Line". Ideally, all companies are on this line placed according to their volatility relative to the market (beta, horizontal axis) and their expected return (vertical axis).

Here the market is considered to be efficient, because if there were an asset that provided an expected return **above** that corresponding to its risk, investors would buy it, selling opposite assets (which provide expected returns **below** that corresponding to their risk). In this way, by supply and demand, the price of assets will adjust to the Capital Market Line.

2.5.3.2. Connection to the Efficient Frontier

As we already saw in Section 2.2 on Portfolio Theory, not all possible portfolios are reasonable. It only makes sense to invest in those that are part of the Efficient Frontier, because any other portfolio has a worse combination of return and volatility.

And now we can connect the Efficient Frontier with the CAPM. Notice the Figure 28, which is a reinterpretation of the Figure 27.

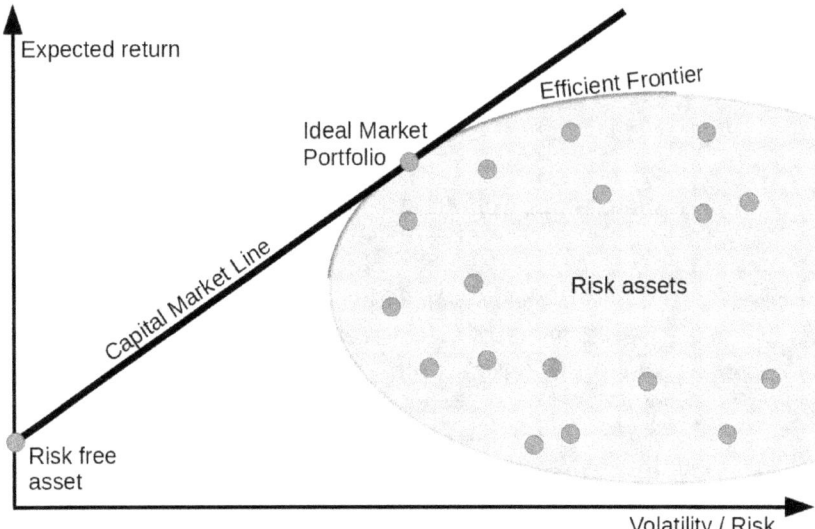

Figure 28. The connection between Modern Portfolio Theory and the CAPM.

Among all the portfolios that represent the risky asset market, only the Ideal Market Portfolio is worth considering. It is the portfolio located where the Capital Market Line meets the Efficient Frontier, the tangent point. Not only because it is a portfolio with a particularly good return/risk ratio, but also because of its effect when combined in a portfolio with the Risk Free Asset.

Any portfolio we can construct is either exactly on the Capital Market Line, or to the right of it. And therefore, for a given return, that portfolio would have higher volatility than the corresponding portfolio on the Capital Market Line (this is a similar argument to the Figure 14).

Bottom line, rational investors only invest in two assets, depending on their need for return/risk: The Ideal Market Portfolio, and the Risk Free Asset, as indicated in the Figure 29.

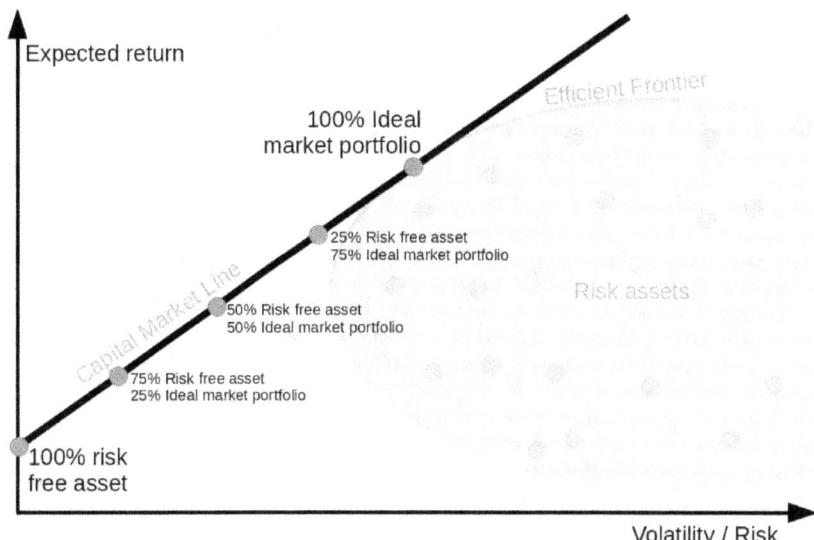

Figure 29. A rational investor only invests in two assets: the Risk Free Asset and in a portfolio representative of the risky asset market. The weights of one and the other depend on the desired return/risk ratio.

Since the Risk Free Asset has no volatility, its correlation with the Market Portfolio is zero, and therefore the combination of the two is a line, the Capital Market Line. This is deduced from the mathematical formula. In other words, when combining in a portfolio two unique assets such as the Risk Free Asset and the Market Portfolio, then the Efficient Frontier of the Portfolio Theory becomes the Capital Market Line. The curve becomes a straight line.

By including the Risk Free Asset, the CAPM model improves on Markowitz's Portfolio Theory, as it allows for higher expected returns for the same risk levels for all Efficient Frontier portfolios. Except for the market portfolio, which is the portfolio that belongs to both the Efficient Frontier and the Capital Market Line.

2.5.3.3. Systematic Risk vs. Specific Risk

Not all risks (volatility) are the same. We can separate the risk of a portfolio into two parts:

- Systematic Risk: This is the volatility of the market as a whole, the volatility of the IBEX if investing only in Spain, or the volatility of the MSCI World if investing globally.

- Specific Risk: This is the volatility added by the assets themselves (the risk of this or that particular company).

Note that when including more assets in the portfolio (see Figure 30), in the case that these assets are not correlated, we can reduce the volatility of the entire portfolio (the total risk).

This reduces the specific risks (of a particular company, an economic sector, a country, etc.), which are the risks that can be eliminated with diversification. However, volatility cannot be completely eliminated, because the Systematic Risk always remains.

And the important thing is that, according to the CAPM model, on average the market only rewards investors for bearing Systematic Risk (the market risk).

It is concluded from this reasoning that diversification should be maximized, because it reduces volatility and does not affect the expected return.

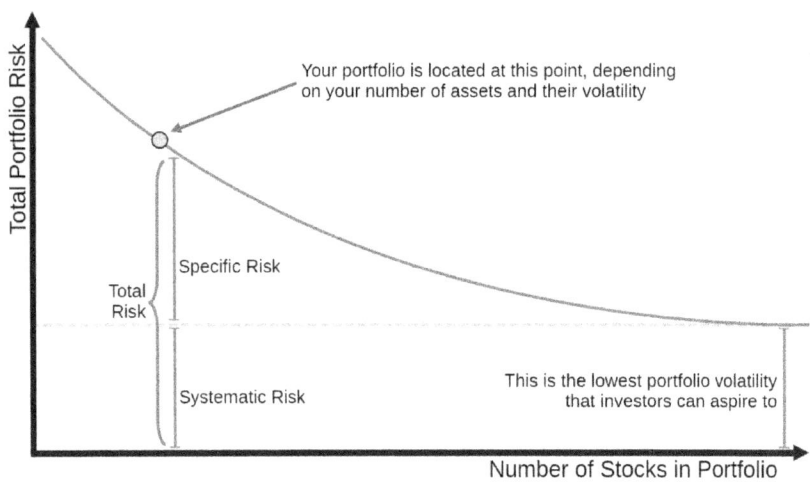

Figure 30. The more assets in the portfolio, the better, because the volatility of the portfolio as a whole will be lower.

2.5.3.4. Portfolio Choice

Once we know that the best portfolios are those on the Capital Market Line, we simply have to choose the best portfolio, the point that represents the most appropriate portfolio.

To do this, the theory goes, you have to find the best possible combination of expected return and risk. This is done using the "indifference curves".

The "indifference curves" are those lines on the Figure 31, which define portfolios with return/risk, for which the investor feels an equal interest. He does not care about one portfolio or another, as long as they are on the same curve. Each investor will have different curves, depending on the risk he can accept and the return he wants to obtain. They are personal.

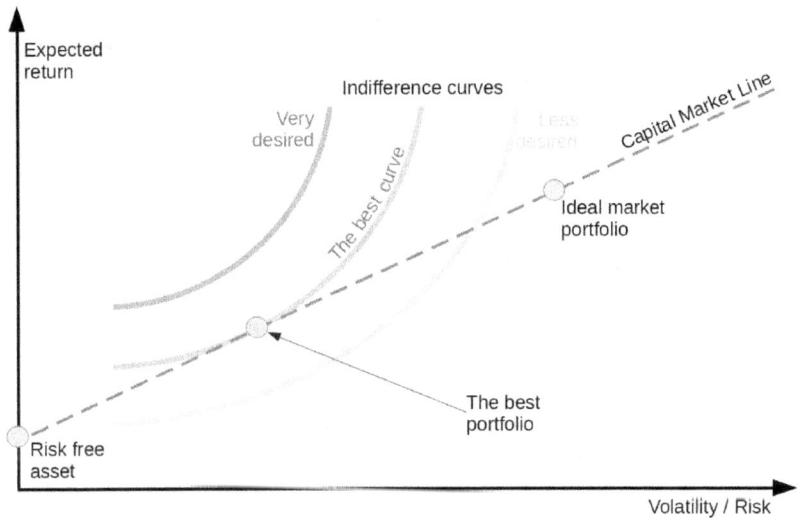

Figure 31. The most appropriate portfolio for an investor is the one that belongs to the indifference curve that touches the Capital Market Line in a single point, the best portfolio.

They are curves, because towards the right zone, towards the higher risk zone, the investor will want to be rewarded with higher returns, and that is why the "indifference curves" become more vertical in the right zone.

The upper left zone (high return and low risk) is "highly desired" by the investor. But the indifference curve that is "very desired" does not cut through the Capital Market Line at any point, so it is not valid.

There is also the "less desired" line, which cuts the Capital Market Line at two points. Those portfolios might work, but we can aim for a better portfolio.

The best indifference curve is the one that touches the Capital Market Line at a single point. And that point is the best portfolio, the one with the best combination of expected return and risk.

Different investors will have different views regarding the return and risk they can accept. As a result, their indifference curves will differ. Thus, although the best portfolio depends on each investor, all portfolios are always part of the Capital Market Line.

2.5.4. Conclusions

It is not worth buying individual stocks. By buying one asset that represents the market in aggregate, and another with the Risk Free Asset, we will get the return/risk ratio we want. And thus we avoid the possibility of the company going bankrupt and losing the investment.

Note that these steps:

- first choose the investor's return/risk level, and
- second define the portfolio with only two assets (Risk Free Asset, and the asset that represents the market),

is the usual procedure followed by the academia, financial advisors, robo-advisors, and the Bogleheads© community.

2.6. Efficient Market Hypothesis

2.6.1. Paper

Title	The Behavior of Stock-Market Prices
Author	Eugene Francis Fama
Publication	The Journal of Business, edited by The University of Chicago Press, volume 38, pages 34-105, January 1965.[24]

> THE BEHAVIOR OF STOCK-MARKET PRICES*
>
> EUGENE F. FAMA†
>
> I. INTRODUCTION
>
> FOR many years the following question has been a source of continuing controversy in both academic and business circles: To what extent can the past history of a common stock's price be used to make meaningful predictions concerning the future price of the stock? Answers to this question have been provided on the one hand by the various chartist theories and on the other hand by the theory of random walks.
>
> Although there are many different havior will tend to recur in the future. Thus, if through careful analysis of price charts one develops an understanding of these "patterns," this can be used to predict the future behavior of prices and in this way increase expected gains.¹
>
> By contrast the theory of random walks says that the future path of the price level of a security is no more predictable than the path of a series of cumulated random numbers. In statistical terms the theory says that successive price changes are independent, identical-

Figure 32. First lines of Eugene Fama's paper "Behavior of Stock-Market Prices" (1965).

2.6.2. Author

Eugene Francis Fama (1939-) is an American economist known for his work on Portfolio Theory, Asset Pricing, and the Efficient Market Hypothesis.

He was awarded the Nobel Prize in Economics in 2013[25], along with Robert J. Shiller (who we will discuss in Section 2.12) and Lars Peter Hansen. He also received the Deutsche Bank Prize in Financial Economics) in 2005, for the development of the concept of market efficiency.[26] He is considered the "father of modern finance" because his works have served to build the foundations of this branch of economics.

He initially studied a degree in Romance languages at Tufts University (Boston).

He subsequently completed an MBA and a PhD at the University of Chicago Business School (now renamed the Booth School of Business). His thesis supervisors were Merton Miller (Nobel Prize in economics in 1990[27] and Harry V. Roberts.

His doctoral dissertation was published as a paper, and it is what we discuss here, the 72 pages of "The Behavior of Stock-Market Prices".

2.6.3. Content

The fundamental idea is that market prices always reflect the real value of that which is traded, because they incorporate all available information. And since all the information is already available, it is not possible to generate alpha, it is not possible to generate return above the market.

Implicitly, the idea of Efficient Markets had been around in the academic community for some time. But it was Eugene Fama, in particular with his 1965 paper, who defined it, and it has therefore remained for posterity associated with his name.

As an example that shows how this topic was being discussed at that time, at congresses and in coffee shop talks, Eugene Fama thanks Benoît Mandelbrot for the conversations they had:

> Many of the ideas in this paper arose out of the work of Benoît Mandelbrot of the IBM Watson Research Center. I have profited not only from the written work of Dr. Mandelbrot but also from many invaluable discussion sessions.

— Eugene Fama, "The Behavior of Stock-Market Prices"

And he cites, through references, many previous authors, such as Louis Bachelier (Section 2.1), the book "The Random Character of Stock Market Prices" (shown in the Figure 8), Harry Markowitz (Section 2.2), M. F.M. Osborne (Section 2.3), Benoît Mandelbrot (Section 2.4), and others.

In the paper he does not use the term "Efficient Market Hypothesis", but he wrote:

> [...] a situation where successive price changes are independent is consistent with the existence of an "efficient" market for securities, that is, a market where, given the available information, actual prices at every point in time represent very good estimates of intrinsic values.
>
> — Eugene Fama, "The Behavior of Stock-Market Prices"

The paper discusses price distributions (as Louis Bachelier and M.F.M. Osborne had done earlier), and the existence or not of mean values and standard deviations. It shows that prices do not follow normal distributions, that there are fat tails, as already indicated by Benoît Mandelbrot.

2.6.3.1. How Efficiency is Achieved

The paper describes the random walk theory (with a quite detailed mathematical description), and makes two separate hypotheses:

1. Changes in successive prices are independent.
2. Prices change according to a probability distribution.

There is an intrinsic value for each asset, which depends on a company's future revenue projections. These political and economic factors affect the company in question, and at the same time also affect other companies.

However, market values, prices, do not necessarily have to coincide with intrinsic values. The difference can be called "noise".

Eugene Fama sees no problem in the fact that the price follows a random walk, and that at the same time the price has a specific intrinsic value.

Intrinsic values are unknown. On the one hand because of the complexity of the world, on the other hand because people may have different opinions and disagree, and furthermore because these intrinsic values vary as news arrive.

Any variation due to a new development, a change in the directive, a new tax, an increase in production... any real or anticipated change modifies the intrinsic value.

In principle, one would think that if new information about a company is independent, and if in addition any source of uncertainty is independent, one would expect that changes in prices would also be independent.

But this is a relatively extreme assumption. There is no reason to assume that estimates of intrinsic values are independent of each other.

For example: The opinion of some individuals or institutions may be highly valued by most investors. That is, their decisions may induce others to change their opinions about the value of a given company.

And there is also no reason to assume that news about a company comes to us independently. Whatever the source of information, as a practical matter we know that good news usually follows good news; and that when there are bad news, it usually comes one after the other.

For these reasons, price changes can be related to each other.

But although there may be dependencies in price generation, as discussed above, there are mechanisms in the market that make price changes independent, as required by the Efficient Market Hypothesis.

There could be sophisticated actors in the market. Sophisticated for two reasons:

1. Some players can be very good at predicting the emergence of new information and estimating its accounting effect on the intrinsic values of companies. These are fundamental analysts.
2. Other players can be very good at studying the statistical behavior of asset prices, and their evolution over time. These are technical analysts.

Let us suppose now that the "noise" in prices is not independent. That the prices of one day depend on the prices of previous days. For example, when a group of people jointly believe that a stock is cheap or expensive, they somehow attract other people to believe the same.

This dependence necessarily generates "bubbles" in the price series. That is, periods of time when the price goes far above or far below its intrinsic value.

But if there are sophisticated players in the market, they can burst the bubbles before they grow too large. They will realize that prices have moved away from intrinsic values, from book values. They will then compare the public price and the intrinsic value they know, and decide to buy if it is cheap, or sell if it is expensive. Forcing a price movement towards its intrinsic value. And thanks to these operations by fundamental analysts, prices will converge to their intrinsic value.

However, in an uncertain world, even sophisticated players like fundamental analysts may not be able to estimate intrinsic values.

This does not mean that we have to accept the existence of bubbles. Their effectiveness in eliminating price dependencies can be reinforced by another mechanism.

Technical analysts can see that the price separates from its intrinsic value with a given trend. They will buy or sell the asset, benefiting from their knowledge to enrich themselves, and as a side effect eliminate the false trend. Even if their knowledge of intrinsic value is vague, as long as they have resources they will do their best to get rich thanks to the wrong price.

In this way, even if there are dependencies in the generation of new information, or inconsistent information, sophisticated players will realize this and exploit it to their advantage. Thus, their operations will tend to make price changes independent, which we can simply call "noise".

And when these sophisticated players react, they sometimes overreact. For example, if the initial price was expensive relative to the intrinsic value, the price may become lower than the intrinsic value. Or vice versa if the initial price was cheap relative to the intrinsic value. On the other hand, the reaction may also fail to converge the price to the intrinsic value. Sometimes it does, sometimes it does not. You do not know, it is noise.

And even if it converges, it will do so with a delay that will not always be the same. That is more noise.

In short, the market can behave as if the price variation were independent, although the initial processes (news, actors in coalition) are not independent.

2.6.3.2. Metaphor of the Twenty Dollar Bill

There is a metaphor, not named in the paper but directly related, that gives an idea of the Efficient Market Hypothesis. It is told by Larry Swedroe (another key person in the retail investor community, with a university degree in finance, MBA, author of 17 books, and one of the most famous Bogleheads©. The story goes like this:[28]

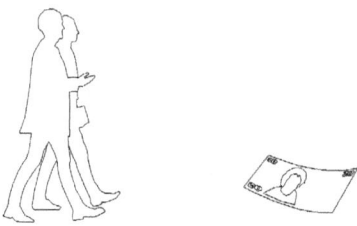

> An economist passionate about the Efficient Market Hypothesis was walking down the street with a friend. The friend stops and says:
>
> — Look, there is a $20 bill on the ground.
>
> The economist turns to his friend and says:
>
> — It can't be. If there were a $20 bill on the ground, someone would have already picked it up.

This joke, implying that the Efficient Market Hypothesis ignores opportunities to get rich, is told by those who believe that markets are inefficient and that investors can therefore outperform the market by taking advantage of mispricing. It us absurd to leave that bill on the floor, isn't it? It is the equivalent of ignoring a stock whose price is undervalued.

Actually, this is a misleading analogy of the Efficient Market Hypothesis. The following version is much more reasonable:

> An economist passionate about the Efficient Market Hypothesis was walking down the street with a friend. The friend stops and says:
>
> — Look, there is a $20 bill on the ground.
>
> The economist turns to his friend and says:

—Wow, it must be our lucky day! You'd better pick it up quick because the market is so efficient that it won't be there for long. Finding a $20 bill lying around happens so infrequently that it would be foolish to spend our time searching for more of them. Certainly, after assigning a value to the time spent in the effort, an "investment" in trying to find money lying on the street just waiting to be picked up would be a poor one. I am certainly not aware of anyone who has achieved their wealth by 'mining' beaches with metal detectors.

When he had finished speaking, they both looked down at the floor and the $20 bill was gone!

This second story is much more realistic. We should not expect inefficiencies in the market, because as soon as they are detected, sophisticated market participants correct them as soon as possible, earning free money. And in doing so, inefficiencies disappear.

The Efficient Market Hypothesis is exceptional because its greatest advocates are not academics with their theories, but its detractors (those who look for inefficiencies) because their actions make markets efficient.

2.6.3.3. Subsequent Summary Paper.

SESSION TOPIC: STOCK MARKET PRICE BEHAVIOR

SESSION CHAIRMAN: BURTON G. MALKIEL

EFFICIENT CAPITAL MARKETS: A REVIEW OF
THEORY AND EMPIRICAL WORK*

EUGENE F. FAMA**

I. INTRODUCTION

THE PRIMARY ROLE of the capital market is allocation of ownership of the economy's capital stock. In general terms, the ideal is a market in which prices provide accurate signals for resource allocation: that is, a market in which firms can make production-investment decisions, and investors can choose among the securities that represent ownership of firms' activities under the assumption that security prices at any time "fully reflect" all available information. A market in which prices always "fully reflect" available information is called "efficient."

Figure 33. First lines of Eugene Fama's paper "Efficient Capital Markets: A Review of Theory and Empirical Work" (1970).

This other paper (see the Figure 33) is a review, a paper providing an overview of the state of knowledge on the subject at that time.

It was presented at the "Annual Meeting of the American Finance Association", with Burton G. Malkiel (the author of the famous book "A Random Walk Down Wall Street") being the chairman during that session of the conference. This paper describes the theory and provides observed data to justify it.

On page 31, Eugene Fama echoes a study about the return of mutual funds in the US during the 10-year period between 1955 and 1964 (by Michael Jensen in 1968). The study compares the return of these funds with the S&P 500 index.

This study is worth being commented here. It was done 60 years ago, with fund return data from 60 to 70 years ago, and shows the same results that similar studies find obtain today.

The general question it asks is: Do fund managers have some skill that makes them get returns above the market? And also another question that may be easier to answer: Can managers earn extra returns that compensate for their costs (purchase, management, holding, etc.), given their return/risk ratio?

The return/risk ratio is important because an investor can choose what return he expects to receive and what risk he wants to take by simply combining two types of assets (we discussed in in the Section 2.5 about the CAPM):

1. The risk free asset (i.e., short-term quality government bonds).
2. The market (in this case, the S&P 500).

The answer is that 89 of the 115 mutual funds analyzed (77%) obtained return/risk ratios worse than the market. And in addition, the aggregate return of the funds after 10 years was -14.6% worse than the market.

For both reasons, an investor would have obtained better returns by simply investing in the market.

But going a step further, it can be argued that the "front-end charge" (a one-time charge applied at the time of initial purchase of the fund) is a reward to the seller, who has to receive his salary from this item.

Since this charge is not actually invested, someone might say that it should not be subtracted from the return on the funds. Would that make any difference?

No. Even ignoring this fee, the return of the funds is not reasonable. In this case, 72 out of 115 the funds (63%) earned return/risk ratios worse than the market, and their average return after 10 years was -8.9% worse than the market.

It does not matter how you measure it, investors do always better if they invest directly in the market.

The Efficient Market Hypothesis states that financial markets are efficient in processing and reflecting all available information, making it impossible for investors to systematically outperform the market based on information already known to the public. Eugene Fama noted that efficiency had three forms:

1. **Weak form**: In this form, market prices reflect all past stock market information, such as historical prices and trading volumes. According to this form, **Technical Analysis** (the study of past price and volume data) cannot systematically generate above market returns because this information is already reflected in stock prices.

2. **Semi-strong form**: This idea states that all publicly available information, including recent news (of a company, or its competitor, or the sector, etc.) and past trading data, is fully reflected in stock prices. Consequently, in addition to Technical Analysis, **Fundamental Analysis** (the study of financial statements and economic factors) also cannot systematically beat the market, because all available information is already incorporated into prices.

3. **Strong form**: The most extreme version of the Efficient Market Hypothesis holds that all information, public and private, is fully reflected in stock prices. In other words, no individual or group possesses information that can systematically produce superior returns. This form of efficiency implies that (in addition to Technical Analysis and Fundamental Analysis) trading on **insider information** would be useless, since this information would also already be reflected in stock prices.

The three levels of market efficiency are cumulative: the weak hypothesis is included in the semi-strong hypothesis, and both in turn are included in the strong hypothesis.

The three levels can be summarized as prices reflect all past information (weak form), current public information (semi-strong form), and current private information (strong form).

2.6.3.4. Efficient Markets vs. Invisible Hand

The validity of the Efficient Market Hypothesis could be considered from two complementary points of view, using the metaphor of the Invisible Hand of Adam Smith (1723-1790):

- A retail investor (or a consumer).
- An active fund manager (or an entrepreneur).

For a retail investor, with limited resources and skills, the market is indistinguishable from an Efficient Market. And this can be compared to Adam Smith's Invisible Hand metaphor. That is, we consumers go out in the street and if we are thirsty we can go into a bar and have a drink. If we want to get a haircut, we can go to a hairdresser. And if our car is broken down, we can go to a garage.

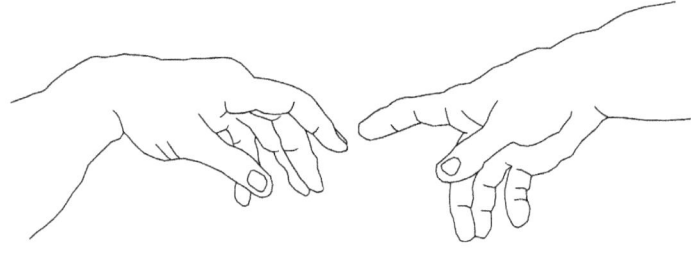

But we probably don't know how to run a bar, nor are we hairdressers or mechanics. Yet we can avoid the "inefficiency" of doing it ourselves, of fermenting our own beer, cutting our own hair, or repairing our own car; simply by trusting professionals.

Someone might criticize that it is foolish to live thinking that we will find a bar, a hairdresser, or a mechanic's shop when we need one. But in practice we know that it is the case, we can trust that there will always be a professional to provide the service. That the Adam Smith's Invisible Hand will be there to solve our need.

In the same way, retail investors do not have to worry about the accounting of companies, the trend of their prices, nor their news in the press. The market simply exists and asset prices make sense. If the price of an asset were clearly incorrect, some market players would step in to buy and sell, on credit if necessary, until the discrepancy is corrected.

Similarly, in a free market, if there were demand in the neighborhood for a barber shop, someone would open a barber shop, providing the service and receiving income in return. As many hairdressing salons as it takes to satisfy the demand, until the inefficiency disappears and the market returns to efficiency. All this is especially valid for an indexed investor, who aspires to receive the right return for the risk taken (as we saw in the Section 2.5 on the CAPM model).

Conversely, if the retail investor buys and sells stocks according to trends or accounting reports, then he is acting as an active manager, and therefore competes with the other active managers. The return he gets on his investment will depend on what he manages to get by competing with the other professionals.

It is the same as if a person opens a business, such as a bar, where the result he gets will depend on how good he is at satisfying the needs of his customers, in competition with the other bars in the area.

Unlike a retail investor, a fund manager cannot accept that the market is efficient, because he is dedicated precisely to finding inefficiencies and making a profit from them. Similarly, an entrepreneur starts a business in the hope of making a profit. How can the market be efficient? The entrepreneur has to set up the business and provide the service, work to be able to get paid, his decisions have a direct impact on his income.

Thus, looking for the needs of society, entrepreneurs create businesses that provide us with services, creating a rich society. And in the same way, investment fund managers search inefficiencies in the market, and with their work they take advantage of them, making large profits, and ultimately generating an Efficient Market from the retail investors' perspective.

In short, people have this dual facet to our lives. In some ways we are consumers (we demand goods and services) and in other ways we are producers (in our work, or setting up a business). Being a producer is hard, because you have to satisfy the needs of the customer or the boss. It is much easier to be a consumer, because when the market works, it is the one who chooses. So the goal is to be a consumer in the aspects of our life in which we do not have good skills, and to be a producer only in what we are better at than others, in our work.

This ties in with the economic concept of "Comparative Advantage" by David Ricardo (1772-1823): that people/companies/countries focus on producing the goods/services they generate with fewer resources than others.

2.6.3.5. Criticism

The Efficient Market Hypothesis is extraordinary because it has called into question how financial markets work, so it is normal that it has received a lot of criticism.

Most financial professionals (fund managers, etc.) consider the Efficient Market Hypothesis to be absurd, while the academic world defends it with papers and studies. Most notably, the evidence in its favor is so strong that the hypothesis has stood the test of time.

Critics give the following reasons about why markets may not be efficient:

1. behavioral biases: errors in judgment, in decision making, and in thinking when evaluating information.
2. Information asymmetry: when one person or group has more or better information than the rest.
3. Market Frictions: anything that interferes with market transactions, including transaction costs, taxes, regulation, and information failures.

A consequence of the hypothesis is that speculative bubbles cannot exist, because a bubble can only occur if the market price of something moves away from its real value. But anyone who remembers the dotcom boom back in 2000, or the real estate boom and the Great Financial Crisis of 2008, will argue that prices were irrational. In fact, a new field of finance, Behavioral Economics, has been developed to study how market participants are inefficient.

With respect to information asymmetry, one of the assumptions of the Efficient Market Hypothesis is that information is immediately distributed throughout the market. In 1965 this seemed ridiculous, but financial services firms soon realized that acting quickly brought them good returns. The sooner they spotted an anomaly and took advantage of it, the sooner they would make a profit. Today, brokers and market makers have gone so far as to connect their servers directly to the exchanges in order to reduce their trade execution times by fractions of a second. In this way, this inefficiency tends to disappear.

As for market frictions, they have been greatly reduced in recent decades. The existence of brokers offering "free" transactions is now normal, and information is transmitted quickly and in large quantities.

Academic papers show that insider trading does provide extraordinary returns. For this reason, in order to promote a level playing field for all players, insider trading is prohibited in developed markets. This makes us realize that markets are not efficient in their strong form. Eugene Fama himself comments in the paper that the strong form is not an "accurate representation of reality", but rather a "reference" for studies and comparison.

Another criticism of the Efficient Market Hypothesis is that certain valuation anomalies persist, even though the hypothesis says they should not. One of these persistent anomalies is that small firms tend to do better than large firms; another is that "value" stocks tend to do better than "growth" stocks.

In 1992, Fama and Kenneth French published a paper demonstrating that these anomalies were real and should be incorporated into financial valuation models. We will see this in Section 2.10 on investment factors.

The Efficient Market Hypothesis remains fundamental within financial theory today, and has profoundly influenced investment strategies, portfolio management, and the understanding of financial markets.

The fact that the weak form (Technical Analysis) does not earn returns above the market is well demonstrated by the data. In any case, great profits are made by "selling" Technical Analysis, not "implementing" it, but that is another matter.

2.6.4. Conclusions

If the Efficient Market Hypothesis is correct, we find ourselves in a situation equivalent to playing a card game in which all the players' cards are on the table, shown face up. In this way all players see all the cards, and since they all apply the same rules of the game, they can all estimate what is going to happen during the game.

The first conclusion of the Efficient Market Hypothesis is that the best investment is to invest in the whole market and as cheaply as possible. That is, index funds offer better returns (risk-adjusted, and after fees) than active investing.

This assumption implies that research and analysis is no better than picking stocks at random. As investors, the best we can accept is the market return. Chasing higher returns is mathematically similar to finding $20 bills lying on the ground.

However, despite the fact that markets are not always efficient, and despite the fact that prices sometimes move away from the real value of assets, the market efficiency hypothesis offers a way of understanding finance.

It is an idealization, like assuming in high school physics that there is no friction on a falling body due to the law of gravity. It is thanks to simplifications like this that problems can be solved, and applications created, that would otherwise be impossible.

These papers by Eugene Fama were instrumental in sparking the indexed inversion revolution. To this day there is still debate as to whether the Efficient Market Hypothesis is valid or not. Perhaps we should not get purist, because the conclusion (that index funds are better investment vehicles than active funds for retail investors and possibly also for institutional investors) continues to be confirmed every 6 months by both SPIVA (see Section 2.23) and Morningstar (see Section 2.24). And furthermore, this conclusion appears to hold even though the Efficient Markets Hypothesis may not be accurate (see Section 2.22).

2.7. The Flap of a Butterfly

2.7.1. Paper

Title	Predictability: Does the Flap of a Butterfly's Wings in Brazil Set off a Tornado in Texas?
Author	Edward Norton Lorenz
Publication	Presented to the "American Association for the Advancement of Science" on December 29, 1972.[29]

The Butterfly Effect

THE FOLLOWING is the text of a talk that I presented in a session devoted to the Global Atmospheric Research Program, at the 139th meeting of the American Association for the Advancement of Science, in Washington, D.C., on December 29, 1972, as prepared for press release. It was never published, and it is presented here in its original form.

Predictability: Does the Flap of a Butterfly's Wings in Brazil Set off a Tornado in Texas?

Lest I appear frivolous in even posing the title question, let alone suggesting that it might have an affirmative answer, let me try to place it in proper perspective by offering two propositions.

Figure 34. First lines of the text by Edward N. Lorenz.

2.7.2. Author

Edward Norton Lorenz (1917-2008) was born in the United States. He studied mathematics at the University at Dartmouth. He graduated in 1938 and then went to Harvard intending to pursue a doctorate.

There he completed a master's degree in mathematics, but then World War II began and he enlisted in the air force, where he worked as a weather forecaster. After the war he went to MIT, where he completed a PhD in meteorology. He remained on staff there until he retired.

He received multiple awards, including the Kyoto Prize in 1991 and the Lomonosov Medal in 2004.

2.7.3. Content

The author asks exactly this question:

> The question which really interests us is whether [...] two particular weather situations differing by as little as the immediate influence of a single butterfly will generally after sufficient time evolve into two situations differing by as much as the presence of a tornado. In more technical language, is the behavior of the atmosphere unstable with respect to perturbations of small amplitude?
>
> — Edward N. Lorenz, "Does the Flap of a Butterfly's Wings in Brazil Set off a Tornado in Texas?"

Exchange the expressions "weather situations", "butterfly", and "tornado"; for "stock markets", "news in the press", and "crisis"; and you will see the importance of this paper.

The author argues:

> How can we determine whether the atmosphere is unstable? The atmosphere is not a controlled laboratory experiment; if we disturb it and then observe what happens, we shall never know what would have happened if we had not disturbed it. Any claim that we can learn what would have happened by referring to the weather forecast would imply that the question whose answer we seek has already been answered in the negative.
>
> — Edward N. Lorenz, "Does the Flap of a Butterfly's Wings in Brazil Set off a Tornado in Texas?"

That is, the stock market is not an isolated experiment where all parameters are kept under control. It is full of unpredictable factors.

If we could make a claim as a result of an experiment, then we could argue that the market is not really unstable. But it is very difficult to make claims in the stock market, remember that it is customary to recognize that "we cannot predict the future" and that "past performance does not assure guarantee results".

Lorenz made a computer program to solve the equations of weather forecasting. He used one of the first existing computers, which allowed him to perform intensive numerical computation. Until then the calculation had been manual, and being able to use a computer allowed him to make cutting-edge research.

He would run the program, which took hours to finish, dump the results with a printer, and then come back to see the result.

One day he repeated the data processing. He executed the same program, and typed the same input parameters himself. However, the result of the program was very different. It had nothing to do with what he expected. What had happened? Lorenz tells his anecdote himself:

> At one point, I decided to repeat some of the calculations to examine what was happening in greater detail. I stopped the computer, typed in a line of numbers that I had printed out a while earlier, and set it running again.
>
> I went down the hall for a cup of coffee and returned after about an hour, during which time the computer had simulated about two months of weather.
>
> The numbers being printed were nothing like the old ones.
>
> I immediately suspected a weak vacuum tube or some other computer trouble, which was not uncommon, but before calling for service I decided to see just where the mistake had occurred, knowing that this could speed up the servicing process.
>
> Instead of a sudden break, I found that the new values at first repeated the old ones, but soon afterward differed by one and then several units in the last [decimal] place, and then began to

differ in the next to the last place, and then in the place before that. In fact, the differences more or less steadily doubled in size every four days or so, until all resemblance with the original output disappeared somewhere in the second month.

This was enough to tell me what had happened: the numbers that I had typed in were not the exact original numbers, but were the rounded-off values that had appeared in the original printout. The initial round-off errors were the culprits; they were steadily amplifying until they dominated the solution.

— Edward N. Lorenz, "The Essence of Chaos", U. Washington Press, 1993, page 134

Despite being a deterministic system, where given the initial conditions and equations we can predict the state at any future time, it turns out that the long-term future state ended up being unpredictable.

And this happens because we do not know the initial conditions with infinite precision, any tiny difference between measurement and reality causes a difference in the model results that increases until it has nothing to do with reality.

This topic had already been addressed by Lorenz in an earlier paper, which contained revolutionary ideas for its time (see the Figure 35).

Deterministic Nonperiodic Flow

EDWARD N. LORENZ

Massachusetts Institute of Technology

(Manuscript received 18 November 1962, in revised form 7 January 1963)

ABSTRACT

Finite systems of deterministic ordinary nonlinear differential equations may be designed to represent forced dissipative hydrodynamic flow. Solutions of these equations can be identified with trajectories in phase space. For those systems with bounded solutions, it is found that nonperiodic solutions are ordinarily unstable with respect to small modifications, so that slightly differing initial states can evolve into considerably different states. Systems with bounded solutions are shown to possess bounded numerical solutions.

A simple system representing cellular convection is solved numerically. All of the solutions are found to be unstable, and almost all of them are nonperiodic.

The feasibility of very-long-range weather prediction is examined in the light of these results.

Figure 35. Edward Lorenz's 1963 paper. It talks about weather forecasting, but we can extrapolate it to the stock market.[30] *Some of the text has been blurred to make it easier to be read.*

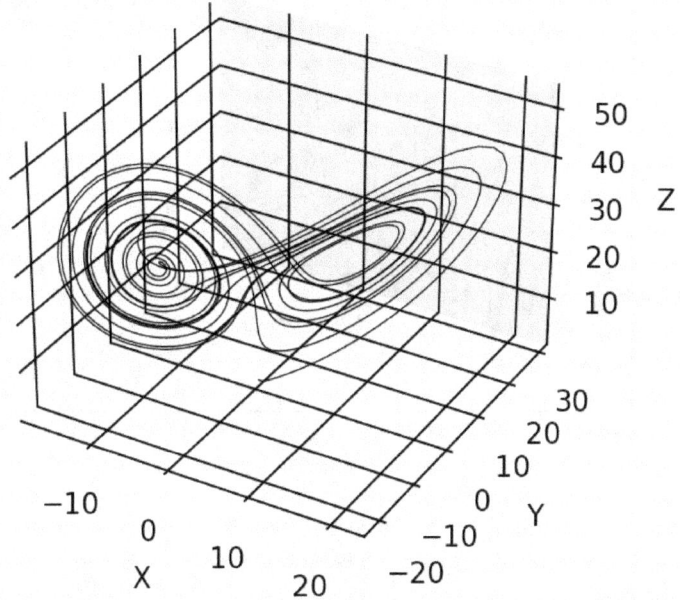

Figure 36. Lorenz attractor, a 3-dimensional figure.

One way to look at this initial value problem is with the so-called Lorenz Attractor. It is a mathematical equation in 3 dimensions, and the most usual is to present its results as in the Figure 36. There it is shown that the function is "orbiting" around two centers, one more to the left and the other more to the right, jumping from one to the other every now and then.

But we do not need now the full complexity of the Lorenz Attractor, just a single axis is enough for our purpose. For example, the Y-axis, shown in the Figure 37. This Y-axis could represent the price of a stock, the wind speed in Cape Canaveral, the heart rate of a person, or anything else.

The model is well known, and can be solved for two similar initial conditions. Suppose the value on the Y-axis is in one case 1.000 and in the other 1.001, just a thousandth of a millisecond difference, all else being equal.

In this case, for 9 seconds the difference is imperceptible. Both lines overlap each other.

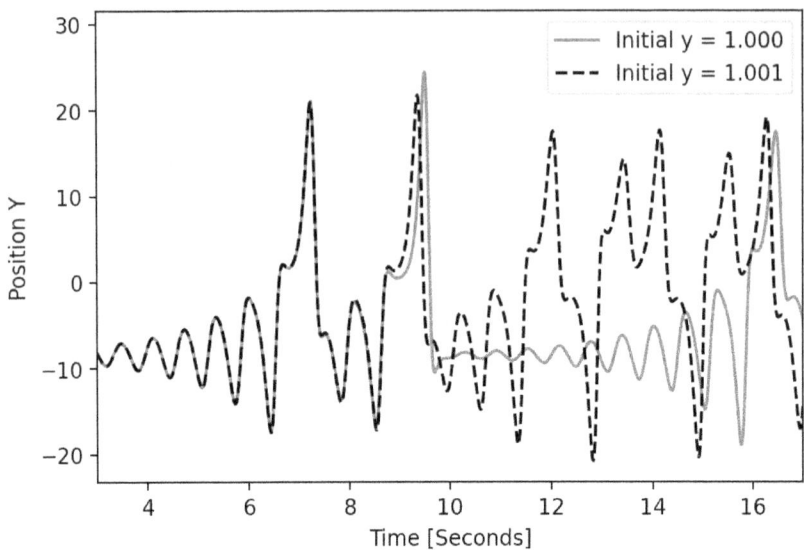

Figure 37. The behavior of the Lorenz equations on the Y-axis. Corresponds to the Figure 36. See text for explanation. It could be a stock price as a function of time.

Between seconds 9 and 10, the difference begins to show. In a way this is what one would want to expect: if the initial difference is a few percent, the final result will differ by another few percent. Proportional amounts.

However, from the 10th second on, the two results have nothing to do with each other. They are not comparable, they are not even proportional.

- The simulation with initial value Y=1.000 (solid gray line) shows regular and increasing oscillations,
- while the simulation with initial value Y=1.001 (black dashed line) presents very irregular oscillations.

This is what chaos is all about: two very similar initial conditions, perhaps a slight rounding of the last decimal place, give completely different results. And this is why neither weather forecasting nor stock market prices are predictable. No matter how deterministic the mathematics are (temperature, pressure... in the case of meteorology; book value, debts... in the case of stock market shares) the future cannot be known in detail.

This is what Lorenz called the "Deterministic Chaos". Even though the laws governing the system (the weather, the value of company shares) are deterministic, totally predictable, the result is chaotic because of initial inaccuracies.

Therefore, financial markets are complex systems, they have random components, and on top of that they have chaotic behavior, whereby small differences in the initial state (flapping of a butterfly) cause very different final situations (tornado). Stock market forecasts can only be accurate up to a certain point.

In addition, economic and financial systems are fundamentally different from those of the natural sciences, since the former are the result of people's interactions. This makes them also modify their attitude according to the conditions around them. This is why deterministic models are unlikely to provide accurate representations of the data.

Lorenz showed that complex chaotic systems are vulnerable to small changes, which can disturb a system away from equilibrium.

Periods of high uncertainty may not be caused solely by the internal dynamics of the system. External factors such as natural catastrophes, earthquakes or floods can also cause market volatility.

This is not an argument in favor of setting aside research because of the limitations of scientific knowledge. It is an argument in favor of being aware of the limitations of knowledge. After all, mankind has come a long way in its understanding of the world, let us hope that we continue further.

2.7.4. Conclusions

Any small difference in estimates of the initial state of the weather (or of the stock market), generates future states that are completely different to each other, like forecasting a tornado or not (or like predicting a financial crisis or not).

This is in line with Mandelbrot's "wild randomness" processes. There are limits to knowledge, we cannot predict the unpredictable.

These ideas of chaos can be applied to the study of the accounting status of a company. If you have done so yourself, surely you had a complex spreadsheet, which attempts to model in detail the future state of the company. The output of the spreadsheet may be the target price of the stock. However, small variations in any of the cells (interest rate, future revenue expectations, etc.) can cause huge changes in the target price. This is the chaos.

It is impossible to forecast the future, so it is better to follow a strategy that does not, such as Harry Markowitz's Portfolio Theory, as we saw in Section 2.2.

2.8. Challenge to Judgment

2.8.1. Paper

Title	Challenge to Judgment
Author	Paul Anthony Samuelson
Publication	The Journal of Portfolio Management, volume 1, series 1, fall 1974.[31]

Challenge to judgment

Perhaps there really are managers who can outperform the market consistently – logic would suggest that they exist. But they are remarkably well-hidden.

Paul A. Samuelson

Figure 38. First lines of the paper by Paul A. Samuelson.

2.8.2. Author

Paul Samuelson (1915-2009) was an American economist.

He applied profound mathematical developments, work for which he is considered one of the founders of modern economics, and was thus one of the most important economists of the 20th century.

He studied at the University of Chicago, just after the Great Depression. He obtained his doctorate at Harvard University. And then he went to MIT as a professor, where he spent the rest of his life. There he became Institute Professor, the highest level within the faculty council.

He was an economic advisor to presidents John F. Kennedy and Lyndon B. Johnson, and a consultant to the US Treasury.

He wrote for years a column in Newsweek magazine together with Milton Friedman, where each represented opposing ideas (Samuelson described himself as a "Cafeteria Keynesian").

He received the Nobel Prize in Economics in 1970[32], and the National Medal of Science (of the USA) in 1996.

2.8.3. Content

This paper is written in a provocative tone. It makes several blunt assertions, such as this:

> [...] the best money managers cannot be demonstrated to be able to deliver the goods of superior portfolio selection performance.
>
> Any jury that reviews the evidence, and there is a great deal of relevant evidence, must at least come out with the Scottish verdict: superior investment performance is unproved.
>
> — Paul Samuelson, "Challenge to Judgment", page 2

The reference to the "Scottish verdict" seems to refer to three possible outcomes of a trial: "conviction", "absolution", or "not proven". A verdict of "not proven" is not an acquittal, but a declaration that insufficient evidence has been presented to the court to obtain a conviction. Thus, Paul Samuelson emphasizes that there is no evidence that active managers provide superior returns.

He argues that outperforming the market is something to be treated with skepticism, because due to the very construction of the market, its average return is the average of investor returns.

He goes so far as to say that most portfolio managers are doing a useless job and should quit.

He suggests that endowments (the foundations of US universities, which invest their own funds) should create a portfolio that tracks the index S&P 500, at least to be able to compare their managers with it, and thus have an opinion of whether their fund managers are successful or not. This text was read by Jack Bogle, who was impressed, and took the baton to create such a benchmark portfolio, as we will discuss later in Section 2.16.

Samuelson gives two relevant arguments about claims made by fund managers.

First of all, about managers' effort "deserving" a reward (not for their results, but for their effort to get their results):

> [...] they simply assert that it stands to common sense that greater effort to get facts and greater acumen in analyzing those facts will pay off in better performance somehow measured.
>
> — Paul Samuelson, "Challenge to Judgment", page 5

And second, on the absence of irrefutable demonstrations:

> [...] they always claim they know a man, a bank, or a fund that does do better. Alas, anecdotes are not science.
>
> — Paul Samuelson, "Challenge to Judgment", page 5

It seems logical that thanks to hard-working, intelligent managers would be able to find stocks that outperform the market. After all, there is always someone who has outperformed the market in the recent past. But Paul Samuelson insists that this proves nothing because "anecdotes are not science".

Paul Samuelson finds no irrefutable evidence for the existence of active managers providing above-market returns:

> What is interesting is the empirical fact that it is virtually impossible for academic researchers with access to the published records to identify any member of the subset with "flair". This fact, though not an inevitable law, is a brute fact.
>
> The ball, as I have already noted, is in the court of those who doubt the random walk hypothesis (that stock prices change in a random, unpredictable manner in response to new information).
>
> They can dispose of the uncomfortable brute fact in the only way that any fact is disposed of — by producing brute evidence to the contrary.
>
> — Paul Samuelson, "Challenge to Judgment", page 7

Here Paul Samuelson's argument (the absence of incontestable arguments) is very similar to the aphorism said by Carl Sagan a few years later in the context of hypothetical extraterrestrial beings visiting Earth:

> Extraordinary claims require extraordinary evidence.
>
> — Carl Sagan, in his 1980 TV documentary Cosmos

At one point, instead of arguing about what to do to "make money", he jokes about what to do to "lose money". And for this, all you have to do is flip a coin, and buy or sell a stock depending on whether heads or tails came up on the coin. Pure chance. In this way the investor is simply transferring his wealth to his broker, via transaction costs, so that in the long term his hope is still to obtain the profitability of the market, but subtracting his enormous costs.

Paul Samuelson goes so far as to refer to Maxwell's Demon, which is an imaginary creature capable of violating the Second Law of Thermodynamics (the law that says that "the entropy — the disorder — of the universe tends to increase with time").

Maxwell's Demon is named after the Scottish physicist James Clerk Maxwell (1831-1879). Although it is a thought experiment, it makes sense to talk about it in this context.

Let us look at the Figure 39. The Maxwell's Demon controls a gate that separates two chambers, A and B. The Demon can open and close the gate at convenience, without doing any work.

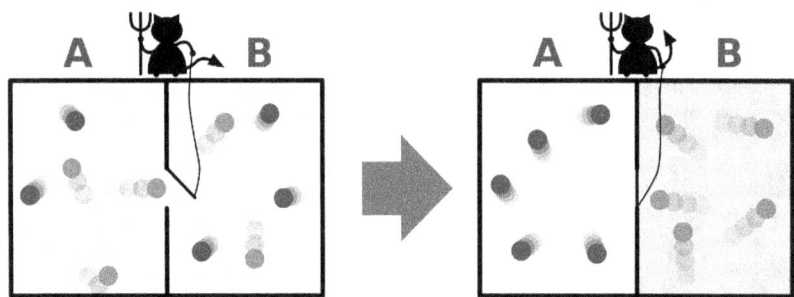

Figure 39. The Maxwell's Demon separating molecules in chamber A or B according to their velocity. It is a famous thought experiment in physics. Source: Wikipedia user Htkym, license CC 2.5.

Inside the chambers there are molecules of a gas. These molecules of gas move at different speeds, some faster and some slower, all mixed together.

The Demon can separate the molecules according to their speed. For example, in the left panel of the Figure 39 the Demon has opened the gate to let a fast molecule pass from A to B.

Later, in the right panel, the daemon closed the gate to prevent another fast molecule from passing back from B to A.

The outcome of this selection is that in chamber A there are only slow-moving molecules, and in chamber B there are only fast-moving molecules.

If this were possible, the Maxwell's Demon would have separated the molecules, ordering them, and thus decreasing the entropy of the universe. But then this Demon would be invalidating the Second Law of Thermodynamics ("disorder always increases"), and therefore its existence is impossible.

And what is the point of all this explanation? Paul Samuelson argues that the existence of fund managers (Maxwell's Demons) capable of discerning good companies (fast molecules) from bad ones (slow molecules), and capable of buying only good companies (managing the gate) is as impossible as denying the Second Law of Thermodynamics.

2.8.4. Conclusions

The history of index funds is often said to begin with Jack Bogle. But we could go one step further, and mark that initial moment when Paul Samuelson published this paper, in 1974.

Samuelson argues that most mutual fund managers fail to beat the market, that those who do so do not persist in successive years, and that therefore most managers should quit their jobs.

Therefore, it makes sense to invest in a highly diversified, low-cost mutual fund with minimal asset turnover.

This is the theoretical justification. Afterwards, someone more practical had to come along to implement these ideas. That person was Jack Bogle, who read the paper (he explicitly cites it as his inspiration[33]), and implemented it in his Vanguard fund (just founded in 1975).

To close the circle, some years later Paul Samuelson said in a public lecture:

> I rank this Bogle invention along with the invention of the wheel, the alphabet, Gutenberg printing, and wine and cheese: a mutual fund that never made Bogle rich but elevated the long-term returns of the mutual-fund owners. Something new under the sun.
>
> — Paul Samuelson, before the "Boston Society of Security Analysts", November 12, 2005

Note: Jack Bogle's personal wealth will be discussed in Section 2.18, where his paper "No Person Can Serve Two Masters" is discussed.

And finally, as a curiosity, Paul Samuelson also contributed with a paper to the book "The Random Character of Stock Market Prices", edited by Paul Harold Cootner in 1967 (see Figure 8).

2.9. Determinants of Portfolio Performance

2.9.1. Paper

Title	Determinants of Portfolio Performance
Authors	Gary P. Brinson, L. Randolph Hood, and Gilbert L. Beebower
Publication	Financial Analysts Journal, July/August 1986, pages 39-44 (reprinted on January/February 1995).[34]

1985–1994

Determinants of Portfolio Performance

Gary P. Brinson, L. Randolph Hood, and Gilbert L. Beebower

A recent study indicates that more than 80 per cent of all corporate pension plans with assets greater than $2 billion have more than 10 managers, and of all plans with assets greater than $50 million, less than one-third have only one investment manager.[1] Many funds that employ multiple managers focus their attention solely on the problem of manager selection. Only now are some funds beginning to realize that they must develop a method for delineating responsibility and measuring the performance contribution of those activities that compose the investment management process—investment policy, market timing and security selection.[2]

Table 1 illustrates the framework for analyzing portfolio returns. Quadrant I represents policy. Here we would place the fund's benchmark return for the period, as determined by its long-term investment policy.

A plan's benchmark return is a consequence of the *investment policy* adopted by the plan sponsor. Investment policy identifies the long-term asset allocation plan (included asset classes and normal weights) selected to control the overall risk and meet fund objectives. In short, policy identifies the entire plan's normal portfolio.[4] To calculate the policy benchmark return, we need (1) the weights of all asset classes, specified in advance,

Figure 40. First lines of the paper "Determinants of Portfolio Performance".

2.9.2. Authors

Gary P. Brinson (1943-) is an American fund manager. He graduated from Seattle University, earned an MBA from Washington State University, and has had a long career in financial firms such as Swiss Bank Corporation and UBS.

The second author, L. Randolph Hood, has an undergraduate degree in economics from John Hopkins University, an MBA in finance and accounting from University of Chicago, and earned a CFA (Chartered Financial Analyst) certification.

Gilbert L. Beebower (1934-2013) graduated in chemistry from Caltech, Pasadena, then served two years in the US Air Force, and subsequently held various positions in financial firms.

2.9.3. Content

This is a seminal paper in the context of asset allocation. Jack Bogle himself wrote about it:

> [This paper] may well be the seminal citation on the subject of asset allocation.
>
> — Jack Bogle, in his book "Common Sense on Mutual Funds" (1999)

This paper starts with strong statements, pointing out the importance of measuring investment effectiveness. It says that when we wish to obtain alpha (by selecting star managers), we unknowingly obtain beta (i.e., the market, as we will see in Section 2.20 on "alpha is beta waiting to be discovered").

> Many funds that employ multiple managers focus their attention solely on the problem of manager selection.
>
> Only now are some funds beginning to realize that they must develop a method for delineating responsibility and measuring the performance contribution of those activities that compose the investment management process: investment policy, market timing and security selection.
>
> — Brinson et al., "Determinants of Portfolio Performance", page 1

This paper does just that, measuring the importance of the following three factors within an investment portfolio:

- The long-term **asset allocation** (the long-term "strategic" asset allocation, the **policy**), which is chosen as a return/risk combination of stocks/bonds (as we saw in Section 2.2 about the Modern Portfolio Theory).

- The **market timing** (the short-term "tactical" asset allocation). Defined as "the underweighting or overweighting of an asset class relative to its strategic weighting, in order to increase return and/or reduce risk."

- The **asset selection** is the selection of specific investments within an asset class (example: which shares of companies for the stock asset class). They define it as "the actual portfolio returns within an asset class (e.g., the actual returns of the common stock and bond segments) in excess of the benchmark passive returns of those classes and weighted by the fund's normal total asset allocation."

The Figure 41 illustrates the conceptual framework used in the paper to study portfolio returns.

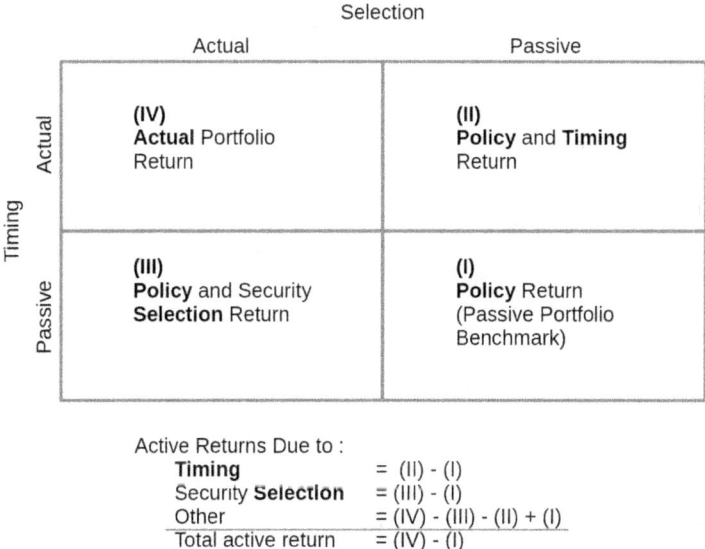

Figure 41. Simplified framework on return. Source: Table 1 from the paper "Determinants of Portfolio Performance".

- Quadrant **(I)** represents the investment policy, the return obtained because of the asset allocation. It is the return that a passive portfolio investing in those assets, and with those proportions, would obtain. The authors calculate it by multiplying the weights defined by the investment policy by their returns.
- Quadrant **(II)** represents the combined effect of asset allocation and timing.
- Quadrant **(III)** represents the combined effect of asset allocation, and asset selection within asset classes.
- Quadrant **(IV)** represents the actual return obtained by the funds.

The paper uses data from 1974 to 1983 (10 years) from 91 US pension plans. The authors calculate pension plan returns by taking into account the following ideas (see the Figure 42):

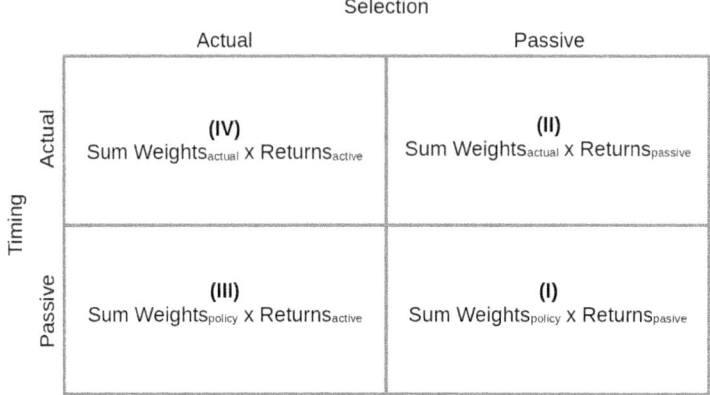

Figure 42. How returns are calculated for each quadrant. Source: Table 2 from the paper "Determinants of Portfolio Performance".

- Asset weights in their portfolios, as specified in their investment policy.
- The actual asset weights in pension plans portfolios (which are not exactly the same as defined in the investment policy).
- The returns of the index funds (passive investing) that correspond to the asset classes in portfolios.
- The returns of actual active funds.

The Figure 43 shows the results obtained by the authors in terms of returns.

The average annualized total return over the 10-year period studied in the paper was **9.01%**, see quadrant **(IV)**.

According to the authors, the average pension plan lost **0.66%** per year for doing market timing, and another **0.36%** per year for doing its stock selection.

The average annualized total return of the plans' investment policy (passive index returns and average weighting) for the sample was **10.11%**, see quadrant **(I)**.

The effect of any other factor on the portfolio return is negligible (loss of **0.07%** per year).

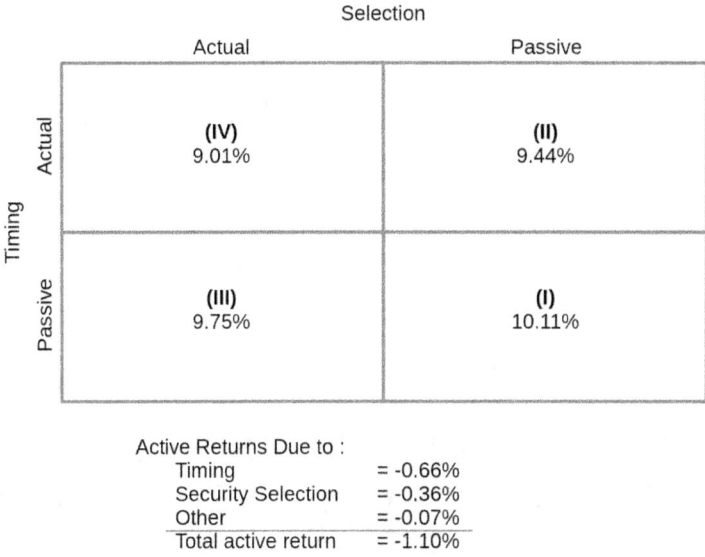

Figure 43. Annualized returns by quadrant. Source: Table 5 from the paper "Determinants of Portfolio Performance".

In addition, the authors construct similar tables for volatility, demonstrating that investment volatility is also primarily due to the chosen asset allocation.

Therefore, the value added by active management is small compared to the return of the asset classes. Most of the return comes from the asset allocation, from being indexed to the assets in the selected proportions.

In authors' words, designing a portfolio requires 4 steps:

1. Deciding which **asset classes** to include (the "strategic" asset allocation) or exclude in the portfolio.
2. Deciding what **weights** those asset classes should have in the portfolio. These are the long-term target weights.

3. "Tactically" modifying the portfolio weights away from the long-term predefined, in an attempt to obtain additional return from short-term fluctuations in asset class prices (**market timing**).

4. The **selection of individual securities** within an asset class to achieve superior returns relative to that asset class (asset selection).

The first two decisions are part of investment policy, and the last two are part of investment strategy.

And the authors conclude by indicating that investment policy is by far the most important, it is the one that investors should choose most carefully.

2.9.3.1. Subsequent Paper by Ibbotson and Kaplan

A few years after the paper by Brinson and his colleagues, Ibbotson and Kaplan published this other paper:

Does Asset Allocation Policy Explain 40, 90, or 100 Percent of Performance?

Roger G. Ibbotson and Paul D. Kaplan

Disagreement over the importance of asset allocation policy stems from asking different questions. We used balanced mutual fund and pension fund data to answer the three relevant questions. We found that about 90 percent of the variability in returns of a typical fund across time is explained by policy, about 40 percent of the variation of returns among funds is explained by policy, and on average about 100 percent of the return level is explained by the policy return level.

Figure 44. First lines of the paper "Does Asset Allocation Policy Explain 40, 90, or 100 Percent of Performance?" by Robert G. Ibbotson and Paul D. Kaplan, year 2000.[35]

This paper was written in order to improve Brinson's previous study. Its objective was to answer the following three questions:

1. What part of the **variability of return over time** is explained by investment policy (the original question that Brinson and his coauthors asked themselves)? In other words, how much of a fund's ups and downs are explained by benchmarks?

2. How much of the **variation in returns between funds** is explained by differences in their investment policies?
3. How much of the **level of return** is explained by the return of the investment policy? In other words, what is the relationship between benchmark return and actual fund return?

Their analysis shows that asset allocation (the "strategic" allocation, the proportions of stocks and bonds decided according to the return/risk ratio of the investor):

1. explains about **90% of the variability of a fund's return over time** (see Figure 45), but
2. it only explains about **40% of the return variation between funds**.
3. Finally, on average, the asset allocation policy ("strategic", long-term) explains about **100% of the level of returns** (explains all!).

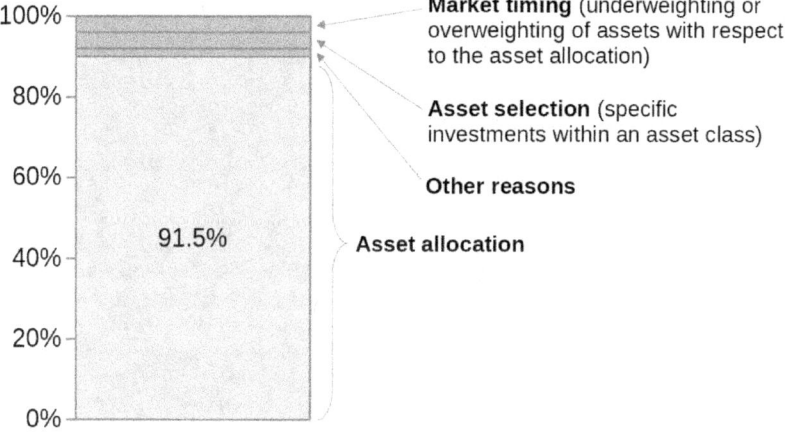

*Figure 45. Factors explaining the **variability of the return** of a portfolio (the answer to the first question the authors asked themselves). By far the most important: Asset allocation. Source: Paper by Ibbotson and Kaplan, after a post by Unai Ansejo.*[36]

2.9.4. Conclusions

The asset class allocation in the portfolio (e.g., stocks/bonds long-term proportions) is the parameter that dominates its return.

This is the most important choice for the investor to make, far above market timing or asset selection within a class.

These papers demonstrate that investors should focus on selecting assets and their weights in the portfolio (stocks, bonds, cash), rather than choosing assets (individual stocks, or sector ETFs) that they believe will outperform the market.

2.10. Fama-French Three Factor Model

2.10.1. Paper

Title	The Cross-Section of Expected Stock Returns
Author	Eugene Francis Fama and Kenneth Ronald French
Publication	The Journal of Finance, published by The American Finance Association, volume 47, number 2, pages 427-465, June 1992.[37]

> **The Cross-Section of Expected Stock Returns**
>
> EUGENE F. FAMA and KENNETH R. FRENCH*
>
> **ABSTRACT**
>
> Two easily measured variables, size and book-to-market equity, combine to capture the cross-sectional variation in average stock returns associated with market β, size, leverage, book-to-market equity, and earnings-price ratios. Moreover, when the tests allow for variation in β that is unrelated to size, the relation between market β and average return is flat, even when β is the only explanatory variable.
>
> THE ASSET-PRICING MODEL OF Sharpe (1964), Lintner (1965), and Black (1972) has long shaped the way academics and practitioners think about average returns and risk. The central prediction of the model is that the market portfolio of invested wealth is mean-variance efficient in the sense of Markowitz (1959). The efficiency of the market portfolio implies that (a) expected returns on securities are a positive linear function of their market βs (the slope in the regression of a security's return on the market's return), and (b) market βs suffice to describe the cross-section of expected returns.

Figure 46. First lines of the paper by Fama and French "The Cross-Section of Expected Stock Returns" (1992).

2.10.2. Authors

We have already seen Eugene Fama in Section 2.6, when discussing the Efficient Market Hypothesis.

Kenneth Ronald French (1954-) is an American economist. He studied mechanical engineering at Lehigh University in 1975, an MBA in 1978, and a PhD in finance in 1983 from University of Rochester.

He has taught at MIT, Yale Business School, and the Booth School of Business of the University of Chicago.

He has served as president of the American Finance Association, is a member of the American Academy of Arts and Sciences (AAA&S), and is a member of the board of directors of Dimensional Fund Advisors.

Fama and French were classmates at the Booth School of Business of the University of Chicago, where Eugene Fama continues to work.

2.10.3. Content

In asset valuation and portfolio management, the Fama-French three-factor model is a statistical model designed in 1992 by Eugene Fama and Kenneth French to describe stock returns.

The three factors are:

1. The return of the market,
2. the extra return of small firms versus large firms, and
3. the extra return of firms with high book-to-market ratios versus firms with low book-to-market ratios.

Book-to-Market

> Book-to-market is a financial metric used to evaluate a company's value. It compares its book value (accounting value) relative to its market value (capitalization).
>
> A high book-to-market ratio means that the market participants consider that the price of stock (its capitalization) should be relatively lower compared to its accounting value.
>
> Therefore market participants do not trust the company. The company may be experiencing difficulties.

Factor models are statistical models that attempt to explain these complex phenomena using a small number of parameters.

The traditional asset pricing model, formally known as the Capital Asset Pricing Model (CAPM), uses a single variable to compare the returns of a portfolio or stock with the returns of the market as a whole. In contrast, the Fama-French model uses three variables.

Fama and French started from the observation that two groups of stocks have tended to outperform the market as a whole:

1. small-cap stocks; and
2. stocks with a high book-to-market ratio.

The CAPM model (single parameter model) explains about 70% of the return of diversified portfolios. And when considering the three-factor Fama-French model, it explains about 90% of the return of diversified portfolios.

The same methodology has been applied by other authors looking for more factors, with the hope of being able to explain 100% of the return of diversified portfolios. But these additional factors are debatable because they represent very small contributions and can hardly be confirmed.

- Fama and French extended the model in 2015 to 5 factors, adding "profitability" (robust-minus-weak, referring to high operating profitability minus low operating profitability) and "investment" (conservative-minus-aggressive, low total asset growth minus high total asset growth).
- Mark Carhart proposed "momentum" (defined as the speed of change of an asset's price) as a fourth factor.
- Cliff Asness, a doctoral student of Eugene Fama and co-founder of AQR Capital), is also a proponent of the "momentum" factor.
- "Low volatility" is another possible factor, much talked about in the wake of the 2008 financial crisis, but of which there is no clear academic consensus. Its proponents argue that it requires a long time to demonstrate its effect, a full business cycle, to appreciate that it reduces losses during bear markets, but lags during bull markets.

Factor investing has received a lot of attention from large fund managers, probably because it allows them to sell financial instruments that are passively managed (low costs), but have high fees like active funds. They are called "smart beta", and managers such as iShares/BlackRock have hundreds of factor ETFs.

This paper shows that small-cap companies, as well as value-style companies, earn higher returns than the other companies. The Table 2 shows the monthly returns (in percentage) of companies organized into different groups.

Table 2. Table V from Fama and French's paper "The Cross-Section of Expected Stock Returns" (1992). Monthly returns (in %), data from July/1963 to December/1990. See text for explanation.

	All	Low	2	3	4	5	6	7	8	9	High
All	1.23	0.64	0.98	1.06	1.17	1.24	1.26	1.39	1.40	1.50	1.63
Small-ME	1.47	0.70	1.14	1.20	1.43	1.56	1.51	1.70	1.71	1.82	1.92
ME-2	1.22	0.43	1.05	0.96	1.19	1.33	1.19	1.58	1.28	1.43	1.79
ME-3	1.22	0.56	0.88	1.23	0.95	1.36	1.30	1.30	1.40	1.54	1.60
ME-4	1.19	0.39	0.72	1.06	1.36	1.13	1.21	1.34	1.59	1.51	1.47
ME-5	1.24	0.88	0.65	1.08	1.47	1.13	1.43	1.44	1.26	1.52	1.49
ME-6	1.15	0.70	0.98	1.14	1.23	0.94	1.27	1.19	1.19	1.24	1.50
ME-7	1.07	0.95	1.00	0.99	0.83	0.99	1.13	0.99	1.16	1.10	1.47
ME-8	1.08	0.66	1.13	0.91	0.95	0.99	1.01	1.15	1.05	1.29	1.55
ME-9	0.95	0.44	0.89	0.92	1.00	1.05	0.93	0.82	1.11	1.04	1.22
Large-ME	0.89	0.93	0.88	0.84	0.71	0.79	0.83	0.81	0.96	0.97	1.18

Book-to-Market Portfolios

The effect of capitalization size is shown vertically (the acronym "ME" refers to "Market Equity"), in 10 rows. The top row ("Small-ME") corresponds to small-cap companies, the bottom row ("Large-ME") to large-cap companies, and all the intermediate cases in between.

The effect of the book-to-market ratio is shown horizontally, in 10 columns. The "Low" (low book-to-market) column refers to "growth" style companies, the "High" (high book-to-market) column to "value" style companies, and all the intermediate cases in between.

There are many values in the table, but we could focus on the gray background row and column.

- Look at the gray background column (the column that combines "All" columns, all book-to-market portfolios), there is a large difference in value: the monthly return is 1.47% for small-cap and 0.89% for large-cap. In this case, small-cap are 0.58% per month better than large-cap.

- Look now at the gray background row (the row that combines "All" market capitalizations). The monthly return is 1.63% for "value" companies versus 0.64% for "growth" companies. Therefore "value" companies have a return 0.99% monthly better than "growth" companies.

- And combining both factors boosts the return. The group of companies with the highest monthly return (1.92%, box with gray background in top right corner) are precisely the small-cap and "value" style companies.

The usual explanation for these extra returns is that the market rewards for investing in riskier assets:

- Smaller companies have a higher risk of failure than larger ones, and so the market rewards those who take the risk of investing in small caps with an extra return.
- And value-style companies, whose stock market capitalization is small compared to their book value, investors consider them riskier than the market aggregate, that is why they are cheap.

This is why investors have to be rewarded with extra return.

Factor investing has generated a lot of discussion. Clearly, past returns show the advantage of investing in small-cap and value-style companies, yet the effect seems to have worn off in recent years.

Factor investing may have been so successful that it has disappeared. Because once the way to earn extra returns is discovered, investors rush in, making the assets expensive, and erasing the effect. This is in line with the Efficient Market Hypothesis: when an inefficiency is discovered, actors try to take advantage of it, until they make the effect disappear, and finally the market becomes more efficient.

2.10.4. Conclusions

Historically, investing in small-cap companies, or in value-style companies, or in both factors simultaneously, has provided extra returns.

The existence of factors in investing makes it possible to argue that in the past there may have been fund managers who have earned above-market returns by quietly making use of them.

However, today it is not clear that factor investing continues to provide extra returns; the effect seems to have disappeared.

Given a typical portfolio, consisting of government bonds and an aggregate of market equities, it may optionally make sense to add small factor components (small-cap, value, or both), which are expected to outperform the market return, at the cost of adding extra volatility.

But consider that this extra return may never appear again. What is certain is that you are going to pay a higher fee, and you are probably going to get just the market return after fees.

2.11. Withdrawal Rates

2.11.1. Paper

Title | Determining withdrawal rates using historical data
Author | William P. Bengen
Publication | The Journal of Financial Planning, volume 7, number 4, pages 171-180, October 1994.[38]

Figure 47. First lines of William P. Bengen's paper "Determining withdrawal rates using historical data" (1994).

2.11.2. Author

William P. Bengen (1947-) is an American financial advisor.[39]

He studied aerospace engineering at MIT and began his professional career along this path. In fact, he is co-author of the book "Topics in Advanced Model Rocketry", published in 1973 and available online.[40]

He then took over the family business, engaged in bottling soft drinks in the New York area, until it was sold in 1987.

Then he went to live in California, where he obtained the Certified Financial Planner (CFP) in 1990. Afterwards he studied for a master's degree in financial planning, in 1993. And finally he created his advisory firm, where he worked until 2013, when he retired.

Something remarkable is how he charged for his consulting services. In his advisory firm he charged by the hour (example: $200/hour), not at a percentage of the investment (example: 1% of the invested wealth, per year), which is the way recommended in the Bogleheads© community, by advisors like Rick Ferri.

2.11.3. Content

This paper is the originator of the 4% Rule and the "Safe Withdrawal Rate" (SWR) concepts.

What he did was to calculate an annuity, corrected for inflation, and constructed with the instruments available to retail investors.

Annuity

> An annuity is a contract between you and an insurance company, where you make one or more premium payments in exchange for a guaranteed income stream. This income is typically paid for the remainder of your life.

The summary of the paper, which is basically what Bengen proposed to his clients, is this:

> Assuming a minimum requirement of 30 years of portfolio longevity, a first-year withdrawal of 4 percent, followed by inflation-adjusted withdrawals in subsequent years, should be safe.
>
> — William P. Bengen, page 2 of his paper

He comments that to consider both the average return and average inflation is not enough to calculate future investment income. This is due to market volatility.

He performed some simulations with various portfolio compositions and portfolio longevities (How long will the portfolio last before all its investments have been exhausted by withdrawals?) to find out the best possible safe withdrawal rates.

2.11.3.1. Simulations

Bengen performs his simulations with historical US data, considering portfolios composed of stocks and government bonds.

His procedure is to initially set the amount to be withdrawn in the first year (the so-called "withdrawal rate"). This amount is typically 4%, but could be 3% or less, or 5% or more.

Example: for an invested wealth of 1 million dollars, a withdrawal rate of 4% implies withdrawing 40 thousand dollars the first year (and the following years correcting for inflation).

The steps of the simulations are:

1. Correct the invested wealth by the return obtained for stocks and bonds during the year.
2. Subtract at the end of the year the amount to be withdrawn from the invested assets.
3. Is the portfolio exhausted?
    - "No": then correct the amount to be withdrawn for inflation, and return to point 1 to simulate another year.
    - "Yes": then end the simulation. The important outcome is the number of years that the portfolio lasted.

Note that the amount to be withdrawn each year is corrected for inflation, because the objective is to maintain constant purchasing power.

The above procedure is the one that William P. Bengen used to generate the Figure 48, which is the justification for the 4% Rule.

He assumed US stock market returns, with US inflation, portfolios composed of 50% stocks and 50% government bonds, and performing rebalancing by the end of the year.

The duration of his simulations was 50 years, with the aim of finding longevities of 30 years or more.

Then, the simulations are run for three withdrawal rates: 3.0%, 4.0%, and 5.0%.

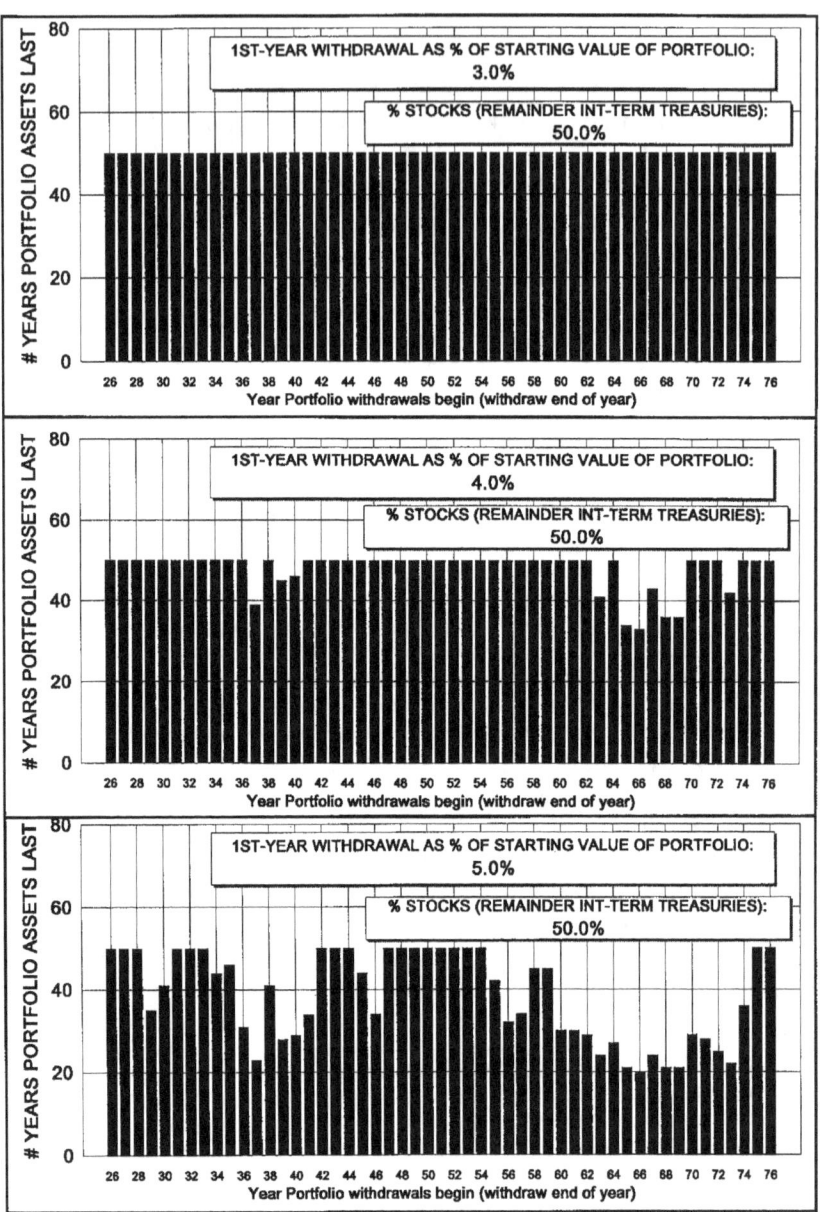

Figure 48. These are Figures 1a, 1b, and 1c from the paper by William P. Bengen. They are 50-year simulations with three different Safe Withdrawal Rates: 3.0% in the top panel, 4.0% in the middle, and 5.0% in the bottom. With actual US returns and inflation data up to 1992. Subsequent returns and inflation are extrapolated (stocks 10.3%, bonds 5.2%, inflation 3.0%). Thus, simulations starting in 1976 use real data up to 1992 and then extrapolated until 2026.

- Portfolios that withdrew **3.0%** of the portfolio value in the first year had no problem, none were depleted in 50 years. This is a relatively small amount to extract from the portfolio. Therefore 3.0% is very low, a quite conservative withdrawal rate.
- Portfolios that withdrew **4.0%** of the portfolio value in the first year had longevities always larger than 30 years. They struggled through the 1929 crisis and the great inflation of the 1970s, but always lasting more than 30 years. Good, this is what Bengen was looking for.
- For portfolios that withdrew **5.0%** of portfolio value in the first year, there are many simulations in which portfolios only lasted for 20 years. Not for all starting years, but for many of them. Therefore 5.0% is too high, a relatively risky value. Higher withdrawal rates exhaust the portfolios even sooner.

Therefore 4.0% is the Safe Withdrawal Rate, the highest possible withdrawal rate without exhausting the portfolio in 30 years (which is typically the minimum reasonable longevity). And this is where the so-called 4% Rule comes from.

Bengen also studies the composition of portfolios, and concludes that mixed stock-bond portfolios are better than just 100% stocks:

> The 50/50 stock/bond mix appears to be near-optimum for generating the highest minimum portfolio longevity for any withdrawal scheme.
>
> — William P. Bengen, page 5 of his paper

If the portfolio is needed to last many years, such as 50 years, better to increase the proportion of stocks:

> I think it is appropriate to advise the client to accept a stock allocation as close to 75 percent as possible, and in no cases less than 50 percent.
>
> — William P. Bengen, page 6 of his paper

For very long periods of time, a higher proportion of stocks is appropriate, because they have the greatest growth potential. When crises come, and there will be some of them, the higher proportion of stocks will help the portfolio to recover sooner.

But increasing the proportion of stocks can be counterproductive because it makes the portfolio more sensitive to crises. A large loss in value, say half, may cause the portfolio to never recover.

On the other hand, a higher proportion of bonds makes the portfolio less volatile, and therefore the duration is more predictable. This gives more security for short periods of time.

In addition, Bengen wonders whether it is worth changing the asset allocation over the years, and his answer is no:

> My research indicates strongly that as long as the client's goals remain the same, there is no need to change the initial asset allocation. It is likely to do more harm than good, as we shall see.
>
> — William P. Bengen, page 7 of his paper

The paper concludes by indicating that the 4% Rule is not a hard and fast rule, but a first step to start talking about the topic, to start planning for retirement, without forgetting each person's needs.

2.11.3.2. Deterministic Chaos

Now we can bring here the ideas of Edward N. Lorenz and his Deterministic Chaos (see Section 2.7), because small variations in the parameters of the simulations can generate huge differences in the final results.

For example, let us have a look at the Figure 48, in particular at the year-to-year differences. In the lower panel (on those who started withdrawing 5% of the initial wealth each year) we see that in 1937 they managed to make the portfolio last for 22 years. However, if they had started the following year, in 1938, the longevity would have been 41 years, almost twice as long.

Similar huge variations are found when starting the simulations in other years, with other withdrawal rates, and depending on the composition of the portfolio (stocks vs. bonds).

And not only regarding longevity. In a similar way, the final value of the portfolio can vary a lot. Depending on small changes in the initial parameters, in 30 years the portfolio can be depleted or increase many times its initial value.

Therefore, we should not be overly concerned about accuracy, about calculating the percentage with all possible digits, such as 3.987%, because there is no perfect figure. Small variations such as starting to withdraw capital a year earlier or a year later, applying the same historical data, generate considerable differences.

In summary, the 4% Rule is simply a reasonable approximation, not an exact figure.

2.11.3.3. Example

Let us look at a simple example of what it would be like to apply the withdrawal rate.

The first step is to select the withdrawal rate, the percentage of the initial portfolio, typically 4%.

At the end of the first year, this amount is withdrawn from the principal.

Then, the value of the portfolio will change, up or down, depending on the behavior of the financial markets.

At the end of the second year, the amount withdrawn from the portfolio is the first year's amount adjusted for inflation. The objective is to keep the purchasing power constant.

Again, the value of the portfolio will have changed according to market returns, but that does not affect the amount to be withdrawn.

In the third and subsequent years, the amount withdrawn in the previous year continues to be updated with inflation.

Note that, on the one hand, the value of the portfolio evolves year by year with the stock market. On the other hand, the value of the amount withdrawn evolves with inflation. Only in the first year the 4% of the portfolio value is withdrawn, the following years will be different percentages of the portfolio.

The advantage of this method is that the amounts withdrawn are predictable and allow the purchasing power to remain constant. The disadvantage is that if the stock market starts with consecutive declines over several years, the invested assets may disappear.

This strategy makes sense if you have largely fixed expenses and want to be able to predict over the long term the amounts that can be taken out of your portfolio.

The Table 3 shows a simple example, a portfolio that does not provide any return (for example because the money is not invested but standing in the bank's current account, which is not very reasonable, by the way). We assume 1 million dollars of assets as initial capital and a withdrawal rate of 4%. Note that the amount withdrawn during the year grows by 5% per year due to inflation. During year 17 this portfolio is exhausted.

Table 3. Practical example of applying 4% withdrawal rate, with 5% inflation, €1 million equity, uninvested (with no return).

Year	Capital at the Beginning of the Year	Amount Withdrawn at the End of the Year
1	1,000,000	40,000
2	960,000	42,000
3	918,000	44,100
4	873,900	46,300
...	...	...
16	136,857	83,157
17	53,700	Equity is depleted during this year

What Bengen did in his simulations is to substitute the central column (capital at the beginning of the year) according to the capital the previous year and the historical returns.

2.11.3.4. Trinity Study

The Bengen paper opened a new field. Soon afterwards, in 1998, another well-known paper was published: "Sustainable Withdrawal Rates From Your Retirement Portfolio". It is written by three authors (Philip L. Cooley, Carl M. Hubbard, and Daniel T. Walz) of Trinity University in Texas. For this reason, the paper is commonly referred to as the "Trinity Study".[41]

> **Sustainable Withdrawal Rates From Your Retirement Portfolio**
>
> **Philip L. Cooley,**[1] **Carl M. Hubbard**[2] **and Daniel T. Walz**[3]
>
> *This study reports the effects of a range of nominal and inflation-adjusted withdrawal rates applied monthly on the success rates of retirement portfolios of large-cap stocks and corporate bonds for payout periods of 15, 20, 25, and 30 years. A portfolio is deemed a success if it completes the payout period with a terminal value that is greater than zero. Using historical financial market returns, the study suggests that portfolios of at least 75% stock provide 4% to 5% inflation-adjusted withdrawals.*
>
> Key Words: *Retirement planning, Retirement wealth adequacy*
>
> Specifying a sustainable withdrawal rate is an important factor to consider in retirement investment planning. The question we address is what percentage withdrawal rate applied to the initial value of a retirement portfolio can be sustained through a payout period? This is an important question since higher withdrawal rates produce greater retirement income from a given portfolio for a more attractive standard of living but are sustainable only for shorter payout periods. Lower withdrawal rates reduce the risk of running out of funds but provide less retirement income from the portfolio. Thus an investor
>
> Of course, different investors have different goals. Some plan to leave substantial amounts of their portfolios to heirs. However, the purpose of withdrawal rate analysis is to provide investors with a planning tool that can be used to evaluate the sustainability of various withdrawal rates. Clearly investors who wish to leave an estate must plan to withdraw a lower percentage annually from their portfolios than those who plan to consume most of the principal. Our analysis is presented so that investors can determine the range of withdrawal rates that is likely to achieve their goals.

Figure 49. First lines of the Trinity Study, "Sustainable Withdrawal Rates From Your Retirement Portfolio" (1998).

This paper is much more formal and detailed than Bengen's, reaching the same conclusions but in a more robust way.

As a curiosity, the procedure followed in the two papers for the calculation is slightly different:

- Bengen: You set the amount withdrawn the first year, and calculate the longevity of the portfolio.

- Trinity Study: Set the number of years the portfolio has to last, and calculate the maximum withdrawal rate that achieves this. Typically, by studying the percentage of portfolios that succeed (i.e., a portfolio is successful if it holds 75% of the simulations). This second approach is the standard procedure today.

Finally, I would like to point out that there is an exceptional source of information about the Safe Withdrawal Rate. It is "Early Retirement Now", which is almost an encyclopedia on the topic. This website has been created by Karsten, a German living in the USA, PhD in economics and CFA certified.[42]

2.11.3.5. Critics

Bengen (and the Trinity Study) present a very good first approach to the retirement problem.

Basically, it is like an annuity, but instead of the service being provided by an insurer, it is self-made.

The fundamental difference is that the insurer can compensate for risks (the longevity of its customers) thanks to having many customers (the life expectancy of one person is uncertain, but the average of many people is predictable).

With the 4% Rule we are providing insurance to ourselves, but with greater uncertainty, because we do not know how long the portfolio has to last, since we do not know the date of our death.

Criticisms that are often made of these studies are:

- The valuation of stock market assets (if the stock market is relatively expensive or cheap) can make future return expectations lower. Therefore, the Safe Withdrawal Rate can be corrected with the CAPE (see the Section 2.12).
- Investor longevity. Studies of the 4% Rule usually assume 30 years of portfolio longevity, but this may be inadequate for someone retiring extremely early, or if life expectancy grows a lot. Therefore, for early retirees the Safe Withdrawal Rate has to be lower than 4%.
- The cost of investments (commissions) and taxes. Again, the Safe Withdrawal Rate has to be lower than 4%.
- The difference of having invested in different countries. The original studies only use data from the USA, which is a country that has done exceptionally well economically during the last century.

2.11.4. Conclusions

Bengen's study, particularly its 4% Rule, is a direct application of Harry Markowitz's Portfolio Theory (Section 2.2).

An individual can build his or her own annuity using instruments available to retail investors. And furthermore, by doing so passively, it requires minimal intervention.

2.12. Irrational Exuberance

2.12.1. Paper

Title	Valuation Ratios and the Long-Run Stock Market Outlook
Author	John Young Campbell and Robert James Shiller
Publication	The Journal of Portfolio Management, published by National Bureau of Economic Research, volume 24, number 2, pages 11-26, Winter 1998.[43]

Valuation Ratios and the Long-Run Stock Market Outlook

Ratios are extraordinarily bearish.

John Y. Campbell and Robert J. Shiller

When stock market valuation ratios are at extreme levels by historical standards, as dividend-price and price-earnings ratios are in the United States today, one naturally wonders what this means for the stock market outlook. It seems reasonable to believe that prices are not likely ever to drift too far from their normal relationships to indicators of fundamental value, such as dividends or earnings. Thus one might expect that when stock prices are very high relative to these indicators, as they are in 1997, prices will fall in the future to bring the ratios back to more normal historical levels.

Figure 50. First lines of Campbell and Shiller's paper "Valuation Ratios and the Long-Run Stock Market Outlook" (1998).

2.12.2. Authors

Robert James Shiller (1946-) is an American economist of Lithuanian immigrant descent. He is a university professor and has authored several best-selling books on finance.

111

He studied at the University of Michigan, where he received his undergraduate degree in 1967. He then went to MIT for his doctorate in 1972. His thesis advisor was Franco Modigliani, who received the Nobel Prize in 1985.[44]

He has taught at the University of Pennsylvania, the University of Minnesota, the London School of Economics, and since 1982 he has been a professor at Yale University.

He has written books on Behavioral Economics, real estate, and risk management. He wrote his best-known book, "Irrational Exuberance", in 2000, warning that the stock market was in a bubble, which could mean imminent losses. He was right, and that helped his book become a New York Times bestseller.

He subsequently wrote about a possible bubble in the housing market, both in academic papers and in The Wall Street Journal in August 2006. This was a year ahead of the Great Financial Crisis, which contributed to his reputation as a discoverer of financial bubbles.

In 2009 he was awarded the Deutsche Bank Prize in Financial Economics for his work on the dynamics of asset pricing, volatility, bubble emergence, and risk.[45]

In 2013 he received the Nobel Prize in Economics, together with Eugene Fama and Lars Peter Hansen. There is a certain paradox in this, because Eugene Fama and he had opposing views on market efficiency. Eugene Fama is the proponent of the Efficient Market Hypothesis (as we saw in Section 2.6), and Robert Shiller had forged his academic profile by pointing out market inefficiencies.

On the other hand, John Y. Campbell (1958-) is an American economist of British origin.[46]

He studied at Oxford, and then continued at Yale University, where he obtained a master's degree and his PhD, directed precisely by Robert Shiller.

He taught at Princeton University and later at Harvard University. He has published a multitude of academic papers and books on finance, and has served as president of the American Finance Association.

2.12.3. Content

The original paper was written in 1998, and tried to explain the stock market situation at that time. The paper subtitle indicates its argument straight away (see the Figure 50), "Ratios are extremely bearish".

In a later update of this paper, in 2001, at that time at the height of the Dotcom crisis, he further argued for the existence of a stock market bubble.

How do Campbell and Shiller find financial bubbles? They claim that there is mean-reversion:

> Thus it seems natural to give at least some weight to the simple mean-reversion theory that when stock prices are very high relative to these indicators, as they have been recently, then prices will eventually fall in the future to bring the ratios back to more normal historical levels
>
> — Campbell and Shiller, page 1 of the paper

And starting from the mean-reversion, they justify that "something must be predictable" about the future:

> If we accept the premise for the moment that valuation ratios will continue to fluctuate within their historical ranges in the future, and neither move permanently outside nor get stuck at one extreme of their historical ranges, then when a valuation ratio is at an extreme level either the numerator or the denominator of the ratio must move in a direction that restores the ratio to a more normal level. Something must be forecastable based on the ratio, either the numerator or the denominator.
>
> — Campbell and Shiller, page 5 of the paper

The Efficient Market Hypothesis (see Section 2.6) says that the future cannot be predicted. But Campbell and Shiller indicate that if the market is "expensive" (measured with a financial ratio), and assuming mean-reversion, then the prediction can be made that at some point the market will go down in price. And if this is so, it invalidates the Efficient Market Hypothesis, because predictions can be made.

This explanation is a rule of thumb with a questionable theoretical basis. What if financial conditions have changed and the ratios are not the same again? Well, let us go ahead and see how they calculate it.

A first step is to use the P/E ratio (Price-to-Earnings ratio) or PER (Price-to-Earnings Ratio), which relates a share price (in dollars) and a cash flow (earnings per share over a given time, typically years, dollars/year).

The P/E ratio has the units of time and can be interpreted as the amount of time the company needs to maintain its current earnings to make enough money to pay for its current capitalization.

They proposed a modification to the P/E, a new ratio that is the average of company earnings over several years:

> A clearer picture of stock market variation emerges if one averages earnings over several years. Benjamin Graham and David Dodd, in their now famous 1934 textbook Security Analysis, said that for purposes of examining valuation ratios, one should use an average of earnings of "not less than five years, preferably seven or ten years". Following their advice we smooth earnings by taking an average of real earnings over the past ten years.
>
> — Campbell and Shiller, page 16 of the paper

With this rationale, they created the CAPE ratio, which stands for "Cyclically Adjusted Price-to-Earnings", which is also known as "Shiller P/E" (Shiller's Price-to-Earnings) or "P/E 10" (when averaged over 10 years).

CAPE is defined as the share price divided by the ten-year average of earnings per share (inflation-adjusted moving average). Not just for the last year, because in that case it would simply be the P/E.

This ratio can be used to determine whether a stock, or group of stocks, is undervalued or overvalued by comparing its current market price to its historical, inflation-adjusted earnings.

The CAPE makes sense because using average earnings over the past decade smoothes out the impact of economic cycles, and thus provides a better picture of the company's ability to generate profits over the long term.

In order to illustrate this argument, the Figure 51 has been created with data taken from Robert Shiller's website. It is equivalent to the well-known CAPE figure that appears in his book "Irrational Exuberance". [47] [48]

Each plot represents a group of starting dates, when the 20-year periods begin. For each plot:

- The horizontal axis shows the CAPE at the beginning of a 20-year period.
- The vertical axis shows the annualized gross return after that 20-year period.

The Figure 51 clearly shows the mean reversion effect. In the months where the CAPE was higher than its historical average (points more towards the right side), the following 20 years the return obtained was lower than the historical average return (points more towards the lower part).

The Dotcom crisis of 2001 (see the period 1984.01 — 2004.02, the last graph at the bottom right) is well appreciated. The CAPE value of the S&P 500 peaked at 44 in December 1999 (that is, 1999.12 in the chart format), then returned to its historical average, near 17.

Looking at the Figure 51 we can deduce that the return earned by investors at the peak CAPE (value 44, on December 1999) was 4% per year over the next 20 years, not a bad figure, but well below the 10% annualized return earned by those who invested when CAPE value was 10.

Let us make a simple approximation with the latest period (1984.01 — 2004.02). We would say that the expected long-term return is 7% for an average CAPE of 25, and that each point difference in CAPE from 25 implies a 0.2% annualized return (lower return at higher CAPE, and vice versa).

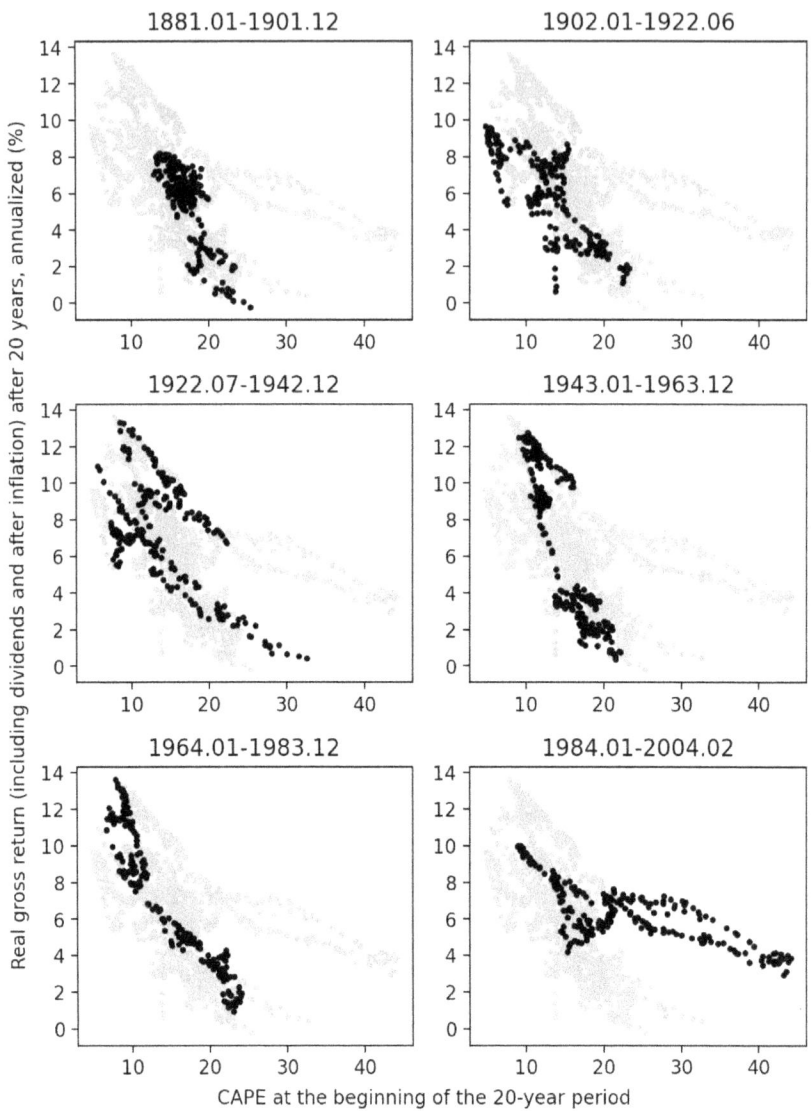

Figure 51. Annualized return of the US stock market (S&P 500) after 20 years, including dividends and inflation, as a function of CAPE at the beginning of that period. The beginning dates of each 20-year period are shown in YYYYY.MM ("year.month") format, with the month being an integer from 01 to 12. Each point represents one month, from January 1881 to February 2004 (note that the last period starts in 2004.02 and ends in 2024.02). For ease of interpretation, these 123 years are divided into 6 periods of about 20 and a half years duration. In the background, in gray color, all the data are shown, and in the foreground, in black color, the data of that period. Note that the higher the CAPE, the lower the return.

In 2014, Robert Shiller expressed concerns that the then prevailing CAPE value over 25 was:

> [...] A level that has only been exceeded since 1881 in three previous periods: the years clustered around 1929, 1999 and 2007. These peaks were followed by significant market declines.
>
> — Robert Shiller, 2014

Robert Shiller wrote his book "Irrational Exuberance", where he detailed the calculation and use of the CAPE. The title refers to that same expression used by Federal Reserve Chairman Alan Greenspan in 1996, regarding the fact that the price of assets in the stock market was much higher than economically justifiable.[49]

> Clearly, sustained low inflation implies less uncertainty about the future, and lower risk premiums imply higher prices of stocks and other earning assets.
>
> We can see that in the inverse relationship exhibited by price/earnings ratios and the rate of inflation in the past. But how do we know when irrational exuberance has unduly escalated asset values, which then become subject to unexpected and prolonged contractions as they have in Japan over the past decade?
>
> — Alan Greenspan, The Challenge of Central Banking in a Democratic Society, 1996-12-05

What at the time was a reasonable assumption, that we were living in a bubble with a CAPE value of 44, ended up becoming the Dotcom crisis. Shiller got it right in predicting the bubble, and that helped make him and his book famous.

Subsequently, during the Great Financial Crisis, the CAPE value reached 47. Note that this CAPE is not shown in the Figure 51, because due to the methodology, we need to wait 20 years to know the final return during the period.

The current CAPE value (August 2024), regarding the S&P 500, is 36. This is a relatively high value, which leads us to believe that returns over the next 20-year period will be lower than historical returns. The current value of CAPE can be found on Robert Shiller's personal website Shiller[48] or on a multitude of webs[50]

During his lecture at the Nobel Prize award ceremony, he argued that markets are not efficient, as opposed to the other prize winner, Eugene Fama.

The Efficient Market Hypothesis postulates that the current value of an asset reflects the incorporation of all price-related information. And since there is an intrinsic value and the price is close to it, the price movement should be relatively smooth. But according to Robert Shiller, the results of market movement are extremely erratic and irrational.

Robert Shiller alluded to John Maynard Keynes' explanation of stock markets to point out the irrationality of people in making decisions. Keynes compared the stock market to a beauty contest in which people, instead of betting on who they find "attractive", bet on "the contestant they think most people find attractive". Which is not the same thing. Thus, Robert Shiller argues that investors do not use complicated mathematical calculations, nor sophisticated economic modeling, when participating in the asset market. Investors are watching other investors, amplifying irregularities.

Robert Shiller believes that more information about the asset market is crucial to improve its efficiency. He argued that a huge data set is needed for the market to function efficiently.

Since the data available on asset markets for the research he conducted was very limited, and is even more limited for ordinary people, he developed the Case-Shiller index that provides information on house price trends. The use of technology can benefit by accumulating data on broader asset classes, which will make the market more data-driven, and thus pricing more efficient.

Robert Shiller studied the effect of "narratives", worldviews that affect how society unfolds.

> How errors of human judgment can infect even the smartest people, thanks to overconfidence, lack of attention to details, and excessive trust in the judgments of others, stemming from a failure to understand that others are not making independent judgments but are themselves following still others — the blind leading the blind.
>
> — Robert Shiller, in his book "Irrational Exuberance"

Finally, CAPE also has a connection to the Safe Withdrawal Rate, because if you start drawing principal from your portfolio when CAPE is high, you may not have to apply the 4% rule, but be even more conservative, like 3.5% (see the Section 2.11).

2.12.4. Conclusions.

Robert Shiller provides a simple conclusion for retail investors:

> [Figure 51] confirms that long-term investors — investors who commit their money to an investment for ten full years — did do well when prices were low relative to earnings at the beginning of the ten years. Long-term investors would be well advised, individually, to lower their exposure to the stock market when it is high, as it has been recently, and get into the market when it is low.
>
> — Robert Shiller, in his book "Irrational Exuberance"

Does this mean that an investor should modify the asset allocation in his portfolio, decreasing the proportion of stocks when CAPE is high?

That may well be the case. But be careful because the market can continue to grow for many years even though CAPE is already high, so the upside can be lost.

This idea of using historical series of financial ratios seems to be a reworking of Technical Analysis. Basically there is a "moving average" (the historical average of the CAPE), and the expectation of future returns is higher if the current value of the CAPE is below that moving average (and vice versa).

As long as history repeats itself, it is fine, but if valuations change over the long term (due to new disruptive technologies, different financial conditions, corporate culture, globalization, etc.), then its predictive power is gone. In fact, it is well proven that Technical Analysis does not generate returns above the market.

As we will find out in the Section 2.25 about the Behavioral Gap by Morningstar, investors who try to guess when to enter and when to exit the market get lower returns than simply buying and holding their assets long-term.

What has to be done is to rebalance the portfolio, keeping the percentages constant, and thus a fraction in relatively safe assets (such as government bonds). In this way, we automatically sell relatively overvalued assets to buy relatively undervalued assets.

2.13. Impact of Size and Skewness

2.13.1. Paper

Title	Why active fund managers often underperform the S&P 500: The impact of size and skewness
Author	David L. Ikenberry, Richard L. Shockley, and Kent L. Womack
Publication	Journal of Private Portfolio Management, volume 1, number 1, pages 13-26, year 1998.[51]

> **Why active fund managers often underperform the S&P 500: The impact of size and skewness**
>
> **Abstract**
>
> The performance of actively managed U.S. equity funds is often naively compared to that of the S&P 500 index. In recent years, this comparison has generally cast an unfavorable impression of active fund managers and has led many investors to embrace index funds.
>
> Systematic deviations from the benchmark are affected by two conventional practices of active fund managers: 1) equally-weighting their positions, and 2) holding small numbers of stocks. These two practices accentuate the statistical characteristics of longer-horizon stock returns and cause active manager performance to deviate predictably from broad-based benchmarks such as the S&P 500.

Figure 52. First lines of the paper "Why active fund managers often underperform the S&P 500: The impact of size and skewness".

2.13.2. Authors

David L. Ikenberry holds a B.A. from Pennsylvania State University (1983), an M.B.A. from Kellogg School of Management of Northwestern University (1985), and a PhD from University of Illinois (1990). He is a former dean of the Leeds School of Business of the University of Colorado Boulder, and currently teaches there.[52]

Richard L. Shockley is a professor of finance at the Kelley School of Business, Indiana University, where he received his PhD in 1984.[53]

Kent L. Womack was a professor of finance at the Rotman School of Management, University of Toronto (Canada). He also worked at Goldman Sachs.[54]

2.13.3. Content

This paper explains why, in general, active managers earn worse returns than their benchmarks, why there are years when active managers seem to do better, and why there are managers who earn huge returns much higher than the market.

Authors begin by arguing that the higher cost of investment for active funds (compared with index funds) is important, because active managers have to pay research and transaction costs, while index funds minimize these expenses (few transactions) or even eliminate them (no market research is done). These costs by active manager imply a reduction in their return (as we will see in Section 2.16 with Jack Bogle).

If cost were the only explanation for the loss of returns for active managers, then every year active managers would underperform their comparable index funds. Although this is observed over the long term, in the short term most active managers outperform their comparable index funds. How is this possible?

Although this is what is observed over the long term, in the short term there are years when a majority of active managers outperform their comparable index funds. How is this possible?

Authors argue that the fact that active mutual funds perform poorly when compared to indexes (such as presented in the SPIVA report, which we will look at in Section 2.23), or to index funds (such as the Morningstar report, which we will look at in Section 2.24), is due to two reasons:

1. Active managers tend to give similar weights in their portfolio to the companies in which they invest.
2. Active managers tend to concentrate their portfolios in a few companies.

2.13.3.1. About Equal Weight Portfolios

Assigning equal weights to portfolio assets is equivalent to underweighting large-cap companies and overweighting small-cap companies. And small-cap companies provide higher expected returns (as we have seen in Section 2.10 with the Fama-French Three

Factor Model), along with higher volatility, to the extent that return and risk go hand in hand.

Authors argue that active managers tend to allocate the same weight to their portfolio assets, even though the capitalization of those companies may be very different.

They give the example that at the end of 1997 the capitalization of the largest companies in the S&P 500 was about 400 times larger than the capitalization of the smallest companies. The authors do the thought experiment of imagining two portfolios composed of 6 assets that are part of the S&P 500 (see Table 4).

1. Active managers usually apply a similar portfolio weight for all assets. Thus, we might expect a portfolio where each of the assets weighs 1/6, which is approximately 16.67% (middle column).
2. In standard indices, their portfolio is weighted by capitalization. In this case we expect weights like those in the last column (the capitalization of the largest companies is assumed to be 400 times larger than that of the smaller ones, 33.25% vs 0.08%).

Table 4. Example of two portfolios combining hypothetical S&P 500 assets (first column). A typical portfolio of an active manager (second column, equal weight for all assets) and a capitalization-weighted portfolio (assuming that large companies have 400 times the capitalization of small companies). The asset weights are very different in the two portfolios.

Hypothetical S&P 500 Companies	(Equal) Weight in Active Manager's Portfolio	Weight by Capitalization Portfolio
#1 (largest capitalization)	16.67%	33.25%
#2	16.67%	33.25%
#3	16.67%	33.25%
#498	16.67%	0.08%
#499	16.67%	0.08%
#500 (lower capitalization)	16.67%	0.08%

It would be very exceptional for an active manager to have an unbalanced portfolio like the weighted by capitalization in the last column. For this reason, by equalizing, managers have to allocate greater weight to small-cap companies, increasing the expected return and volatility relative to their benchmark.

2.13.3.2. About Asset Concentration in Portfolios

The second factor why managers deviate from the index is more subtle and relates to the statistical nature of returns over the long term.

In the short term, such as one day or even one week, the stock market returns approximate normal distributions (symmetric, bell-shaped distributions, as we saw in Section 2.1 with Louis Bachelier).

However, in the long run, this symmetry disappears. In almost every year, the returns of individual stocks show considerable rightward skewness (i.e., a few stocks earn huge returns). This effect is not new, we have already discussed it in the Section 2.3 with M.F.M. Osborne.

According to the authors of this paper, the asymmetry of returns occurs for two reasons:

1. First, limited liability truncates stock losses. You cannot lose more than what you have invested. Unless you go leveraged, but that's another issue.
2. Second, upside returns are unlimited. In any given year, several individual stocks can provide extraordinary returns. For example, it is not uncommon to see the price of ten or more S&P 500 stocks more than double.

This skewness is problematic for active fund managers because they typically only invest in a small subset of the stocks that make up the index.

Assuming the bias is toward positive returns, one would expect the **median** stock return (the value that leaves half the stocks below and half the stocks above it) to be lower than the **average** return of the set. See Figure 53 for a visual explanation.

That is, typical active managers tend to get the **median** return of the market (because they tend to "miss out" the few outperforming stocks). But index investors hold all the stocks in their portfolio, so their return is exactly the market **average**.

This is why index funds outperform active funds: because the market average return is higher than the market median return.

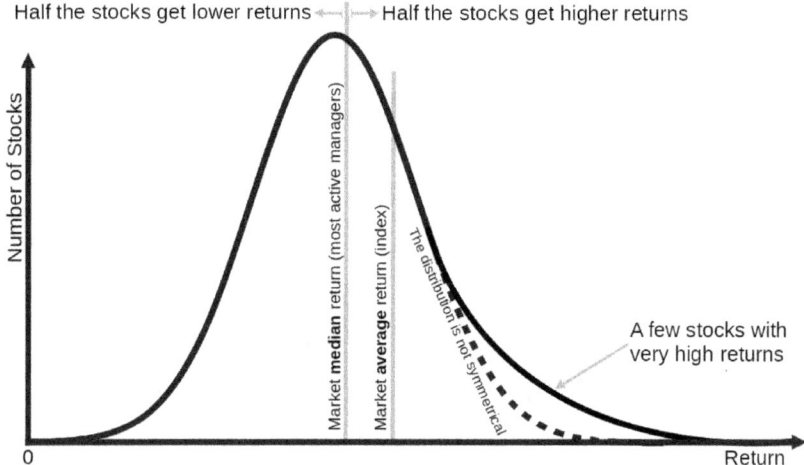

*Figure 53. The distribucion of stock returns is not symmetrical, there are a few stocks that provide very high returns. These high-returns move the market **average** return toward higher values. However, the **median** return is relatively insensitive to extreme values and stays at lower returns.*

Note that this bias hurts active fund managers even before taking into account costs and other factors.

To illustrate this idea more clearly, consider the following example. Suppose we have a 500-stock index, such as the S&P 500, but all of them with the same capitalization, as shown in the Figure 54.

Over the course of the year, 499 of the companies in the index provide 0% return, while company number #1 (representing only 1/500 of the index capitalization) has an exceptional year with a 500% return.

Among the 500 stocks in the index, 499 will underperform the benchmark; and 1 company will outperform it. The total return of the index (average return) is 1% (= 500% x 1/500).

At the beginning of the year, fund managers select 50 stocks from the 500 stocks that make up this index to form their portfolios. Let us also assume that the managers select these stocks without any skill, that they choose them randomly.

At the end of the year, we will have two types of managers: those who were lucky enough to include the winning stock in their portfolio (stock #1, the one with the 500% return), and those who did not include stock #1. As shown in the Figure 55.

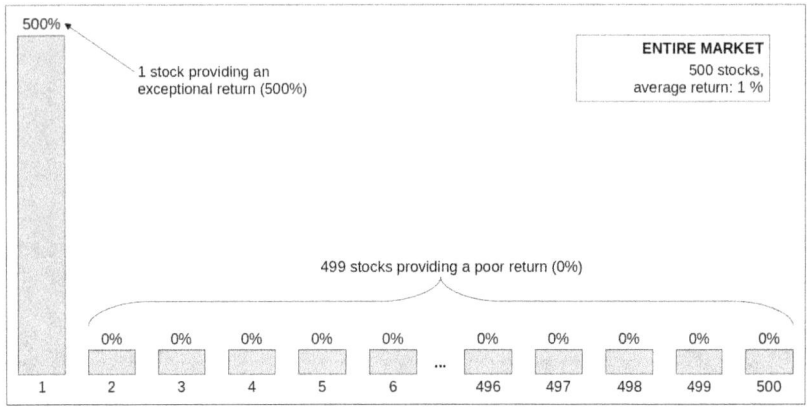

Figure 54. Suppose a stock market composed of 500 companies of equal capitalization. 499 companies provide no return during the year, but one of them gives 500%. Therefore the market aggregate provides a 1% return.

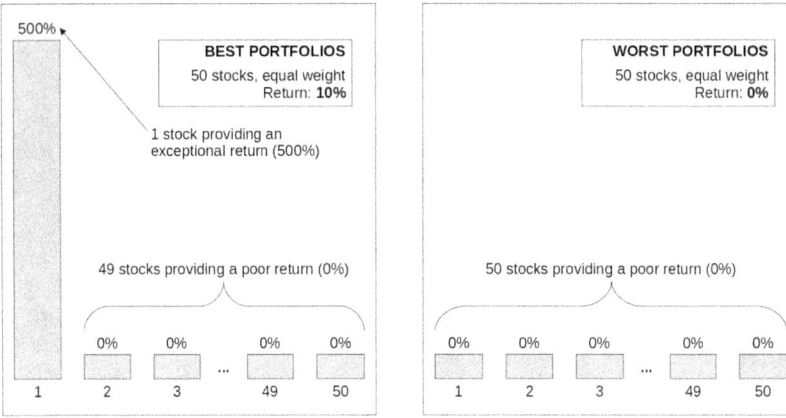

Figure 55. We can form two groups of mutual funds that invest in 50 stocks. The "best portfolios" will be those that include the best company (#1), and the "worst portfolios" will be those that do not.

The "best managers" of the year will "beat the market" with portfolio returns of 10% (= 500% x 1/50), while the "worst managers" will underperform the benchmark, with portfolio returns of only 0%.

But the probability of investing in the best stock (which is 1 in 500), with portfolios of 50 stocks, is 10% (= 50 / 500). Therefore, it is unlikely to become one of the best managers. And overall, most managers (90%) earn below-market returns. See the Figure 56.

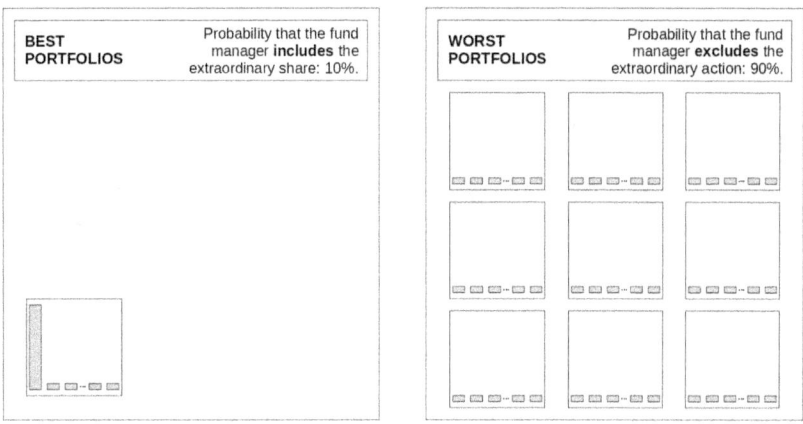

Figure 56. Statistically, the "best portfolios" are only 10% of all possible portfolios, and the "worst portfolios" the remaining 90%.

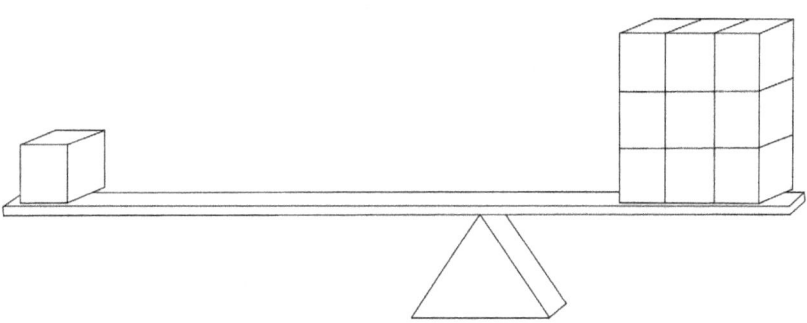

Figure 57. The asymmetry in mutual fund returns behaves like a lever. A single weight (a successful active fund getting a high return) far from the leverage point (market average) counteracts many weights (many active managers having poor returns) near the leverage point.

The conclusion of this argument is shown in the Figure 58, where the three groups of portfolios that we have discussed (the "best portfolios", the "worst portfolios", and the portfolio composed of exactly all the assets in the index, the indexed portfolio) are presented in a very clear way.

The outcome is shocking: in this example, the index fund (1% return) outperforms 90% of these active funds (those earning 0% returns).

This example is a huge oversimplification, but nevertheless it illustrates the potential impact that positive skewness can have on average manager returns.

Figure 58. Investing in the entire market (index fund) provides a 1% return, which is not as great as the return of the best active portfolios (10%), but is nevertheless better than the 0% return earned by 90% of active portfolios.

Most years skewness tends to be positive, and so in most years skewness works against managers with concentrated portfolios.

However, skewness is not constant from year to year, and if it shifts toward low returns, that year it can favor managers with concentrated portfolios.

2.13.4. Conclusions

Most active funds, most years, will underperform their benchmarks. And this is not just because of costs, but also because stock returns are not symmetric, most returns are low and only a few of them are exceptionally high.

In addition, managers tend to overweight small-cap companies, resulting in relatively higher volatility in their portfolios than in the market.

2.14. A Multifractal Walk Down Wall Street

2.14.1. Paper

Title	A Multifractal Walk Down Wall Street
Author	Benoît Mandelbrot
Publication	Scientific American, volume 280, issue 2, pages 70-73, February/1999.[55]

> **A Multifractal Walk Down Wall Street**
>
> "The geometry that describes the shape of coastlines and the patterns of galaxies also elucidates how stock prices soar and plummet."
>
> by Benoit B. Mandelbrot
>
> Individual investors and professional stock and currency traders know better than ever that prices quoted in any financial market often change with heart-stopping swiftness. Fortunes are made and lost in sudden bursts of activity when the market seems to speed up and the volatility soars. Last

Figure 59. First lines of the paper by Benoît Mandelbrot.

2.14.2. Author

We have discussed this author previously, in Section 2.4, when talking about "fat tails" and how randomness can be wilder than the one described by normal distributions.

2.14.3. Content

This paper is interesting for being a critique of the whole of the Modern Portfolio Theory. The title itself is a reference to the book "A Random Walk Down Wall Street" by Burton G. Malkiel, published in 1973, and which served to popularize the random walk hypothesis among retail investors.

But before discussing this paper, let us begin by describing fractals. In fact, we can ask ourselves the question Mandelbrot asked in another paper that he wrote in 1967: How long is the coast of Britain?

How Long Is the Coast of Britain?
Statistical Self-Similarity and Fractional Dimension

Abstract. *Geographical curves are so involved in their detail that their lengths are often infinite or, rather, undefinable. However, many are statistically "self-similar," meaning that each portion can be considered a reduced-scale image of the whole. In that case, the degree of complication can be described by a quantity*

Figure 60. Mandelbrot's paper on the length of the coast of Britain, published in Science, volume 156, year 1967, pages 636-638.[56]

This may seem like a simple question. You would think that all you have to do is look at a map, run the coastline with a ruler, and add up the distances.

However, it is a more complex problem than it appears. It depends on the length of the details we are considering, the length of the ruler we use. A coastline is not a straight line, and the shorter the length of the ruler, the longer the ability to go into gulfs and peninsulas. As an example, see the Figure 61.

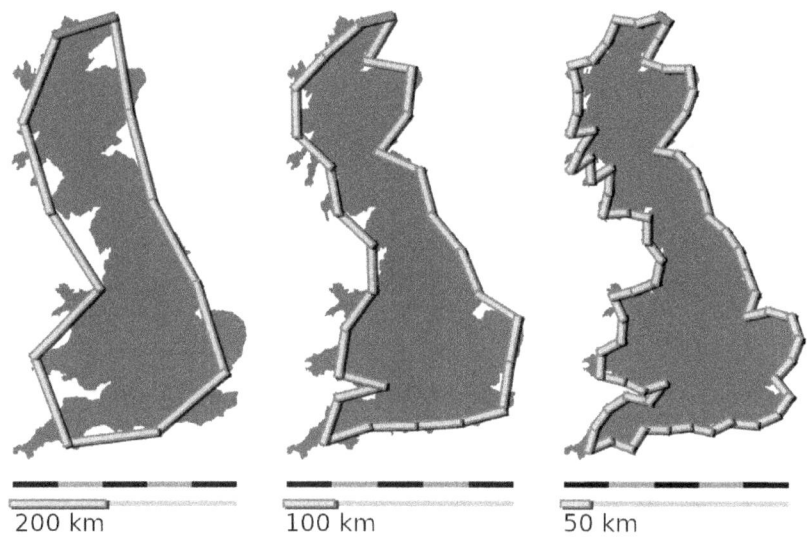

Figure 61. The length of the coast of Great Britain depends on the length of the ruler we use to measure it. The smaller the ruler, the greater the ability to measure the details, and therefore the longer the length of the measured coastline.[57]

Using a 50 km ruler, we will measure a longer length of coastline than using a 200 km ruler. But we could use a 1 km ruler, which would allow us to better follow the details of the coastline, increasing the measured length. Or better, a 10-meter ruler, to be able to trace even the small coves. And following this strategy, why not a 1 cm ruler? Or better yet, an atomic-sized ruler. The smaller the ruler, the greater the distance measured.

This brings us to the paradox that "the instrument affects the measurement". There is no single answer, we can only say "the length of the coast is X when using ruler Y". Because no matter how small the ruler is, the measurement of the coast length will always fall short.

What characterizes fractals is "autosimilarity". The fact that each of the parts is itself a fractal. No matter how much you fractionate a fractal, the smaller parts still show complexity, and so on to infinity, over infinitely small distances.

We could say that it is a "recursive" problem, in the mathematical or programming context, because each time you increase the resolution to observe greater detail of the rugged coastline, you find that the small features of the terrain have intricate detail. And each time you zoom in, more detail appears, and so on *ad infinitum*.

Each time you decrease the ruler, the measured length changes. And not a little, but a lot, "wildly". It is impossible to give an exact figure for the length of the coast. This is a general property of fractals derived from their self-similarity. On the one hand they are beautiful and regular, but on the other hand they are a "wild randomness" (as Mandelbrot says).

If fractals are present everywhere, as Mandelbrot believed, then the world is a place dominated by extremes where our intuitions about mean values and normality will lead us to inaccurate approximations.

As an example of a famous fractal, the Figure 62 shows the "Mandelbrot Set". This is perhaps the most studied of the fractals. It is a very complex geometric figure that arises from relatively simple mathematical rules.

In the real world the self-similarity of fractals can be found in rivers, which, starting from their mouths, divide into tributaries, each with the characteristics of rivers, getting smaller and smaller, until they become streams, and we could go on to flows of water molecules sliding along the earth's surface. On the other hand, the branches of a tree also look like a tree themselves.

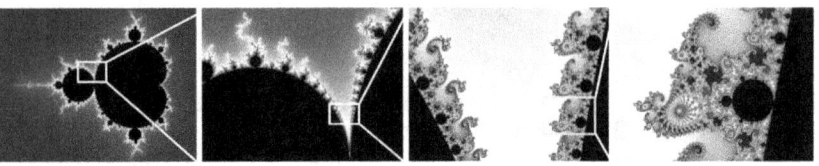

Figure 62. Fractals are geometric structures that show complexity at any scale. Starting from the first image on the left, an enlargement of each image is shown to its right. This process could continue indefinitely.[58]

Fractals justify that price charts exhibit complexity at all scales, whether in fraction of seconds, days, or years. From this it can be deduced that there are emergent properties, which are specific to each scale, and do not apply to the others. Like physics, whose laws explain the behavior of atoms. But when those atoms combine with each other, emergent properties arise, which is chemistry, that goes beyond the laws of physics. And when chemistry comes into action, biology emerges, with new emergent properties that are not deduced from the previous scale (for example: what is life?).

Mandelbrot writes in his paper:

> The mathematics underlying portfolio theory handles extreme situations with benign neglect: it regards large market shifts as too unlikely to matter or as impossible to take into account. It is true that portfolio theory may account for what occurs 95 percent of the time in the market. But the picture it presents does not reflect reality, if one agrees that major events are part of the remaining 5 percent. An inescapable analogy is that of a sailor at sea. If the weather is moderate 95 percent of the time, can the mariner afford to ignore the possibility of a typhoon?
>
> — Benoît Mandelbrot, "A Multifractal Walk Down Wall Street", page 1

On the other hand, Mandelbrot suggests a way to simulate price data series, using fractals, in which the price curves repeat themselves at smaller and smaller scales. These curves are visually closer to the actual market behavior. The Figure 63 and the procedure described in the following paragraphs show this way of creating the price curves.

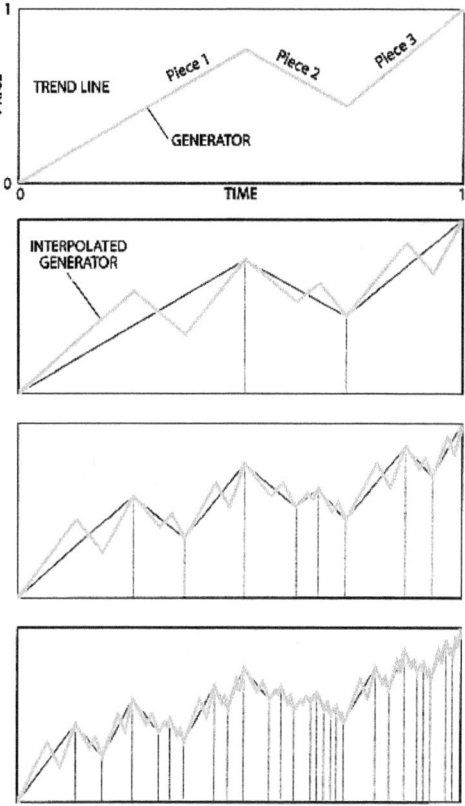

Figure 63. Generation of a realistic price curve using fractals, specifically their self-similarity property. Source: Illustration 1 in Benoit Mandelbrot's paper.

1. In the top panel we find the initial pattern that will be repeated successively, the **generator**. On the vertical axis, the stock **price** is shown, and on the horizontal axis the **time**. This initial pattern is composed of three **pieces**.

2. In the second panel, each **piece** in the upper figure is replaced by the initial **generator**. The vertical lines indicate the beginning and end of each interpolated **piece**. This **generator** expands or contracts on the horizontal axis and on the vertical axis to match its start and end points. If the **piece** line is decreasing, the **generator** is vertically inverted.

3. In the third panel, the same procedure is repeated as was done in the second panel. In this case, the **pieces** of the second panel are replaced by the initial **generator**.

4. In the fourth panel, the procedure is repeated (and it would be repeated indefinitely if we were to show more panels). Note that the first **piece** of the fourth panel (and of the previous panels) is the initial **generator**, just compressed in time.

Modifying the generator, the initial pattern, yields different price curves. In particular, Mandelbrot suggests modifying the length of the segments in time, keeping the starting and ending point. If a segment is made relatively short in time, when it is replaced by the generating curve it will be forced to have an enormous variation in a very small space of time. This generates the "wild randomness" that Mandelbrot is interested in.

In the paper, Mandelbrot explains that Portfolio Theory is based on premises that he considers baseless. For these two reasons:

1. The theory assumes that price changes are statistically independent of each other (i.e., that today's price has no influence on tomorrow's price). It follows from this point that it is impossible to predict future prices.
2. Price changes are assumed to follow normal distributions, defined by mean values and standard deviations. Extraordinary events are not considered.

Mandelbrot is skeptical that today's price is independent of tomorrow's price, i.e. that future prices cannot be predicted. But if the reality is as Mandelbrot suggests, then one would expect mutual fund managers to earn above-market returns. In particular, one would expect "persistence", i.e. that good managers are good managers for many years in a row. And yet, what is actually observed is that there is no persistence, good managers one year are different from good managers next year (see report SPIVA in Section 2.23). This contradicts Mandelbrot's first criticism.

The criticism that price volatility does not follow a normal distribution is important. To avoid having problems with volatility, it is best to be a long-term investor, buy&hold, so that volatility affects as little as possible (because the volatility between the buying price and the selling price in the distant future is irrelevant to us).

On the other hand, if this "wild randomness" exists, it is in the interest of professional managers to benefit from it, by buying when prices go down a lot, and selling when they go up a lot. This way of acting is a force that tends to minimize this volatility.

A passive investor gets his fair return from his share of being invested in the world economy. Whether there is "wild randomness" in the short term, that is a secondary issue.

Finally, Mandelbrot's criticisms are empirical laws. He is referring to what is observed in nature, what has happened in the past. And it is fine to take that into account, but it is not a law of nature. It is not like the law of gravity, which we all know is always true. An empirical rule is not the same as a law of nature. And Mandelbrot speaks of empirical rules as if they were laws of nature.

2.14.4. Conclusions

Mandelbrot's criticism of Portfolio Theory is important and has to be considered. However, a passive investor should not worry.

The fact that forward prices cannot be predicted is well documented, and is confirmed every 6 months in each new SPIVA report.

Against "wild randomness", the best is to minimize the number of trades and stay invested in the market.

And beware of trading stocks. Because one can expect to make frequent small gains, but it is possible that a negative event that we thought was exceptional (and which was not so exceptional) can cause us to lose everything all at once.

2.15. Trading Is Hazardous To Your Wealth

2.15.1. Paper

Title   Trading Is Hazardous to Your Wealth: The Common Stock Investment Performance of Individual Investors

Authors   Brad M. Barber and Terrance Odean

Publication   The Journal of Finance, volume 55, number 2, pages 773-806, April 2000.[59]

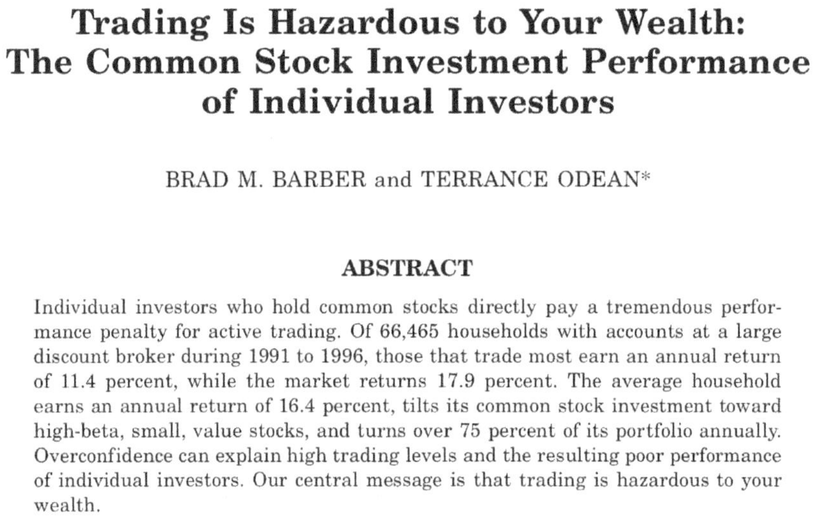

Trading Is Hazardous to Your Wealth: The Common Stock Investment Performance of Individual Investors

BRAD M. BARBER and TERRANCE ODEAN*

ABSTRACT

Individual investors who hold common stocks directly pay a tremendous performance penalty for active trading. Of 66,465 households with accounts at a large discount broker during 1991 to 1996, those that trade most earn an annual return of 11.4 percent, while the market returns 17.9 percent. The average household earns an annual return of 16.4 percent, tilts its common stock investment toward high-beta, small, value stocks, and turns over 75 percent of its portfolio annually. Overconfidence can explain high trading levels and the resulting poor performance of individual investors. Our central message is that trading is hazardous to your wealth.

Figure 64. First lines of the paper "Trading Is Hazardous to Your Wealth" by Brad M. Barber and Terrance Odean.

2.15.2. Authors

Brad M. Barber[60] is professor emeritus of finance in the School of Management at the University of California, Davis. He earned a degree in economics from the University of Illinois, a PhD in finance from the University of Chicago in 1991, and an MBA also from the University of Chicago.

Terrance Odean (1950-) is a professor of finance at the Haas School of Business, University of California, Berkeley. Terrance began a university degree, but dropped out before finishing. Later, at the age of 37, he enrolled at the University of California, Berkeley. Initially planning to study psychology, he ended up pursuing a degree in statistics. There he was taught by Daniel Kahneman (who won the Nobel Prize in economics in 2002), and after a conversation with him, decided to pursue a PhD in finance.

2.15.3. Content

The paper starts off strong, with its title being a direct reference to the well-known phrase "smoking is bad for your health". And the summary just after clarifies it, stating that individual investors lost return by excessive trading.

The study involved analyzing the returns earned on the stock investments of 66,465 US households during the six years ending January 1997.

Their **gross returns** (before taking transaction costs into account) earned by these investors have been, on average, the **market aggregate**.

However, their **net returns** are **poor** (after taking into account the bid-ask spread on the exchange order book, and the commissions paid by these investors). The market average provided a prodigious annualized return of 17.9% those years, but retail investors only earned 16.4% (average per invested capital).

Overall, the average return for retail investors underperforms a market index by 1.1% per year (average per investor).

But if we consider the fact that, in average, retail investors overweight their investments in small-cap, value-style stocks... then we need to compare them to a more appropriate benchmark. And when comparing with similar benchmarks, the result is even worse, 3.7% annually lower.

The Figure 65 shows the results of this paper. Columns are presented in groups of three:

- The lighter gray columns are the gross returns, before costs.
- The black columns are the net returns, after accounting for costs.

- The darker gray columns show the portfolio turnover. That is, the percentage of assets in the portfolio that are sold to buy others. In this case, monthly turnover.

On the other hand, the figure is subdivided into three panels, from left to right:

1. In the left panel, they order retail investors **according to the turnover of their portfolios**, from the lower to the largest.
2. The middle panel shows an **average investor**, obtained by combining all the investors from the left panel.
3. The right panel shows the return of an **index fund** tracking the S&P 500 (in this case, from Vanguard). Since costs are minimal, the difference between gross and net returns are also minimal.

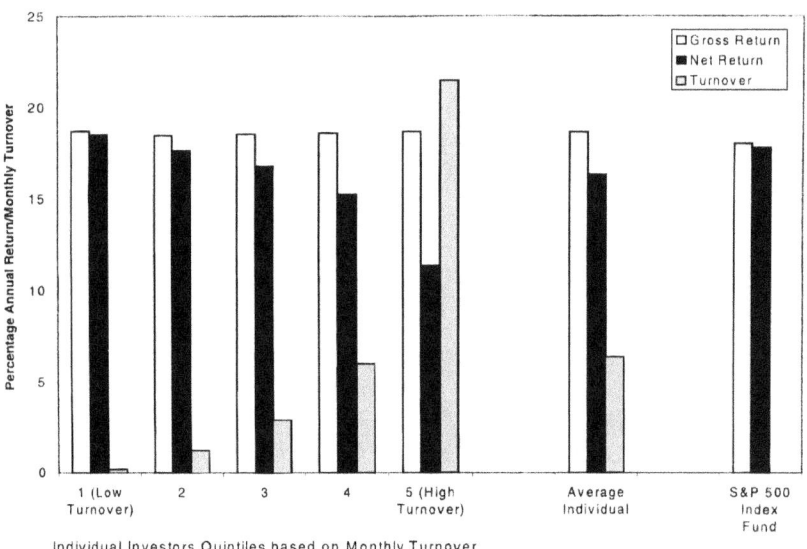

Figure 65. Figure 1 from the paper "Trading Is Hazardous to Your Wealth" by Brad M. Barber and Terrance Odean. See text for explanation.

The Figure 65 is best understood thanks to the following two figures extracted from it. When investors buy and sell more frequently, and thus have a higher portfolio turnover, then they obtain lower net returns. The inverse relation between turnover and return is obvious. This is all despite the gross expected being the same for all groups.

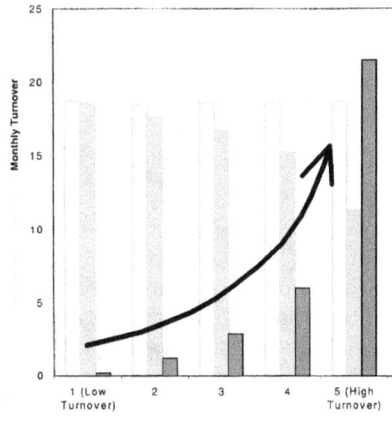

Figure 66. When the portfolio turnover is higher...   *Figure 67. then the net return is lower.*

The most dramatic evidence is provided by the 20% of the most frequently traded investors (labeled as column 5 in the charts).

With an average monthly turnover of over 20%, these investors completely revamp their stock portfolios more than twice a year.

The gross returns earned by these high turnover investors are basically the market aggregate, but their net returns are poor.

The monthly net return is 5.5% per year lower than that of a market index.

But it is even worse, because if we assume that the average high turnover investor overweights small-cap and value-style stocks in their portfolio (as do other retail investors), then the return is even worse. The authors calculate that they lose 10.3% per year.

These results are also directly applicable to mutual funds, not only to retail investors (as we will see in Section 2.25, dedicated to the Behavioral Gap report). Therefore, professional managers are not doing much better than the retail investors in this paper.

The Efficient Market Hypothesis could be the explanation for these results. Exceptional information that would allow investors to earn high returns is very scarce. This is why active managers fail to outperform passive managers. And that is why this paper is another argument in favor of passive investing.

On the other hand, behavioral finance models that incorporate this investor overconfidence provide an even stronger prediction: Active investment strategies earn lower returns than passive investment strategies. Overconfident investors overestimate the value of the private information available to them, leading them to trade too actively and, consequently, to underperform.

The paper concludes by stating that:

- Retail investors trade too much in the stock market. On average they buy and sell more than 75% of the portfolio annually.
- Transaction costs are high. When the paper was written (year 2000), the authors estimated transaction costs (in a hypothetical case of doing a full cycle of selling everything to buy it back, to come back to the initial asset allocation) of 3% in broker commissions and 1% in bid-ask spread. The return loss observed in retail investors is similar to this cost estimation.
- Retail investors overweight small-cap and value-style companies.

In the authors' words:

> It is the cost of stock trading and its frequency, not the assets in the portfolio, that explains the poor return on investments.
>
> — Barber & Terrance, "Trading Is Hazardous To Your Wealth", page 4

2.15.4. Conclusions

The more you trade in the market, the worse the return you get. Therefore the more passive the investment, the better.

In the context of behavioral finance, investors are overconfident, which leads them to trade more than they should, and thus have higher expenses, which ultimately lead to worse returns.

2.16. An Index Funds Fundamentalist

2.16.1. Paper

Title	An Index Fund Fundamentalist
Authors	John Clifton Bogle
Publication	The Journal of Portfolio Management, volume 28, number 3, pages 31-38, Spring 2002.[61]

An Index Fund Fundamentalist

Goes back to the drawing board.

John C. Bogle

In 1997, I prepared a study of the returns for the mutual funds in each of the nine Morningstar "style boxes," a matrix with large-, mid-, and small-capitalization funds on one axis and value, blend, and growth funds on the other (Bogle [1998]). For the five-year period 1992 through 1996, the study presents powerful evidence that the low-cost quartile of funds in each box had earned not only higher returns than those in the high-cost quartile, but also returns that significantly exceeded the cost differential.

Figure 68. First lines of the paper "An Index Fund Fundamentalist".

2.16.2. Author

John Clifton Bogle (1929-2019), usually known as Jack Bogle, was an American investor, entrepreneur, and philanthropist.

He was the founder of The Vanguard Group, and is known among retail investors for being instrumental in popularizing index funds. He has written 13 books on investing where he expounded his ideas, such as promoting "investing instead of speculation", encouraging the long term over the short term, and reducing fees as much as possible.

Jack Bogle studied economics and then did his doctoral dissertation at Princeton, in 1951, with the title "The Economic Role of the Investment Company", where he already laid out the ideas he worked on all his life. For example:

- "Investment funds cannot claim to be above the market average".
- "Future [investment] growth can be maximized by reducing sales charges and management fees".

However, his seminal contribution to the world of index funds is not academic, but the founding of The Vanguard Group. This is the financial company that made index funds accessible to retail investors, creating the Vanguard 500 Index Fund in 1975, which is considered the first index mutual fund.

At Vanguard he committed to his ideas and struggled for 40 years, while Wall Street treated him with derision for "not trying to beat the market, and accepting mediocre returns". But in the end, he succeeded.

And it wasn't just investors in Vanguard's managed funds who benefited. Over the past decades it has forced the financial industry to lower its fees, so that all investors have benefited. He has contributed so much that even Forbes magazine ran an obituary on the day of his death titled "Jack Bogle is gone, but he's still saving investors $100 billion [100 thousand million dollars] a year [in fees]".[62]

There is a web site with many of his papers and talks (https://johncbogle.com), and there are many groups of retail investors who call themselves Bogleheads©, who share their ideas and keep their spirit alive. You can find them for example in these online forums:

- https://bogleheads.org (in English, focusing on USA, but in having also many international groups).[63]
- https://bogleheads.es (in Spanish, focusing on Spain).

Regarding his philanthropic work, during his years as a director of Vanguard he gave half of his personal income to charity, in particular to Blair Academy (where he studied high school) and Princeton University. And in addition, in 2016 Princeton created the Bogle Fellowship for supporting students.[64]

It has also had multiple recognitions. In 1999 Fortune magazine deemed him "one of the four investment giants of the 20th century". And in 2004, Time magazine recognized him as "one of the 100 most influential people in the world".

2.16.3. Content

This is a representative paper by Jack Bogle, which allows us to talk about him and the ideas that made him famous. It is an extension of another paper published a few years earlier (hence its subtitle "Goes back to the drawing board").

It consists of a statistical treatment of the returns obtained by US mutual funds, as documented in Morningstar, from July 1, 1991, to June 30, 2001. There are 634 mutual funds.

All returns are distributed into the 9 groups of the Morningstar classification, according to whether the companies are Large/Mid/Small capitalization (capitalization is constant in each row), and according to whether they are Value/Mixed/Growth style (style is constant in each column). See the Table 5. This table is used to classify assets, in this case shares of listed companies, and to be sure that we are comparing homogeneous funds.

Table 5. Morningstar investment style table; with capitalization by rows, and investment style by columns; used to sort mutual funds into groups.

Capitali-zation	Investment Style		
	Large Cap. Value	Large Cap. Mixed	Large Cap. Growth
	Mid. Cap. Value	Mid. Cap. Mixed	Mid. Cap. Growth
	Small Cap. Value	Small Cap. Mixed	Small Cap. Growth

In each box of the Table 5 there are about 70 funds.

In each box, funds are ordered according to their cost (their TER, "Total Expense Ratio"), and 4 groups (quartiles) are made with about 18 funds each. The first quartile contains the funds with lower costs, the second a little more expensive, the third a little more expensive, and the fourth the funds with higher costs.

What we are interested in is to look at the cost effect, and this is best seen in the difference in returns between the first quartile (low cost) and the fourth (high cost).

The paper demonstrates that the return obtained by the investors is directly related to the cost of the fund in which he invests (its TER). On average, expensive funds obtain lower returns than funds with lower costs. And this is a general rule, valid for all categories, as shown in the table Table 6.

Table 6. Annualized returns over the 10 years that ended on 30/June/2001. Funds are grouped by fund capitalization size, style, and fund cost quartile. The fourth column is the subtraction of the returns of the second (low-cost fund quartile) minus the third (high-cost fund quartile). It corresponds to Table 2 of the "An Index Fund Fundamentalist" paper.

Fund Category	Low-Cost Quartile	High-Cost Return	Low-Cost Advantage
Large-Cap, Value	14.8%	12.8%	2.0%
Large-Cap, Blend	14.7%	10.9%	3.8%
Large-Cap, Growth	14.2%	11.2%	3.0%
Mid-Cap, Value	15.3%	12.5%	2.8%
Mid-Cap, Blend	15.4%	14.2%	1.2%
Mid-Cap, Growth	14.7%	12.5%	2.2%
Small-Cap, Value	16.8%	12.0%	4.8%
Small-Cap, Blend	15.6%	11.3%	4.3%
Small-Cap, Mixed	15.4%	14.5%	0.9%
All Funds	14.5%	12.3%	2.2%

This result (the higher the cost, the lower the return to the investors) is counterintuitive. Aren't the best managers supposed to be more expensive because they are better professionals and provide higher returns? Well, the answer is no.

And furthermore, one might think that the expected return is "the market return minus costs". If this were so, the difference in returns in the Table 6 would be comparable to the difference in costs (typically 1.2%, with the annual cost of cheap funds being 0.6% and expensive funds 1.8%). But it is even worse, because losses are greater than 1.2% per year. Managers subtract value even above their fees.

All this was without taking into consideration the "survivorship bias", because the funds that get closed (usually the most expensive ones with very bad returns) are not part of the statistics. Bogle estimates that the returns of expensive quartile funds can worsen by another 2% per year when this survivorship bias is taken into account. Additional to the 2.2%/year advantage of low-cost funds!

There are similar tables with risk-adjusted returns, and with the Sharpe Ratio[65]. Expensive quartile funds are always worse than low-cost quartile funds, for all market segments.

The paper goes a step further and asks if someone wants to invest according to a particular segment of the market, according to capitalization and style (according to the Table 5), it makes the most sense to do so using index funds.

> Index funds eliminate the risks of individual stocks, market sectors and manager selection, leaving only stock market risk.
>
> — Jack Bogle, Vanguard founder

The paper concludes with:

1. Higher returns are associated with lower cost funds.
2. Indexing works for all market segments. Supposedly large-cap stocks are efficient, and there should be differences with non-efficient markets (small-cap, etc.). But there are no differences.

Since the Efficient Markets Hypothesis has been heavily criticized (we already saw this in Section 2.6 with Eugene Fama), he humorously proposes to refer to the "Cost Matters Hypothesis". And this is an argument that has not been refuted so far.

> The grim irony of investing is that we investors, as a group, don't get what we pay for, we get precisely what we don't pay for. So if we pay nothing, we get everything [all the return].
>
> — Jack Bogle, Vanguard founder

2.16.3.1. The Importance of Cost

The following thought experiment helps understand the effect of investment cost on net returns.

Let us imagine that we throw two 6-sided dice and add up the results. We can assume that the Table 7 and the Figure 69 represent the return of mutual funds over the year. Most funds earn an average return (the mean value is 7), and a few earn either very high returns (12) or very low returns (2).

Table 7. Combinations of rolling two dice and adding up the result.

Dice Sum	Dice Combinations	Number of Combinations
2	1+1	1
3	1+2, 2+1	2
...	...	...
7	1+6, 2+5, 3+4, 4+3, 5+2, 6+1	6
...	...	...
11	5+6, 6+5	2
12	6+6	1

Next, suppose we subtract "-2" from the sum of the dice, which is the equivalent of the investment cost. This causes the distribution to shift to the left, as shown in Figure 70.

Finally (see Figure 71), "after subtracting -2" there are very few rolls that exceed the average value "before subtracting -2". They are the runs that initially added up 10, 11, and 12 do so (black columns); which after subtracting "-2" are 8, 9, and 10. That is 6 cases out of the 36 possible. In other words, only 17% of the cases exceed the average, and the rest, 83%, do not.

The same is true for mutual fund returns, which after accounting for their costs, very few outperform their benchmark. Their returns before fees look good, but after fees they are below the average.

It is not that half of mutual funds earn returns above the index and half below. It is that far fewer outperform the index, because the bell-shape of the return distribution implies that very few funds outperform the average. There are few high returns in the tail (the black columns in Figure 71).

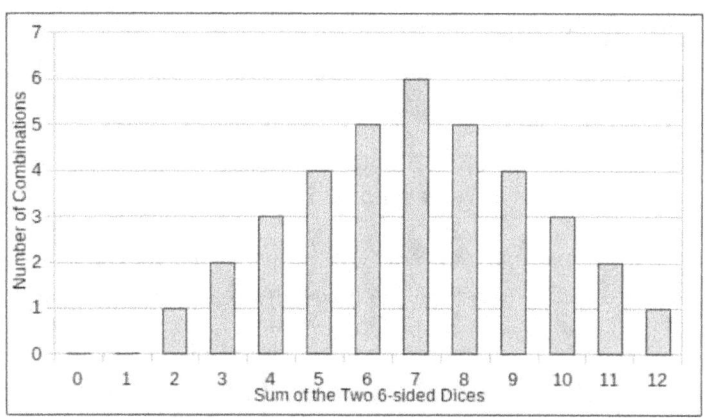

Figure 69. Combinations of rolling two dice and adding up the result.

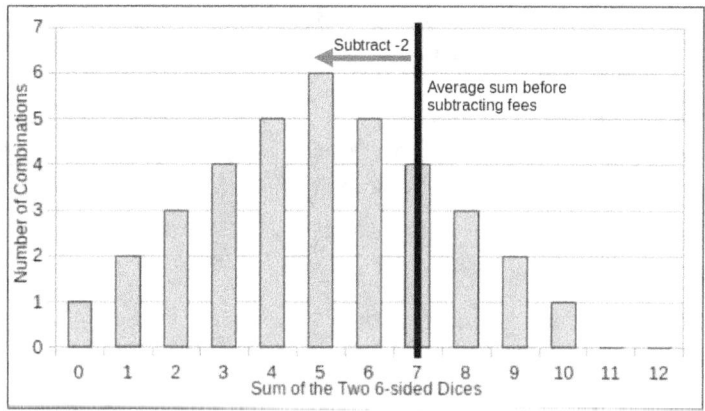

Figure 70. Effect of subtracting -2 from the sum of two dice.

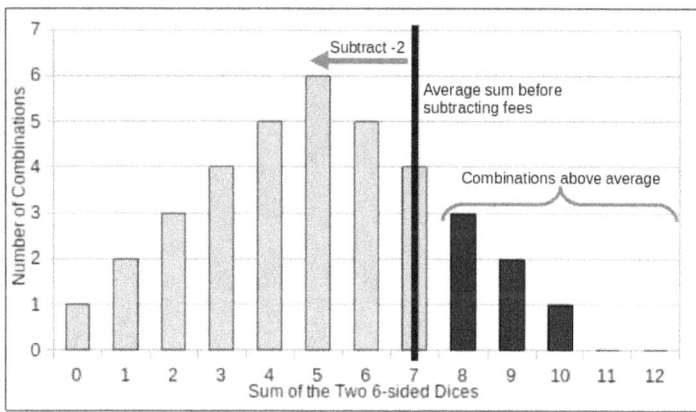

Figure 71. After subtracting -2, there are very few rolls (black columns) that exceed the initial average value (i.e., adding up more than 7).

2.16.4. Conclusions

Jack Bogle was an exceptional person.

His academic contribution highlighting the cost of an investment as a predictor of its return is remarkable.

But he has also been a great communicator of basic investment ideas among the general public, with great common sense, having written 13 books and having conducted many interviews.

And on top of that, he was able to make the theory a reality. With all the difficulties that this implies, he created a company whose objective was to keep the costs of his clients as low as possible, minimizing its budget. And this company has now survived five decades, is the second largest fund manager in the world, and competes on an equal footing with Wall Street managers.

Jack Bogle deserves the podium of honor for having been perhaps the person who has contributed the most to the world's retail investors.

2.17. Disagreement, Tastes, and Asset Prices

2.17.1. Paper

Title	Disagreement, Tastes, and Asset Prices
Author	Eugene Francis Fama and Kenneth Ronald French
Publication	Journal of Financial Economics, volume 83, number 3, pages 667-689, 2007.[66]

> **Disagreement, Tastes, and Asset Prices**
>
> Eugene F. Fama and Kenneth R. French[*]
>
> Abstract
>
> Standard asset pricing models assume that (i) there is complete agreement among investors about probability distributions of future payoffs on assets, and (ii) investors choose asset holdings based solely on anticipated payoffs; that is, investment assets are not also consumption goods. Both assumptions are unrealistic. We provide a simple framework for studying how disagreement and tastes for assets as consumption goods can affect asset prices.

Figure 72. Summary of the paper by Fama and French "Disagreement, Tastes, and Asset Prices" (2007).

2.17.2. Authors

We already discussed Eugene Fama and Kenneth Ronald French in Section 2.6 (on the Efficient Market Hypothesis) and Section 2.10 (on Factor Investment).

2.17.3. Content

Is indexed investment growing too much? Maybe. But this does not have to be negative. On the contrary, it can even be positive for all investors.

The CAPM model (which we have already seen in Section 2.5) assumes that investors know the return distribution of assets. However, the CAPM model fails to explain the returns of certain asset groups (as we already saw in Section 2.10 on the Fama-French Tree Factor Model).

The Behavioral Economics tries to explain this, and it considers "disagreements" (over- or under-reacting in the markets), or different "tastes" (of investors towards assets).

Let us look at these two sets of explanations.

2.17.3.1. Disagreement

Suppose there are two types of investors:

- the well-informed group (A), who know the distribution of asset returns, and.
- the misinformed group (D), who misperceive the distribution of returns. Moreover, they do not know that they are misinformed.

We can now assume that misinformed investors cause market prices to be inefficient, making the CAPM model meaningless.

The Figure 73 shows the portfolios of different groups of investors.

- Informed investors hold in aggregate the portfolio T, tangent to the Efficient Frontier and part of the Capital Market Line. This is the most rational portfolio.
- Poorly informed investors hold in aggregate the D portfolio, with return/volatility properties worse than the T portfolio of informed investors.
- The aggregate of the market (well-informed and misinformed investors) is the M portfolio. This portfolio is a combination of T and D. Applying the Modern Portfolio Theory, M lies on a curve. It is located according to the return, volatility, and correlation properties between the T and D portfolios. The M will be closer to T or to D, depending on whether there is more capital invested in T or in D.

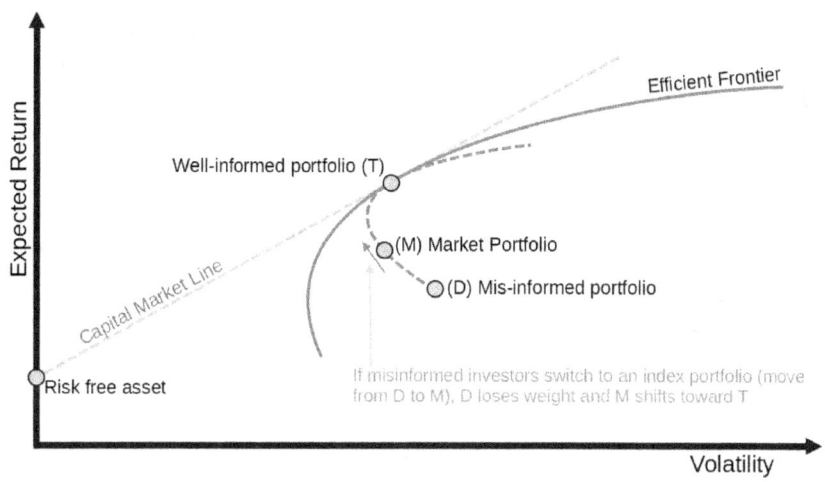

Figure 73. Portfolios as a function of their volatility and expected return. Source: figure 1 of the paper by Fama & French (2007).

Note these three ideas:

1. Well-informed investors get better returns/volatility than misinformed investors (because they invest in the portfolio T). In fact, well-informed investors get alpha at the expense of misinformed investors.

2. If misinformed investors decide to get indexed to the market (they move from holding portfolio D to portfolio M), then the market becomes more efficient. This happens because less capital is invested in D portfolios (misinformed), then portfolio T (well-informed) is proportionally larger than D, and portfolio M (the aggregate between T and D) shifts toward portfolio T (notice the arrow next to M).

3. T portfolios (informed investors) perform better than M portfolios (market-indexed). But this is only before fees and taxes. After fees and taxes, informed investors fail to outperform indexed investors (as we have seen in Section 2.16 on the effect of costs on fund returns).

There is a widespread belief among practitioners that active investment managers contribute to rational prices, and that prices are less rational if active managers switch to a passive market portfolio strategy. This is often the justification for the existence of active managers (as we will see in Section 2.21 on "Passive Investing Is Worse Than Marxism"). This argument is used despite the fact that active managers obtain systematically poor performances (as we will see in Section 2.23 on the SPIVA report and Section 2.24 on the Morningstar Barometer).

In this model, the price effects of misinformed managers are like those of other misinformed investors: trading based on bad beliefs makes prices less rational. From which authors deduce that:

> And the world is a better place (prices are more rational) when misinformed investors acknowledge their ignorance and switch to a passive market portfolio strategy.
>
> — Fama & French, "Disagreement, Tastes, and Asset Prices", page 7

2.17.3.2. Tastes

In addition to disagreement among active investors, we have the effect of different investor interest in assets.

A common assumption in asset pricing models is that investors only care about the returns on their portfolios. But this is not true; investment assets are also commodities.

Let us see that there are two groups of investors:

1. Some investors, called group A, evaluate assets based solely on economic returns. In other words, investors in group A do not have preferences for specific assets, such as consumer goods.
2. Investors who do have such tastes are called group D. Investors in group D derive direct utility from their holdings. This utility is more important to them than the asset returns.

Examples of this utility obtained by D-investors are abundant:

- "Socially Responsible Investing" (e.g., refusing to own shares of tobacco companies or arms manufacturers) is a form of preferring assets as consumption goods that are unrelated to returns.
- Loyalty or desire to belong, which leads to the utility of holding employer stock, favorite sports team, etc.; which are reasons unrelated to the return characteristics of stocks.
- National bias, i.e., the fact that investors hold more assets from their home country than what Portfolio Theory proposes.

- Finally, there may be investors who prefer a particular investment style. For example, they may prefer growth companies, and therefore avoid value companies.

Even if employees have no appreciation for the company's stock as a consumption good, incentives and subsidies that require an employee to hold the stock for a certain period of time affect portfolio decisions in the same way as "taste" for the stock.

And the effect of capital gains taxes can block buy and sell transactions, to avoid paying taxes for them.

In this way, investors' differing tastes or appetites for assets ends up affecting the composition of portfolios, moving asset prices away from their rational values.

If these investors with particular tastes were indexed, they would get better portfolios.

2.17.4. Conclusions

The conclusion of this paper goes against common sense: that the growth of indexed management can increase the efficiency of markets. This happens in the case of misinformed investors switching from active management to indexed management.[67]

The fact that indexed management is growing does not imply that markets will become less efficient. This would only happen if well-informed active managers switch to indexed management.

Moreover, if the costs of accessing information are low, a few active managers will be sufficient to maintain market efficiency.

2.18. No Person Can Serve Two Masters

2.18.1. Paper

Title	The Fiduciary Principle: No Man Can Serve Two Masters
Author	John Clifton Bogle
Publication	The Journal of Portfolio Management, volume 36, number 1, pages 15-25, fall 2009.[68]

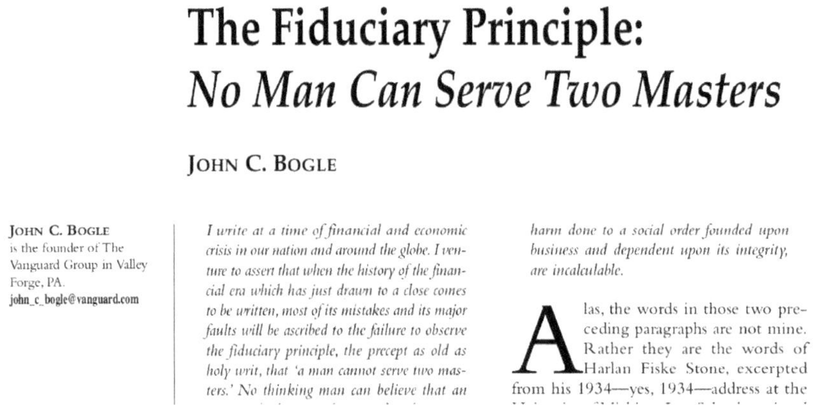

The Fiduciary Principle:
No Man Can Serve Two Masters

JOHN C. BOGLE

JOHN C. BOGLE
is the founder of The Vanguard Group in Valley Forge, PA.
john_c_bogle@vanguard.com

I write at a time of financial and economic crisis in our nation and around the globe. I venture to assert that when the history of the financial era which has just drawn to a close comes to be written, most of its mistakes and its major faults will be ascribed to the failure to observe the fiduciary principle, the precept as old as holy writ, that 'a man cannot serve two masters.' No thinking man can believe that an harm done to a social order founded upon business and dependent upon its integrity, are incalculable.

Alas, the words in those two preceding paragraphs are not mine. Rather they are the words of Harlan Fiske Stone, excerpted from his 1934—yes, 1934—address at the

Figure 74. First lines of the paper "The Fiduciary Principle: No Man Can Serve Two Masters" by Jack Bogle.

2.18.2. Author

We have previously discussed this author in Section 2.16 ("A Fundamentalist of Index Funds"), when explaining that, counterintuitively, mutual funds with lower costs provide higher returns to their unitholders.

2.18.3. Content

Vanguard, the company founded by Jack Bogle, has a unique peculiarity (we are referring to the parent company in the United States, not the subsidiary in the European Union).

The structure of Vanguard is exceptional, firstly because the company is owned by its funds, and secondly these funds are owned by their unitholders. That is, the unitholders of Vanguard's funds are the owners of Vanguard. Vanguard has no external investors (as it would have if it were a listed company), only its unitholders. Thanks to this structure, the manager reinvests any profit, any cost savings, in the fund itself, in its unitholders.

This is not a minor detail, because Vanguard manages a whopping 9.3 trillion US dollars in 2024 (9.3 "million million" dollars), making it the second largest mutual fund manager in the world, only behind BlackRock.

The average TER of Vanguard funds in the US is 0.09%, while the US industry average is 0.54% (6 times more!).

And that is because managers cannot "serve two masters", they either serve the unitholders (providing market return at minimum cost) or they serve the owners (the owners of the management company, providing them with capital appreciation and dividends).

The fact that the Vanguard funds distribute their profits to the unitholders, and not to the owners and management, has clearly visible effects. Let us look at the fortunes of the chairmen of the world's largest fund management companies:

- In 2019, Edward C. Johnson III, chairman of Fidelity Investments, was estimated to have a fortune of $7400 million.
- Larry Fink, chairman of BlackRock, would have a fortune of $1000 million in 2022.
- Jack Bogle, as former chairman of Vanguard, had a fortune estimated at $80 million in 2019.

Notice that Jack Bogle's fortune is about 100 times less than Edward C. Johnson III's, and about 10 times less than Larry Fink's. These are not differences of 10% or 20%, nor larger differences of 100%, they are even bigger, huge differences, which indicate that something exceptional is happening.

In an European context they are considered "millionaires", but in American English the difference is even more evident, because Jack Bogle is a **millionaire** while the other managers are **billionaires** (1000 millions).

These differences in the top management of the companies are largely due to the fees that Vanguard investors have saved.[69]

2.18.3.1. Asset Managers that Provide Many ETFs of the Same Index

As an example of the different behavior of fund managers, we can take the case of iShares in Europe. This fund manager (a subsidiary of BlackRock, mentioned above) offers multiple UCITS ETFs (UCITS refers to "Undertakings for Collective Investment in Transferable Securities", the "passport" to operate funds throughout the European Union).[70]

In 2005 they launched their "iShares MSCI World UCITS ETF", with a TER of 0.50% per year (see the first row of the Table 8).

In 2009 they saw that it was doing well and that they had room to lower the TER. But instead of that they decided to launch a new ETF (part of their "Core" low-cost ETF segment) with a lower TER of 0.20%/year.

This second ETF tracks exactly the same index (the MSCI World), same UCITS regulation, also domiciled in Ireland, of optimized physical type, and holding about 1440 stocks (of the 1429 stocks that make up the MSCI World in July/2024).[71]

Table 8. The 2 iShares ETFs that track the MSCI World index. Source: their factsheets on May/2024.

ISIN	ETF Name	Launch Date	TER	Return in 2023	Assets [M$]
IE00B0M62Q58	iShares MSCI World UCITS ETF	2005	0.50%	23.55%	7100
IE00B4L5Y983	iShares **Core** MSCI World UCITS ETF	2009	0.20%	23.86%	76500

As expected, the difference in annual return between the two ETFs is roughly the difference in their costs: 0.30% per year (0.50% minus 0.20%, see the penultimate column of the Table 8).

In 2009 the expensive ETF had many more assets under management than the low-cost one, but over the years gradually the assets have been flowing from the expensive ETF to the low-cost one.

For any new unitholder the rational thing to do is to buy the low-cost ETF (as we saw in the Section 2.16 on the importance of cost). But many initial unitholders are still stuck in the expensive ETF. This happens because there are unitholders who are not aware of the existence of a low-cost option, or because switching may entail even higher costs for them (e.g. because of high capital gains and having to pay taxes on it).

So, in this way the fund manager keeps its clients captive.

This 0.30% annual difference in cost has generated iShares some $21 million in 2023 ($7100 million assets under management x 0.30%/year). This was free money for iShares.

In 2024 iShares continues to offer its MSCI World UCITS ETF at a cost of 0.50% (the most expensive in the market), while offering its other ETF for 0.20%, and at the same time there are managers offering the same index for up to 0.10% (five times cheaper!).[72]

Therefore, we see that this is a good example where managers had to choose between providing the best service to their unitholders, or providing profitability to their owners. And they have chosen their owners.

2.18.4. Conclusions

The fact that investors own Vanguard's funds changes managers' incentives. And it does so for the better. A good idea that should be implemented in more places.

If somebody from Vanguard reads this, please, consider bringing to Europe the structure that you implemented in USA.

2.19. False Discoveries in Mutual Fund Performance

2.19.1. Paper

Title	False Discoveries in Mutual Fund Performance: Measuring Luck in Estimated Alphas
Authors	Laurent Barras, Olivier Scaillet, and Russ Wermers
Publication	The Journal of Finance, volume 65, number 1, pages 179-216, February 2010.[73]

False Discoveries in Mutual Fund Performance: Measuring Luck in Estimated Alphas

LAURENT BARRAS, OLIVIER SCAILLET, and RUSS WERMERS*

ABSTRACT

This paper develops a simple technique that controls for "false discoveries," or mutual funds that exhibit significant alphas by luck alone. Our approach precisely separates funds into (1) unskilled, (2) zero-alpha, and (3) skilled funds, even with dependencies in cross-fund estimated alphas. We find that 75% of funds exhibit zero alpha (net of expenses), consistent with the Berk and Green (2004) equilibrium. Further, we find a significant proportion of skilled (positive alpha) funds prior to 1996, but almost none by 2006. We also show that controlling for false discoveries substantially improves the ability to find funds with persistent performance.

Figure 75. First lines of the paper "False Discoveries in Mutual Fund Performance".

2.19.2. Authors

Laurent Barras[74] is a professor at the University of Luxembourg. He has published many scientific papers and articles in general magazines such as the New York Times and Forbes. He received his PhD in finance from the Swiss Institute of Finance, associated with the University of Geneva.

Olivier Scaillet[75] is a professor of finance at the University of Geneva and the director at the Geneva Finance Research Institute in

Switzerland. He received a PhD in applied mathematics from the University of Paris-Dauphine.

Russ Wermers is a professor of finance and director of the Center for Financial Policy at the Smith School of Business at the University of Maryland. He earned a PhD from the University of California, Los Angeles.

2.19.3. Content

In this study the authors look for the alpha generated by mutual funds.

Alpha refers to the return that an investment fund obtains above the market return.

The risk taken by the fund manager is taken into account, because if he takes relatively high risks, he is also expected to obtain a relatively high return (as we saw in section Section 2.5 on the CAPM model).

Since the authors do not see an easy way to analyze the funds one by one, they do statistics with a large dataset. They take data about monthly returns of US mutual funds between January 1975 and December 2006. They take into account luck, because it can make a bad manager get high returns in a particular year. And vice versa, a good manager can have a bad year.

After their statistical analysis, the result of the paper is shown in the Figure 76. They find the following three groups of funds, according to the return generated by their managers:

- Skilled: 0.6% of funds provide positive alpha. These are managers with real skill in selecting excellent assets. Exactly what any investor wants.
- Zero-alpha: 75.4% of funds do not provide any alpha. These are funds that provide alpha before accounting for costs, but their costs are similar to their generated alpha, so after taking them into account the net return they earn is basically the same as the market. These active funds are, in practice, equivalent to index funds.
- Unskilled: 24.0% of the studied mutual funds had negative alpha.

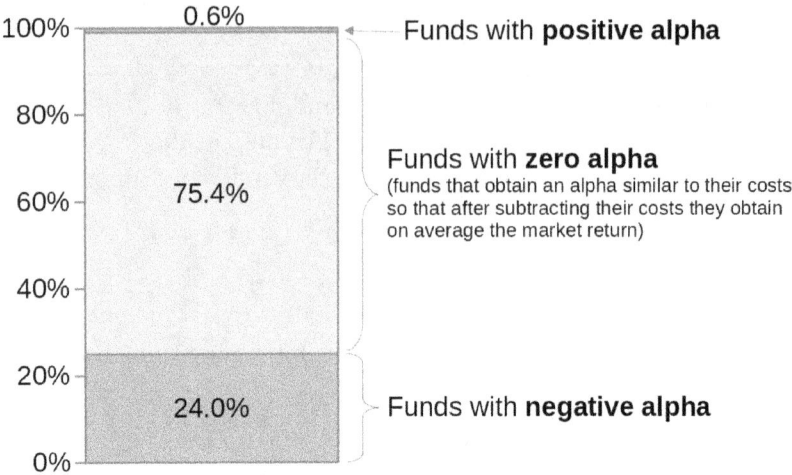

Figure 76. Conclusions of the paper "False Discoveries in Mutual Fund Performance".

The number of good managers is so small that it may not be real, perhaps it is simply a rounding error. In their own words:

> ...only 0.6% [of the fund managers] are skilled, being statistically indistinguishable from zero.
>
> — "False Discoveries in Mutual Fund Performance", page 4

In the study (from 2008), they also found a higher proportion of funds providing positive alpha when they analyzed older, pre-1996 data. However, from 2006 onward, positive alpha managers virtually disappeared. It follows that over time it is more difficult to extract alpha from the market, as if alpha is disappearing (we will see this in Section 2.20, on the paper "Is Alpha Just Beta Waiting to Be Discovered?").

This shrinking alpha seems to be a consequence of the Efficient Market Hypothesis, because as we have seen in Section 2.6 (and specifically in the "Metaphor of the Twenty Dollar Bill"), any inefficiency tends to disappear as soon as the market participants discover it and try to earn the free money.

Another interesting result is that, although the financial industry argues that fund costs for investors have been reduced by increased competition, over the last few decades (the authors refer between

1980 and 2000) there are large groups of investors that did not enjoy these fee reductions. According to the authors this may be due to two reasons:

1. Investors have not learned yet that they pay too much (and this is a good argument for books that make financial outreach like this one).
2. Investors are forced to invest in expensive funds,
   - because they are the only funds offered to them by their brokers, or
   - because unwinding the existing investment would mean paying too much capital gain taxes.

2.19.4. Conclusions

Managers who provide positive alpha are rare. Perhaps even non-existent (the authors say "indistinguishable from zero").

The percentage of managers providing positive alpha seems to have declined over the years, and now it has virtually disappeared.

Surprisingly, there are still investors paying very high fees, which necessarily leads to negative alpha.

The most sensible thing to do seems to be to avoid looking for managers that provide alpha, and simply buy the market, accepting the return it provides.

2.20. Is Alpha Just Beta Waiting to Be Discovered?

2.20.1. Paper

Title   Is Alpha Just Beta Waiting To Be Discovered?

Author   Adam Berger, David G. Kabiller, Brian Crowell

Publication Journal of Investment Strategy, volume 5, number 1, pages 21-29, year 2010.[76]

Is Alpha Just Beta Waiting To Be Discovered?
What the Rise of Hedge Fund Beta Means for Investors

By **Adam Berger, David Kabiller** and **Brian Crowell**
AQR Capital Management

Adam Berger is vice president and head of portfolio solutions. He joined AQR in 2007 after 11 years with Goldman Sachs where he most recently served as a senior research strategist in asset management. Prior to this, Berger worked in the equities division of Goldman Sachs and in the firm's pension services group. He holds an AB in Philosophy, magna cum laude, from Harvard

Alpha is shrinking, and it's good news for investors. This idea may seem paradoxical. But alpha is really just the portion of a portfolio's returns that cannot be explained by exposure to common risk factors (betas). With the emergence of new betas, the unexplained portion (alpha) shrinks – alpha gets reclassified as beta. The rise of a group of risk factors we call hedge fund betas makes this transformation especially relevant today. Hedge fund betas are the common risk exposures shared by hedge fund managers pursuing similar strategies. We believe these risk factors can capture not just the fundamental insights of hedge funds, but also a meaningful portion of their returns.

Figure 77. First lines of the AQR paper "Is Alpha Just Beta Waiting To Be Discovered?" (2010).

2.20.2. Authors

Adam Berger is a vice president at AQR, has worked at Goldman Sachs, graduated from Harvard University, earned an MBA from Wharton Business School, and is CFA certified.

David G. Kabiller is a founding partner of AQR, worked at Goldman Sachs, got a degree in economics from Northwestern University, where he also earned an MBA), and is CFA certified.

Brian Crowell works at AQR, previously at UBS, has a degree in chemistry, an MBA from the University of Chicago, and is CFA certified.

All of them work for AQR Capital Management, a US-based hedge fund.

AQR was founded by four friends who met at the University of Chicago, where they were pursuing their doctorates. Among others Cliff Asness (we talked about him before, in the Section 2.10, because he was a PhD student of Eugene Fama, and he is one of the proponents of the "momentum" factor) and David G. Kabiller

AQR has a close relationship with the financial academic world, and for example they are the creators of the Pandas library[77], well-known for performing data analysis in Python.

2.20.3. Content

The paper begins with an outlandish, counterintuitive statement:

> Alpha is shrinking, and it's good news for investors.
>
> — "Is Alpha Just Beta Waiting To Be Discovered?", page 1

The general idea is that alpha is the part of a portfolio's return that cannot be explained by exposure to risk factors (the betas). And eventually, with the emergence of new betas, this unexplained return (alpha) is further reduced. In short: Over time alpha becomes beta.

The paper takes for granted that this occurs in conventional assets (stocks and bonds), and that it is also obvious to all players in the markets (in fact, the disappearance of alpha we have already discussed it before in Section 2.19, when looking at the alpha generated by funds). So the paper really goes one step further and focuses on applying this idea to hedge funds.

The authors consider that there is no chance for a retail investor to gain alpha by trading in the stock market. On the one hand because they have to compete against professional fund managers, but on the other hand because hedge funds use unconventional techniques to squeeze out as much alpha as possible.

Some summary thoughts from the paper:

- Alpha should not be considered as the return of active management, but rather as a return source that is not associated with any common risk factor (see the Table 9).
- As new risk factors emerge, alpha explains a smaller portion of portfolio returns. This means an improvement in the transparency of financial markets.
- The reclassification of portions of alpha into beta is a continuous evolution that is part of the history of financial innovation.

Table 9. Definitions of alpha and beta. Source: Figure 1 of "Is Alpha Just Beta Waiting To Be Discovered?".

	Alpha	**Beta**
Colloquial definition	Returns generated by active managers	Returns from passive market exposure.
Economic definition	Returns that cannot be explained by exposure to common risk factors	Returns from exposure to one or more common risk factors

Alpha and beta are concepts taken from Portfolio Theory, in particular the Capital Asset Pricing Model (CAPM, see Section 2.5).

This definition makes it clear that alpha is not "the return from active management", but "the return that cannot be explained by betas".

This in turn means that as new risk factors are discovered and popularized, the returns attributable to alpha decrease and some of that alpha is reclassified as beta. This transformation does not mean a decrease in returns. The reduction in alpha is offset by an increasing part of the returns attributable to beta. This is shown visually in the Figure 78.

The reclassification does not necessarily mean lower returns for investors. In fact, if the new factor reduces investment costs, it may result in a higher expected net return.

Before the advent of capitalization-weighted stock indexes more than half a century ago, any investor who used a manager to construct a portfolio of stocks had to attribute the results to the manager's skill.

Thus, all portfolio returns above the risk free asset return were considered alpha.

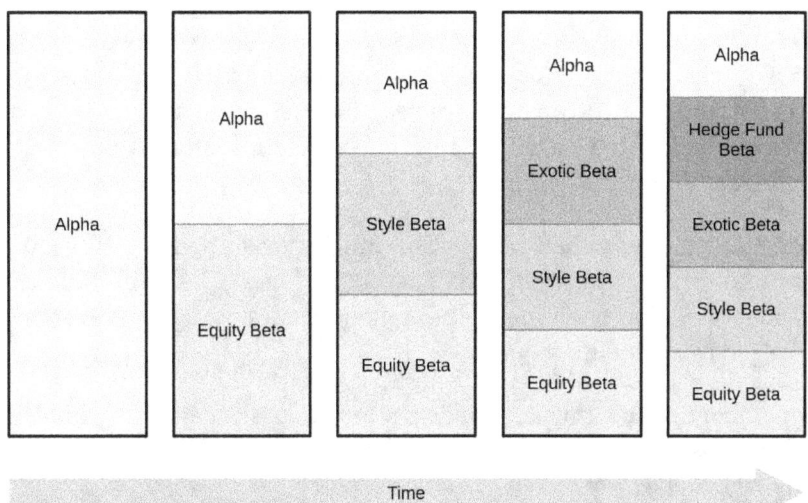

Figure 78. Over time, a growing proportion of returns can be explained as beta. First traditional betas (e.g. S&P 500, Lehman Aggregate), then style betas (e.g. Russel value and small-cap indices), then exotic betas (e.g. commodities, real estate), and now hedge fund betas. Source: Figure 1 from the paper "Is Alpha Just Beta Waiting To Be Discovered" (2010).

As time went by, it became clear that these portfolios' success or failure was tied to the overall performance of the stock market.

There were boom cycles in which most portfolios performed well, and bust cycles in which most portfolios performed poorly. Thus, with capitalization-weighted stock market indexes such as the S&P 500, investors had a better way to explain their managers' returns. Then they could attribute a large portion of portfolio performance to market beta.

After considering the impact of beta, the portion of returns attributed to alpha was significantly reduced.

Nevertheless, some active managers continued to beat the market return, generating alpha. Although investors were realizing that many managers were following similar strategies to beat the market. For example, some managers overweighted small-cap companies, while others overweighted companies trading with low

165

price/earnings or price/book ratios. Both groups tended to outperform the broad stock market indexes over the long term.

The three-factor model of Eugene Fama and Kenneth French (referring to Fama and French's 1993 paper, see the Section 2.10) drove greater acceptance of size- and value-based portfolios. The emergence of small-cap and large-cap indexes, and value and growth indexes codified these ideas into betas that investors could use to understand portfolio returns.

For managers who had beaten an equity market benchmark simply by holding a portfolio of small-cap or value stocks, this discovery turned what had been their alpha into a beta (although not everyone realized this immediately).

If investors could invest in indexes at low cost, managers could no longer justify high fees for market-beating portfolios simply by buying small, cheap stocks.

More recently, investors have diversified their portfolios across a broader range of assets than traditional developed markets. Many of these new investments (commodities, real estate, equities, emerging market debt, etc.) fall into the category of "other market betas", or investments whose returns can be explained by exposure to less traditional risk factors. Like traditional betas, they are often associated with long-term exposure to one or more markets.

This history demonstrates that, as financial theory evolves, what once seemed like uncorrelated and somewhat mysterious alpha tends to become the return associated with exposure to a relatively understandable risk factor. Today, the betas of hedge funds are simply the latest (albeit most complex) step in this story.

The paper also argues that there are price trends due to biases and weaknesses of participants who are not purely seeking to maximize their profits (who have other objectives by being in the stock market).

The Figure 79 shows the life cycle of a trend as described by the authors. Initially a "catalyst" occurs, for example a positive earnings release, a supply shock, or a change in demand. That is, a change in the fundamental value of a stock, a commodity, a currency, or a bond. This change in fundamental value is immediate. The market price then rises due to the catalyst, but initially does not react strongly enough. There are tendencies in investor behavior (anchoring to initial value, following the crowd, and over-reacting), and frictions in the market (costs, etc.), which make the price discovery process imperfect.

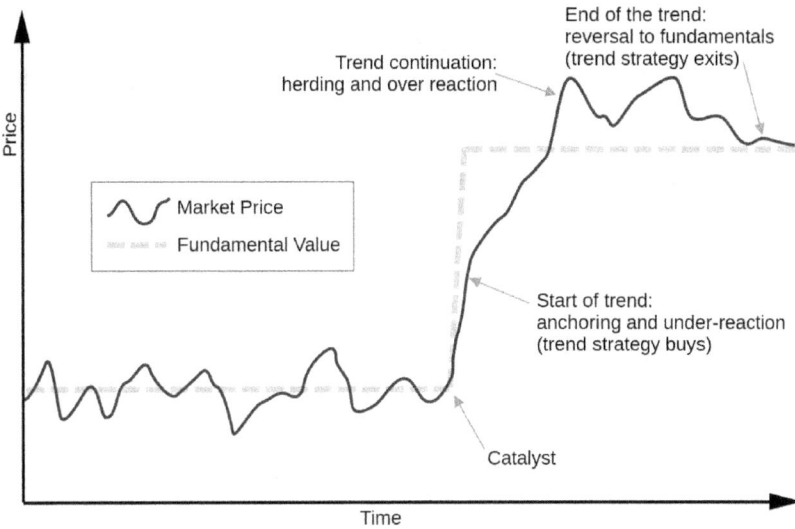

Figure 79. The life cycle of a price trend. Source: Figure 4 from the paper "Is Alpha Just Beta Waiting To Be Discovered" (as updated in 2012). Originally from "Understanding Managed Futures".

According to the authors, strategies such as these are already described, standardized, and systematically implemented by the hedge Funds, and are therefore already beta. They are hedge fund investment styles, just as investing in small-cap companies can be another style in the context of stocks.

2.20.4. Conclusions

What were once investment strategies considered to provide alpha, exceptional returns, today are encapsulated and sold as everyday products. Today buying market beta is like buying a kilogram of salt: it is cheap, there are multiple suppliers, and the product is indistinguishable between any of them.

Now that the old alpha that could be received from the market is already packaged as beta, does it make sense for a retail investor to chase the alpha, the returns generated by active managers? Buying beta from the market provides the same expected return (before costs), but it is practically free.

This is the umpteenth justification for passive investing. The most reasonable thing to do for a retail investor is just to buy the market to receive its beta. And if someone wants a somewhat higher expected return, buy some other asset class (another beta) provided encapsulated in a low-priced index fund. But that's not alpha, it is just the expected reward for taking a higher risk.

Let us leave the professionals looking for alpha, and we retail investors get the beta they provide at low cost.

2.21. Passive Investing Is Worse Than Marxism

This is a report against passive investing that was much commented on. Its title says it all.

2.21.1. Paper

Title	The Silent Road to Serfdom: Why Passive Investing is Worse Than Marxism
Authors	Inigo Fraser-Jenkins, Paul Gait et al.
Publication	This is a report published in August 2016 by the financial firm AllianceBernstein and addressed to its clients.[78]

23 August 2016

Fund Management Strategy

The Silent Road to Serfdom: Why Passive Investing is Worse Than Marxism

Inigo Fraser-Jenkins
+44-207-170-5134
inigo.fraser-jenkins@bernstein.com

Paul Gait
+44-207-170-0599
paul.gait@bernstein.com

Policy makers should care about active fund management because of the role it plays in allocating capital in the economy. This action is a force for social good and indeed comprises the social function of active management (and for that matter of sell side equity research). This note aims to help asset managers and asset owners make this social case for active management to policymakers.

Figure 80. First lines of the report "The Silent Road to Serfdom: Why Passive Investing is Worse Than Marxism".

This is not a scholarly paper because it is not published in a formal journal and has not been approved in peer review. However, it is relevant because it is a well-known critique of passive investing, and from time to time it comes up again to public discussion.

2.21.2. Authors

The authors are ten members of the firm AllianceBernstein, with extensive experience, CFAs, masters, etc.

The first author is Inigo Fraser-Jenkins, co-head of the Institutional department at AllianceBernstein, and with a long career in finance.

He has a bachelor's degree in physics and two master's degrees: one in history and philosophy of science, and the other in finance.[79]

The second author is Paul Gait. He studied a bachelor's degree in natural sciences, a master's degree in experimental & theoretical physics, he attended the Cavendish Laboratory in 1999 to undertake postgraduate research in the department of theoretical condensed matter, and finally he got an MBA in finance. He worked at McKinsey and afterwards joined Sandford Bernstein.

2.21.3. Content

The title of the paper is a reference to "The Road to Serfdom", the famous book written by Friedrich Hayek in 1944, in the context of the World War II and the raise of socialism and fascism. In it, Hayek writes about the danger of tyranny that inevitably results from government control of economic decision-making through central planning. Hayek was awarded with the Nobel Prize in Economic Sciences in 1974.[80]

2.21.3.1. Argument

This study argues that the growth of passive investing is a risk to the economy.

The justification for the subtitle comes from considering companies according to their efficiency in asset allocation:

1. "Capitalist society with functioning capital markets". This is the ideal, because it can allocate capital from declining industries into new economic sectors. It is talking about Joseph Schumpeter's Creative Destruction idea.
2. Marxism. In this case we have an economy where a central agency plans where to allocate resources. This central agency seeks a good for society. Whether it is the best possible good is debatable, but at least it has a goal.
3. "Capitalist society with predominantly passive capital markets". This is what worries the authors, that in this case no one is thinking about how to allocate assets. There is a decision vacuum, no one is responsible. And such a society, they argue, cannot thrive.

They argue against this third case:

> A supposedly capitalist economy where the only investment is passive is worse than either a centrally planned economy or an economy with active market led capital management.
>
> — "The Silent Road to Serfdom", page 1

Both in capitalist markets and under Marxism, there are agents who are optimizing resources for a real economy goal. But passive investment is worse than both because it does not even follow a real economy objective, they say it is nihilistic.

And the authors elaborate on the social function of investment:

> What is the social function of active management in equity markets [...]?
>
> [...] it is even more important than normal to demonstrate that there is indeed a social function. A field of endeavour that performs no social function is ultimately unsustainable if it has a cost that is imposed on the rest of society. Any such activity will, in the ultimate analysis, simply be regulated out of existence.
>
> However, there is a clear and distinct task that active management [...] performs. This is in the allocation of capital either directly through the raising of capital in primary markets or else indirectly in the information discovery process. This is a laudable task and needs to be recognised.
>
> — "The Silent Road to Serfdom", page 3

If most investors were passive, then there would be no incentive to Joseph Schumpeter's Creative Destruction, because all entrepreneurial projects would find funding on the stock market, even those that deserve to fail.

A common argument in the active vs passive debate is that when passive equity is in the majority, this will create opportunities for active managers to gain alpha. However, the authors consider this to be wishful thinking because:

1. It is unclear when this inflection point will be reached.
2. Passive investing continues to grow.

3. Active and passive management scale differently. Passive management is more efficient the larger it gets (since its expenses are relatively constant, as it grows expenses represent a smaller percentage of its assets, lower TER). On the other hand, active managers are no longer profitable when they manage too many assets (because inefficiencies disappear when they are exploited, or for example because small-cap companies have a very limited capitalization available). This is why, if passive management continues to grow, then in the future it will have even more advantage over active management.

The authors ask themselves: How to defend active investing from the rise of passive strategies? They are concerned that strategies that were purely active in the past are now packaged as "smart beta" and offered as ETFs (as we have seen in Section 2.20, "Alpha is just beta waiting to be discovered"). Simple, transparent, and cheap; active managers must compete with these new products. And that is worrying.

The report goes on for 47 pages reinforcing these arguments. They pay attention to their vocabulary: their objective is "social", they have a "social function", active management is a "social good", that provides "social benefits", there are "social arguments", etc.

They talk at length about many different topics, like society, Marxism, the Soviet Union, the book of Genesis, San Isidoro de Sevilla, the Salekhard-Igarka railroad by the Arctic Circle, even the need for the existence of asset markets with ever-increasing prices in order to pay future pensions.

2.21.3.2. Target

This is a report by AllianceBernstein distributed to its clients, but it really targets lawmakers and regulators, asking them to "protect active managers" because it is "a force for social good".

The authors have written this report in the hope that their clients will influence lawmakers and regulators. That is why the title is so provocative.

While the paper does not go so far as to call for government help for Wall Street, it does recommend that:

> [Lawmakers and regulators] may wish to consider the broader benefits of a functioning active asset management industry to society as a whole so that when policy initiatives are undertaken they do not explicitly undermine active management.

— "The Silent Road to Serfdom", page 40

2.21.3.3. Critique

According to their view (the view of a multinational financial company), the financial sector is a kind of NPO (NonProfit Organization) that manages the assets of the unitholders, and the unitholders are generous philanthropists who donate their assets for a social good.

They are benefactors with other people's money.

As we have discussed, the returns of mutual funds, in aggregate, are the market return minus their fees (see the Section 2.16 on Jack Bogle). Because as we have seen, in the short term fund management is a "zero-sum" game. That is why index funds outperform active funds, because of their lower fees. However, from AllianceBernstein they don't believe that argument, and justify their existence for the common good:

> A given investment in active may or may not be the best decision for an individual particular investor but for the system overall there is a benefit in the efficient allocation of capital.

— "The Silent Road to Serfdom", page 3

At times it seems that we are reading the report of an NPO, and not that of a financial multinational.

Curiously, the company criticizes passive funds, but it promotes them. Among the products they offer there are 2 ETFs that track indexes created by them.[81]

> If you look at this product [the two new ETFs], the real innovative feature is that you can basically use the passive process and the passive infrastructure out there to run a fund that uses very active ingredients.

— Robert van Brugge, chief executive officer of AllianceBernstein

And there is another inconsistency in their arguments. Reading their 2015 Annual Report[82] to the US regulator (the SEC), we find that they have been using index funds since at least 2013 (3 years before this report about Marxism). This report to the SEC contains 30 references to the word "passive". And much of the management they were doing, both in equities and fixed income, was already passive back then.[83]

Reading their reports you also find that 63% of their equity management underperformed their benchmarks over the previous 3 years.[83]

There is currently a gigantic transfer of wealth from actively managed mutual funds (which charge high fees and offer relatively poor returns) to index funds (with tiny fees and statistically better returns). For most unitholders, the rational choice is to choose index funds.

This text is the cry for help from a firm like AllianceBernstein that provides sell side equity research. They see their future in jeopardy.

According to the report, the growth of equity in index funds should theoretically cause stocks to move in the same direction, preventing the proper allocation of capital, because both the price of stocks and economic sectors would move in unison. The flaw is that the research does not demonstrate this. They themselves show figures trying to find correlation (Figure 4 of their report), but do not find it.

2.21.3.4. Jack Bogle's commentary

Jack Bogle wrote in The Wall Street Journal, 2 years before the AllianceBernstein) report, the following article (which is adapted from his book "Stay of Course"):

This article is closely related to the "Silent Road to Serfdom" article, because it lays out the same challenges. In this article, moreover, Jack Bogle suggests possible solutions.

In it, Jack describes his beginnings at Vanguard, the creation of what was arguably the first publicly available index mutual fund (the "Vanguard 500 Index Fund" on December 31, 1975), and the difficulties he went through.

THE WALL STREET JOURNAL.

English Edition ▾ | Print Edition | Video | Audio | Latest Headlines | More ▾

WEEKEND INVESTOR

Bogle Sounds a Warning on Index Funds

The father of the index fund says it's probably only a matter of time before they own half of all U.S. stocks; 'I do not believe that such concentration would serve the national interest'

By John C. Bogle
Nov. 29, 2018 10:15 am ET

Figure 81. First lines of Jack Bogle's article in The Wall Street Journal.[34]

He attributes the following comment to the president of Fidelity:

> I can't believe that the great mass of investors are [sic] going to be satisfied with just receiving average returns. The name of the game is to be the best.Vanguard
>
> — Attributed by Jack Bogle to the president of Fidelity, in reference to the newly created first index fund at Vanguard

He argues about the risk of asset concentration in a few asset managers. He gives an example regarding index funds, because in 2016, 81% of their assets were held by only 3 asset managers: 51% Vanguard, 21% BlackRock, and 9% State Street Global.

This is due to barriers to entry. These managers have the scale factor in their favor: the cost of managing index funds is largely independent of the amount of assets under management. Thus, when the assets under management are huge, the cost as a percentage of those assets is very small. New managers, starting with small assets, cannot compete with the existing giants.

For this reason, the problem will not be solved simply by competition between managers.

This leads to a concentration of power in the management companies, which sit on the boards of all the companies and therefore have enormous voting power.

Jack Bogle proposes several ideas to solve the problem, including:

- Fragment the fund managers to reduce their concentration.
- That index fund managers disclose their voting policies to boards of directors, and that there be public documentation of each engagement with company directors. Thus increasing transparency. In this way, unitholders will be able to index with manager X, Y, or Z; knowing that each makes different decisions and seeks to satisfy different groups of clients. This route is the one that the fund managers seem to have taken.

Jack Bogle ends by saying that index funds are a great invention, which has allowed ordinary people to participate in stock market returns, and that it would be a bad idea to ban them.

2.21.4. Conclusions

The criticism that purely passive capital markets cannot allocate resources properly is certainly a powerful one.

However, it is hard to believe that we will get there, because then most investors would be accepting "average returns", rather than "exceptional returns". And ego abounds among investors.

And in the case of passive investment being in the majority, it remains to be demonstrated that a tiny number of active investors (large Wall Street institutional investors, hedge funds, with leveraged investments, etc.), for example 1%, would not be able to generate asset prices with their sales and purchases.

The criticism of Jack Bogle is perhaps more worrying. If index fund managers were a majority on all boards of directors of listed companies, then we would have an enormous accumulation of power in very few hands. That is uncharted territory within capitalism as we know it.

2.22. Shooting the Messenger

This is not an academic paper, but a report carried out by Standard and Poor's (S&P, the famous global credit rating agency). Although it is not a formal paper, it is very relevant because it is done by experts in the field, and because it is heavily publicized, encouraging discussion that ultimately improves the arguments.

2.22.1. Report

Title	Shooting the Messenger
Authors	Anu R. Ganti and Craig J. Lazzara
Publication	S&P Dow Jones Indices, November 2022.[85]

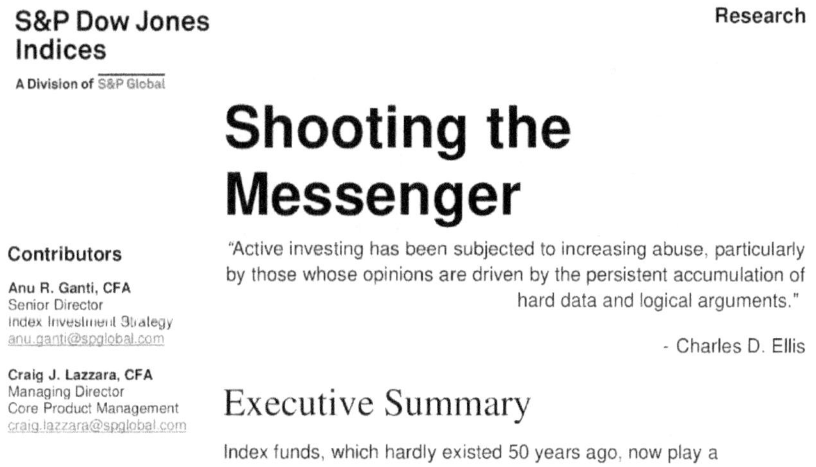
S&P Dow Jones Indices

A Division of S&P Global

Research

Shooting the Messenger

Contributors

Anu R. Ganti, CFA
Senior Director
Index Investment Strategy
anu.ganti@spglobal.com

Craig J. Lazzara, CFA
Managing Director
Core Product Management
craig.lazzara@spglobal.com

"Active investing has been subjected to increasing abuse, particularly by those whose opinions are driven by the persistent accumulation of hard data and logical arguments."

- Charles D. Ellis

Executive Summary

Index funds, which hardly existed 50 years ago, now play a

Figure 82. First lines of the report "Shooting the Messenger".

2.22.2. Authors

The authors are Anu R. Ganti (senior director of Index Investment Strategy within S&P Dow Jones Indices) and Craig J. Lazzara (managing director of Core Product Management, also working at S&P Dow Jones Indices). Both have earned the prestigious CFA (Chartered Financial Analyst) certification.

Craig Lazzara also participates in the SPIVA reports (discussed in the Section 2.23).

2.22.3. Content

As seen in the opening lines of the paper (see Figure 82), the authors start with a touch of humor. Charles D. Ellis (CFA, known for supporting passive investing and writing the book "Winning the Loser's Game") wrote the following text[86] where he said, among other things, that:

> Active investing has been increasingly abused, especially by those whose opinions are guided by the persistent accumulation of solid data and logical arguments.
>
> — Charles D. Ellis, "The Loser's Game", 1975

And this is what this report does, to provide arguments showing what difficulties are facing active investors. In this paper the authors discuss the three reasons why indexing works:

1. the professionalization of management,
2. the cost, and
3. the asymmetry of returns.

As they explain, none of these reasons is likely to be reversed, or even reduced, so the growth of indexing seems destined to continue.

Let us look at these three arguments one by one in the following subsections.

2.22.3.1. Professionalization of Investment Management

Active management is a "zero-sum game". There is no natural source of superior returns; the only source of returns for investors with "above average" skills is the returns they extract from "below average" investors. "Investors" in this sense encompasses not only professional managers, but any owner of assets in the market. They may be investors who are unaware that they are in a zero-sum game. In fact, they may not even be aware that they are part of a game and that they stand to lose.

However, if professionals become the dominant force in a market, and amateur investors become less important, the game changes, because professionals are now competing with each other.

In the United States, for example, professionals started to dominate beginning in the mid-1970s:

> Gifted, determined and ambitious professionals have entered investment management in such numbers over the past 30 years that it may no longer be feasible for any of them to profit from everyone else's mistakes with sufficient frequency and magnitude to beat the market.
>
> — Charles D. Ellis, "The Loser's Game", 1975, page 19

It is important in this discussion to distinguish between **absolute** and **relative** skill.

Absolute skill in active investing requires managers to access information and evaluate, based on some combination of fundamental, technical and quantitative metrics, the difference between a stock's current price and its true intrinsic value.

Criticizing the performance of active managers is not meant to impugn the level of their skills. But managers do not operate in a vacuum. **Absolute** skill may be necessary to succeed as an active manager, but it is not sufficient. It is **relative** skill that determines results.

It is not enough to be good at valuing companies; a successful active manager must be better than his competitors.

If investment management is not unique in this respect, it is at least very unusual. An average doctor may be able to cure a sick person, and an average lawyer may be a perfectly adequate source of legal representation for his client. However, investment management is different: an investment manager of average skill is of no value to his unitholders.

> Investing is unusual, in that the collective judgment of all the participants (weighted by the amount of money they control) is ... available for free ... If a professional investor is to earn excess returns for his client, being good is insufficient, he must be exceptional.
>
> — Hal Arbit, paper "The Nature of the Game", published by Journal of Portfolio Management, Fall 1981, pages 5-9

The difficulty is compounded when we consider what happens when, over time, the assets of active managers are transferred to index funds. Presumably, the least capable active managers lose the most assets under management. This means that the quality of surviving active managers increases as assets move to passive alternatives, making competition for returns harder. Active managers are finding it increasingly difficult to stay above average as index funds weed out weaker competitors.

Fama and French gave a more mathematical explanation about this in his paper from 2007 (see Section 2.17).

2.22.3.2. Cost

Low cost is the simplest explanation for the success of passive management. We already saw this in the Section 2.16, when discussing Jack Bogle.

Let us imagine a market in which all portfolios are actively managed and in which a passive alternative is inserted. This passive alternative buys a proportional share of each company in the market.

Since the passive portfolio owns a proportional share of each company's capitalization, its portfolio will be identical to the aggregate portfolio of the active managers. Therefore, before costs, passive portfolios and active portfolios will have the same return.

We are talking about the aggregate of active managers, because if there are excellent managers, there are also disastrous ones, but all together they form the market as a whole, and the passive manager buys that resulting market.

However, the costs of active managers (research, trading, management fees, etc.) are inherently higher than those of passive managers. And so:

> Measured correctly, the average actively managed dollar should have a lower return than the average passively managed dollar, net of costs. Empirical analyses that appear to refute this principle are guilty of incorrect measurement.
>
> — William Forsyth Sharpe, "The Arithmetic of Active Management", published in "Financial Analysts Journal", January/February 1991, pages 7-9

To illustrate the importance of costs, consider that the average expense ratio of active US equity mutual fund managers in 2021 was 0.68%, versus only 0.06% for their passive competitors. This 0.62% difference (more than 10 times more expensive!) gives investors an automatic advantage in choosing a passive manager over an active one. The growing popularity of index funds, coupled with industry consolidation and economies of scale, has the potential to further drive down the costs of passive funds.

Regarding costs, the Figure 83 shows that indexed investing allows investors a saving (considering that indexed investors receive an equal or better service than active investors). And it is not a small saving, considering that the US GDP was around 23 trillion (23 million million) dollars in 2021, 403 billion (403 thousand million) dollars represented 1.7% of that amount. That's about $1200 accumulated per US citizen.

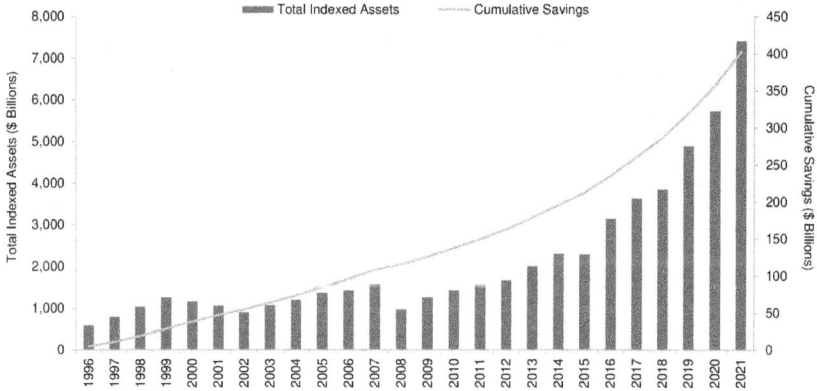

Figure 83. The cumulative fee savings by investors amount to about $403 billion (403 thousand million). Data from S&P Dow Jones Indices as of December 31, 2021. Source: exhibit 9 in report.

In other words, thanks to the tiny improvement in mutual fund TER, indexing has provided cumulative savings to society equivalent to 1.7% of all goods and services provided by the US in 2021. Imagine the interest of the active investment industry in "recovering these losses".

Perhaps the best way to see the importance of cost is to realize that the expected return of a particular asset is the return of its asset class (example: stocks, bonds). And that therefore, if that asset class makes sense for the portfolio, it makes the most sense to buy the entire class (i.e., with maximum diversification), in the appropriate proportion of the portfolio. And since the expected returns of different mutual funds from different managers are the same, regardless of whether they are actively or passively managed, then it only makes sense to buy the cheapest fund, which with few exceptions will be a passive fund.

It is like buying a kilogram of salt in the supermarket. Although different brands sell it at different prices, the service the salt will provide will be basically the same. Price is the only parameter to differentiate each product.

2.22.3.3. Returns Asymmetry

This effect has been known for many years, and has been discussed in the Section 2.13 on portfolio size and the asymmetry of returns.

In a normal distribution the observations are symmetrically arranged around their mean value. But the distribution of stock returns is not a normal distribution, it is skewed toward positive assets. That is: the mean return is usually larger than the median (the median being the value that leaves half of the returns to its left, and half to its right).

For example, there is a natural tendency for stock returns to be skewed, as a stock can only go down by 100%, while it could appreciate much more than that (e.g. 200%). Large positive assets can drag the average level of the distribution above its midpoint.

We observe this in the Figure 84, which represents the distribution of the cumulative returns of the assets that make up the S&P 500 over the past 20 years. The median return was 88%, much less than the arithmetic mean of 358%. Importantly, the positive skew in equity returns illustrated by the chart is not simply a chance artifact of a small number of years: in the 31 years between 1991 and 2021, the mean of the S&P 500 stocks outperformed the median 27 times.

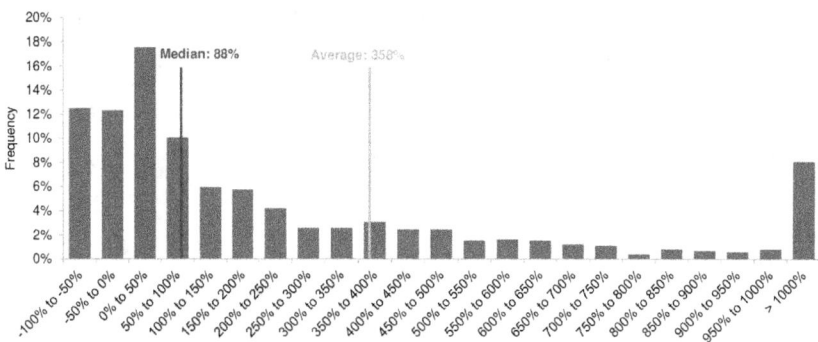

Figure 84. The returns of the stocks that are part of the S&P 500 are highly asymmetric. Data from S&P Dow Jones Indices for the period from 31/Dec/2001 to 31/Dec/2021. The "frequency" (vertical axis) refers to the percentage of S&P 500 stocks that showed that return during the period. Source: exhibit 6 in report.

If stock returns would follow a normal distribution, a randomly chosen stock would be just as likely to offer an "above average" return as an "below average" return. But when the distribution is skewed, selection is much more difficult. Of the 975 assets that were part of the S&P 500 at some point between 2002 and 2021, only 253 outperformed the average return.

In other words, the probability that a randomly chosen stock will deliver an above-average return is worse than choosing "heads or tails" at the flip of a coin, it is 26% (253 stocks out of 975 stocks) and not 50%. And so, when fewer assets outperform the average, active management is more difficult.

Active managers exacerbate the effect of skewed returns because of their tendency to manage relatively concentrated portfolios.

Theoretical Example: Returns vs Diversification

This is a similar example to the one presented in the Section 2.13.3.2 ("About Asset Concentration in Portfolios"), but there we were interested in a single case (portfolios composed of a fixed number of stocks), and here we follow the evolution of returns as diversification increases.

We consider a simple example that presents asymmetric returns. See Table 10. We have a market with five stocks, one of which (E) far outperforms the others. We assume that at the beginning of the year

183

the capitalizations of the stocks are identical, so that the total market return is 9% (sum up the returns and divide by 5), driven by the excellent return of the E security.

Table 10. Hypothetical returns of 5 stocks during one year. It is only an example. It is data that will be used afterwards in Table 11.

Stock	A	B	C	D	E
Return	5%	5%	5%	5%	25%

From these five stocks (A, B, C, D, and E) we can form portfolios with 1, 2, 3, 4, and 5 stocks; as shown in Table 11 (upper rows are less diversified portfolios, lower rows are more diversified portfolios). We assume for simplicity that all stocks have the same weight (they are equal-weighted portfolios).

The portfolio with 5 stocks, all the stocks in the market, is the market portfolio.

Since there are five stocks, there are five possible portfolios composed of a **single stock** (see the first row of numbers in the table). Four of them have a return lower than that of the market aggregate.

- The portfolio that exceeds the market return (9%) is composed 100% by E (return: 25%) and therefore its alpha is 16% (=25%-9%).
- The four portfolios that do not outperform the market (9%) earn returns of 5%, and thus their alpha is -4% (=5%-9%).

Table 11. More concentrated portfolios are more likely to earn returns below the market average. All stocks in each portfolio have the same proportion. Hypothetical data, it comes from Table 10.

Number stocks in portfolio	Number of portfolios	Average portfolio return	Probab. outper- formance	Alpha of the best portfolios	Alpha of the worst portfolios
1	5	9%	20%	16.0%	-4.0%
2	10	9%	40%	6.0%	-4.0%
3	10	9%	60%	2.7%	-4.0%
4	5	9%	80%	1.0%	-4.0%
5	1	9%		Market Portfolio	

Similarly, there are also five possible portfolios of **four stocks** (ABCD, ABCE, ABDE, ACDE, and BCDE), four of which outperform (return: 10%) the market as a whole (all portfolios containing stock E).

Given that the market return, according to our assumptions, is 9% (which is the average return of the 5 stocks), the average return of the portfolios is always 9%: if the market gives us 9%, it does not matter how we divide it. What changes is the distribution of the returns among the portfolios. Diversifying with more stocks increases the probability of outperformance.

The intuition here is simple and is shown in the Figure 85: a manager's picks are more likely to underperform than outperform, simply because there are more underperforming stocks than outperforming stocks to choose from. Since returns are skewed toward positive values, more concentrated portfolios are unlikely to outperform the market average.

The greater the number of stocks in the portfolio, the better.

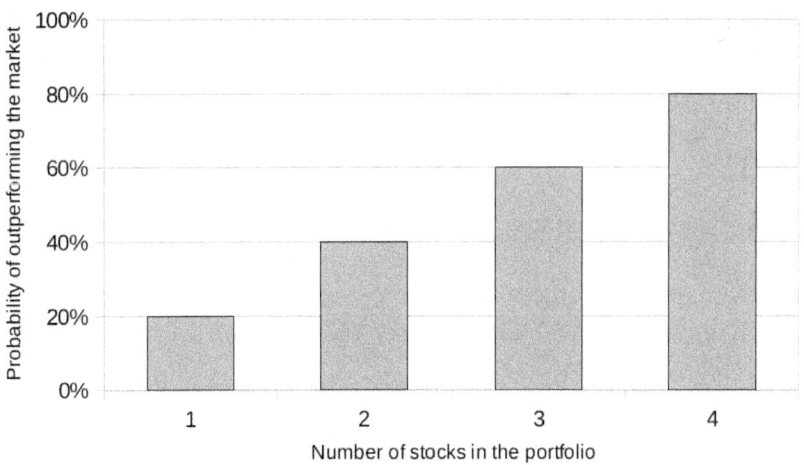

Figure 85. Probability that an equal-weighted portfolio will outperform the market. Assuming a market with 5 stocks as indicated in the Table 10 and the Table 11 (this diagram is simply the first and fourth columns of the latter table). A portfolio with few stocks is unlikely to outperform the market (although when it does, it will do it with a very high return).

2.22.4. Conclusions

Note that at no point have we mentioned the "market efficiency", which can be defined as (taken from the paper discussed in the Section 2.6.3.3):

> [An efficient market is] a market in which prices always "fully reflect" the available information.
>
> — Eugene Fama, "Efficient Capital Markets: A Review of Theory and Empirical Work", published in the Journal of Finance, May/1970, pages 383-417

Obviously, if markets fully reflect available information, market prices will reflect true value, making asset selection unprofitable.

The challenge for detractors of the Efficient Markets Hypothesis is that it is easy to find *a posteriori* evidence of times when price did not correspond to real value, for example during the tech bubble of the late 1990s. But it is not easy *a priori*.

And while the efficiency hypothesis may be sufficient to defend index funds, it is not necessary. Even if we recognize that prices do not always reflect fair value, the factors we have identified (professionalization of management, cost and asymmetry) will continue to challenge active managers relentlessly.

The factors behind active managers' returns underperforming their indices are robust and sustainable over time. Investment management will remain professionalized, active costs will always exceed index costs, and almost every year most active managers will underperform in most markets.

2.23. SPIVA: S&P Indices vs Active

Let us now look at some periodic reports analyzing the mutual fund industry, the SPIVA reports.

2.23.1. Report

Title	There are various reports
Authors	S&P Staff (from Standard and Poor's)
Publication	Periodically, on the S&P website.[87]

There are multiple reports SPIVA, typically by country, and updated every 6 months. Here we look at some of them and extract the most relevant figures and texts.

2.23.2. Authors

The acronym SPIVA refers to "Standard and Poor's Indices vs Active". These are several series of periodical comparisons between indexes and active investment funds prepared by the S&P company.

Standard and Poor's is not just a financial company, they are the ones who created and maintain indexes such as the S&P 500. These SPIVA studies use firsthand financial data, and are signed by highly educated authors, with certificates such as the CFA and doctorates in finance.

2.23.3. Content

The aim of these SPIVA reports is to contribute to the active vs passive debate. In particular because:

- Active managers argue that, with sufficient skill, it is possible to systematically outperform the market (i.e., outperform their benchmark).
- Academic studies argue, as we are reading in this book, that it is not possible to systematically outperform the market.

To add arguments to the debate, these reports study the returns of mutual funds and compare them with their benchmarks.

To make sure that funds are compared with their relevant benchmarks (to avoid comparing "apples with oranges"), funds are segmented into small groups, either by country, size of company capitalization, investment style (value, mixed, growth), fixed income or equity, etc.

In addition, these reports correct for "survivorship bias", i.e. they take into account funds that closed during the period.

These reports are public and freely available online. Let us have a look to a few of them:

1. SPIVA US Scorecard
2. SPIVA Europe Scorecard
3. SPIVA Institutional Scorecard
4. SPIVA Persistence Scorecard

2.23.3.1. SPIVA US Scorecard Year-End 2022

S&P Dow Jones Indices
A Division of S&P Global

SPIVA

SPIVA® U.S. Scorecard

Summary

Contributors

Tim Edwards, PhD
Managing Director
Index Investment Strategy
tim.edwards@spglobal.com

Anu R. Ganti, CFA
Senior Director
Index Investment Strategy
anu.ganti@spglobal.com

Craig J. Lazzara, CFA
Managing Director
Core Product Management
craig.lazzara@spglobal.com

Joe Nelesen, PhD
Senior Director
Index Investment Strategy
joseph.nelesen@spglobal.com

Davide Di Gioia
Chief SPIVA Engineer
Index Investment Strategy
davide.di.gioia@spglobal.com

The S&P 500® finished 2022 with a -18% total return, its worst performance since 2008, and fixed income markets offered little diversification benefit: the iBoxx $ Liquid Investment Grade also fell 18%. Both asset classes suffered as yields rose in response to a surge in domestic inflation, accompanied by an aggressive series of rate hikes by the U.S. Federal Reserve.

Declining markets *can* make active management skill more valuable, and **our 2022 scorecard identifies several fund categories in which a majority of active managers outperformed.** However, in the largest and most closely watched category, **U.S. large-cap equities, a slim majority underperformed.** On the positive side, this was the lowest underperformance rate since 2009 and the fourth best across more than two decades of our annual SPIVA Scorecards. Less positively, 2022 was characterized by several specific and unusual active tailwinds that may not persist.

Figure 86. First lines of the report "SPIVA US Scorecard Year-End 2022".

This report contains a lot of information, both in tables and diagrams. Let us focus for example on US equities, see the Table 12.

Table 12. Percentage of US-domiciled equity funds that underperformed their benchmarks (based on absolute return). It is part of Table 1a of the "SPIVA US Scorecard Year-End 2022" document.

		Percentage of Funds Underperforming their Benchmark		
SPIVA Category	**Benchmark**	**1 Year**	**5 Years**	**20 Years**
Large-Cap	S&P 500	51%	87%	95%
MidCap	S&P MidCap 400	63%	65%	94%
SmallCap	S&P SmallCap 600	57%	71%	94%

Mutual funds which claim to invest in large-cap companies (according to their own documentation), are compared to the S&P 500 index. This index represents *grosso modo* the 500 largest US companies.

During the last year documented in this report, 2022, 51% of the large-cap funds had returns below the S&P 500 (and thus 49% of the funds outperformed the S&P 500). This is almost "half and half", like flipping a coin and trying to predict whether it comes up heads or tails.

However, after 5 years the statistics are much clearer, 87% of managers do worse than their benchmarks. And over the long term, after 20 years, the result is very clear: 95% of managers do worse than their benchmarks.

One could argue that active managers may not excel in markets that are efficient (in the context of the Efficient Market Hypothesis), such as large-cap, where there are many other active market participants operating and therefore assigning prices. But active managers would outperform their benchmarks in the case of markets that are inefficient, such as small-cap stocks. Well, as we can see in the Table 12, active managers focusing on small-cap stocks do not outperform their benchmarks either. Whether the markets are efficient or not, it does not seem to affect.

A Comparison with Chess

Let us compare the difference between active vs index funds with chess players, particularly their ELO points, which are the scores assigned to players to assess their relative abilities.

A player with a 95% chance of beating another player is considered to have about 500 more ELO points. And typical ELO points are: 1000 for an apprentice, 1500 for an average club player, 2000 for a good national player, and 2500 for the world champion.

Investing in an active fund knowing that you are going to underperform your index with 95% probability is equivalent to:

- You are in a chess club, then a person walks in the door saying that "I just learned yesterday to play chess" (ELO 1000), and starts a game with an average club player (ELO 1500).

- In a similar way, the average amateur in the club (ELO 1500) has a 95% of losing when playing against a top national player (ELO 2000).

Who do you think would win each game? If you had to bet, who would you bet on? Because the active vs passive decision is basically the same.

The Table 13 shows study similar to the Table 12, but in this case applied to fixed income. Again, the results are very similar. Active managers earn returns below their benchmarks, and this is especially noticeable over the long term.

Table 13. Percentage of US-domiciled fixed income funds whose returns underperformed their benchmarks (based on absolute returns). It is part of table 11a of the "SPIVA US Scorecard Year-End 2022 document."

SPIVA Category	Benchmark	Percentage of Funds Underperforming their Benchmark		
		1 Year	5 Years	15 Years
Intermediate Duration Government Bonds	iBoxx $ Domestic Sovereigns & Sub-Sovereigns 1-10 Y	95%	89%	91%
High Yield Bonds	iBoxx $ Liquid High Yield	53%	72%	81%
Inflation-Linked Bonds	iBoxx TIPS Inflation-Linked	30%	87%	100%

Note the amazing "inflation-linked bonds" category, where 100% of the funds underperformed their benchmark after 15 years. All of them.

2.23.3.2. SPIVA Europe Scorecard Year-End 2022

S&P Dow Jones Indices
A Division of S&P Global

SPIVA

SPIVA® Europe Scorecard

Contributors

Anu R. Ganti, CFA
Senior Director
Index Investment Strategy
anu.ganti@spglobal.com

Tim Edwards, PhD
Managing Director
Index Investment Strategy
tim.edwards@spglobal.com

Maya Beyhan, PhD
Senior Director, ESG Specialist
Index Investment Strategy
maya.beyhan@spglobal.com

Inaugurated in 2002, the S&P Indices versus Active (SPIVA) U.S. Scorecard has since been extended to Australia, Canada, Europe, India, Japan, Latin America, South Africa and the Middle East & North Africa (MENA), allowing investors to experience the active versus passive debate on a global scale. First published in 2014, the semiannual SPIVA Europe Scorecard reports on the performance of actively managed funds domiciled across Europe.

For the first time, the 2022 edition of the SPIVA Europe Scorecard expands the universe of actively managed funds to include fixed income categories.

Figure 87. First lines of the report "SPIVA Europe Scorecard Year-End 2022".

We have previously seen the SPIVA report on the US, and this one applies the same methodology to European-domiciled mutual funds.

The Table 14 is part of this report. It shows that the results obtained with US-domiciled funds are repeated for European-domiciled funds.

Table 14. Percentage of European domiciled equity funds that underperformed their benchmark indexes (based on absolute return). It is part of table 1a of the "SPIVA Europe Scorecard Year-End 2022" document. The acronym BMI refers to "Broad Market Index", broad indices aim to represent 99% of the relevant market capitalization.

SPIVA Category	Benchmark	Percentage of Funds Underperforming their Benchmark		
		1 Year	5 Years	10 Years
European Equities	S&P Europe 350	87%	91%	90%
Eurozone Equities	S&P Eurozone BMI	68%	87%	95%
Spanish Equities	S&P Spain BMI	75%	86%	81%

Note that the number of years with data is limited in Europe, with only 10 years instead of the 20 years in the US.

2.23.3.3. SPIVA Institutional Scorecard Year-End 2022

S&P Dow Jones Indices
A Division of S&P Global

SPIVA

SPIVA® Institutional Scorecard

Contributors

Tim Edwards, PhD
Managing Director
Index Investment Strategy
tim.edwards@spglobal.com

Anu R. Ganti, CFA
Senior Director
Index Investment Strategy
anu.ganti@spglobal.com

Craig J. Lazzara, CFA
Managing Director

Summary

In this report, we add institutional accounts to the mutual funds analyzed in the S&P Indices versus Active (SPIVA) U.S. Scorecard. We aim to provide the institutional community with the ability to judge managers' true skill without the possible distortions that fees may create and to illustrate the similarities and differences between the performance of open-end funds and segregated institutional accounts across categories.

Figure 88. First lines of the report "SPIVA Institutional Scorecard Year-End 2022".

One of the arguments that may concern a retail investor is whether institutional investors have better instruments at their disposal. Instruments that are, for example, cheaper (we already have discussed the importance of the fees), and thus can outperform their benchmarks. We will see that this is not the case.

The Figure 89 shows some results from this report (it contains many more tables and figures).

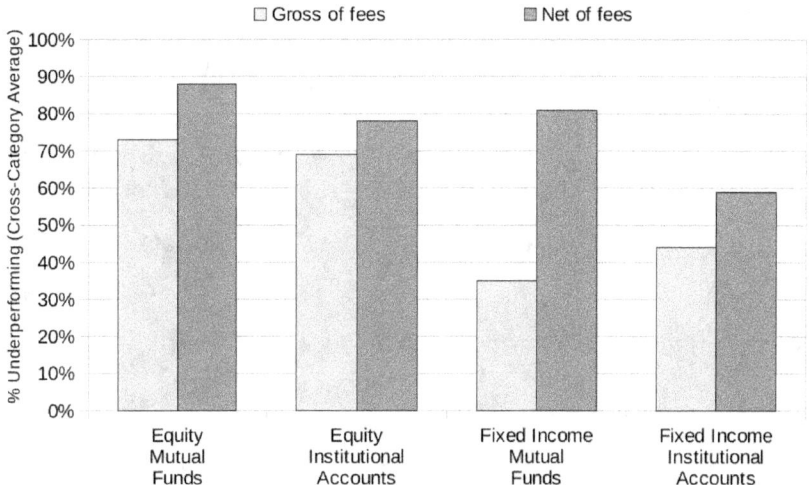

Figure 89. Percentages of US-domiciled funds and institutional accounts that underperform their benchmark after 10 years. This is Figure 1 of the report "SPIVA Institutional Scorecard Year-End 2022". Higher is worse.

We see that:

- Institutional accounts consistently outperform mutual funds available to retail investors (in this figure, for both equities and fixed income), which can be explained by their lower fees.
- The effect of fees can also be seen in that, before fees, the results are better for all categories. But all of them worsen after fees are paid. In particular in fixed income, because before fees both funds and institutional accounts outperform their indices, but after paying fees most of them underperform their indices.
- Overall, after paying fees (light gray in the Figure 89 columns), both mutual funds and institutional accounts underperform their indexes. Therefore, the advantage of institutional accounts over retail investors is limited.

2.23.3.4. SPIVA Persistence Scorecard Year-End 2022

Do excellent active managers keep on outperforming their benchmarks in the long term?

The Table 15 shows two categories of mutual funds: large-cap and small-cap. Their returns have been tracked for 5 consecutive years. And just for comparison, the last row is the case in which funds have a 50% probability to succeed each year, random like flipping a coin.

Table 15. Persistence of US-domiciled equity funds that remain in the top half of returns. It is part of table 2 of the document "SPIVA Persistence Scorecard Year-End 2022".

Category	Fund Count at Start	Percentage of Initial Funds Persisting in the Top Half (Best Returns)			
	Dec/2018	Dec/2019	Dec/2020	Dec/2021	Dec/2022
Large Cap	366	63%	55%	16.9%	1.37%
Small Cap	263	64%	53%	6.1%	2.66%
Random	-	50%	25%	12.5%	6.25%

The 629 funds in this table have been chosen because they have been excellent during **1 year**. From **December/2017** to **December/2018**, these funds were the best half of all funds in their category, the funds with higher returns. These are the initial funds.

The following year we look for the funds that, being part of the **initial group** (they had 1 good year), have earned returns in the 12 months to **December/2019** that put them in the better half of all funds in their category. These are the funds that have persisted for **2 years** with excellent results.

The following year we look for funds that, being part of the **previous group**, have achieved returns in the 12 months to **December/2020** that place them in the top half of the funds in their category. These are the funds that have persisted for **3 years** with excellent results.

And it is repeated for **December/2021** (funds that have persisted **4 years**) and for **December/2022** (funds that have persisted **5 years**), looking for funds that have been in the top half all those years consecutively.

As you can see, as the years go by, fewer and fewer excellent managers persist. This is one of the reasons why regulators (like the SEC in USA) created the advertisement rule that makes compulsory to insert warnings like "past performance does not guarantee future results" in investment advertisements.[88]

But let us look at the Figure 90, because it is a bit clearer.

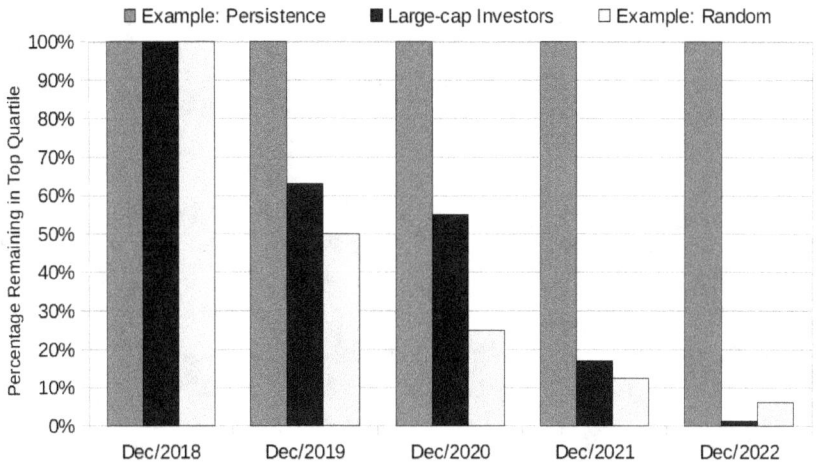

Figure 90. persistence of US-domiciled large-cap funds that remain in the top half of returns (data from Table 15). Compared to hypothetical excellent managers who maintain high returns every year (always 100%), and randomly (each year persist half of the previous).

The Figure 90 shows an example (the performance of large-cap fund managers, domiciled in the US, investing also in the US) compared to two benchmarks:

- Hypothetical persistent excellent managers, that succeed every year, being always in the top half of returns. Therefore, every year they have a 100% chance of being among the best (light gray columns).

- Hypothetical manager where the probability of being in the top returns group every year is pure chance. Like flipping a coin and getting heads or tails. Each year half of the funds persists in the excellent group, and the other half obtains poor results. So of the initial 100%, after the first year only 50% remains, the next year 25%, then 12.5%, and by the fifth year 6.25% of the initial funds remain (gray columns).

Ideally, one would expect good managers to persist over time. Once an excellent manager is found, in successive years he will continue being great. And in this way, stock market investment consists of looking for these excellent managers.

For sure, we do not want managers that perform well or poorly every year with the same probability as flipping a coin.

Look closely at the Figure 90. The active fund managers (black columns), are they closer to persistent excellent managers (dark gray columns) or closer to flipping a coin (light gray columns)?

There is little doubt, they look very much like random.

This does not mean that active managers invest the assets at random, without thinking, "rolling a dice". No, what happens is that active managers compete with each other. And once there is a very competitive ecosystem of excellent professional managers, the difference in returns between a slightly better and a slightly worse manager is indistinguishable from chance.

It is like an Olympic race (see the Figure 91). These are runners who have qualified for the Olympics, so they are all excellent.

We could calculate the average speed for all the runners, and thus compare runners with this benchmark, to know who was relatively faster and who was relatively slower.

Figure 91. Active fund managers compared to runners.

But those runners who are slower than the average are not bad runners. It is just that they are being compared with a benchmark made up of all the Olympic runners, and that average speed is very fast.

They could be "slow" runners among the excellent ones, but certainly much faster than the average Joe.

Similarly, active managers who do not outperform their benchmark are not necessarily bad, it is just that their benchmark is quite good, at Olympic level.

In fact, professional managers are much better investors than the average person. Let us take a better look at this in the next section.

2.23.3.5. About Chance and Michael Jordan

This text presented here is based on a post by Craig Lazzara in Indexology Blog.[89]

In the short term, the active vs passive debate is largely a matter of chance. But randomness is compensated in the long term, and after a few years the conclusion to this debate is clear.

An example to explain this is to assume a basketball competition between an amateur (an unskilled basketball player) and Michael Jordan, arguably the greatest player in history. Just a few rounds of free throw shooting. Does the amateur have any chance of beating Michael Jordan?

To give an objective answer, we need to know the probability of making free throws. Let us suppose:

- Michael Jordan has a 90% probability of scoring, and hence a 10% probability of missing.
- The amateur has a 30% chance of scoring, and a 70% chance of missing.

The Figure 92 shows the possible outcomes after a round of free throw shooting.

These are the three possible cases:

1. Let us suppose the amateur scores his first shot (30% probability), and Michael Jordan misses his (10%). The probability of this happening is 3% (=30%x10%). Incredible, in this case the amateur would be beating Michael Jordan!
2. The opposite case would be that Michael Jordan scores his shot (90%), and the amateur misses (70%). This would happen 63% (=90%x70%) of the time, which is the result we all expect.
3. And the rest, 34% of the cases, is the probability of a tie. Both missing or both scoring.

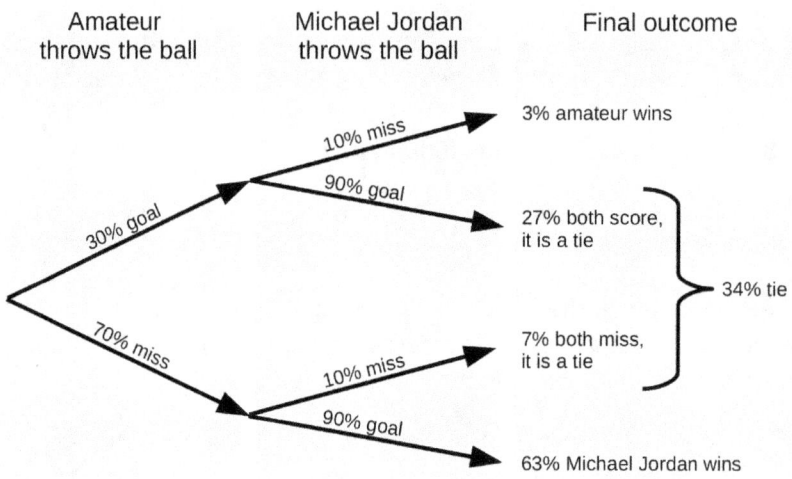

Figure 92. Probabilities of a round of free throw shooting. Both an amateur and Michael Jordan throw each one a ball into the basket.

Although Michael Jordan is exceptional, there is a 37% chance that he will not win: either because the amateur beats him (3% chance of the amateur making a basket and Michael Jordan missing) or because the two tie (34%, either missing or hitting).

If the competition were to end here, in the first round, there is a 37% chance that the amateur would feel like a winner for not having been beaten by Michael Jordan!

However, one round of pitching is not enough to know the quality of a player. Let us see in the Table 16 what happens when considering a second and a third round (this is easily calculated with a spreadsheet).

Table 16. Possible outcomes of a free throw competition between an amateur and Michael Jordan. There are three rounds, each one like in Figure 92. Figure 93 presents this data in a visual plot.

	Probability		
Outcome	**One Round**	**Two Rounds**	**Three Rounds**
Amateur wins	3%	2%	1%
Tie	34%	15%	8%
Michael Jordan wins	**63%**	**83%**	**91%**

The Table 16 shows that amateurs get better results when there are few rounds. Because in short periods of time, randomness dominates.

On the other hand, Michael Jordan needs to throw some rounds to make it obvious that he is a better player. Skilled players prove it in the long run.

And why is this important? Because there is a direct relationship between this basketball example (Table 16) and the probability of a mutual fund underperforming its benchmark (e.g. the Table 12 on US-domiciled equity funds, or the Table 14 on Europeans).

- Where the term "amateur" is used, replace it with "active fund".
- Where it says "Michael Jordan", replace it with "benchmark".

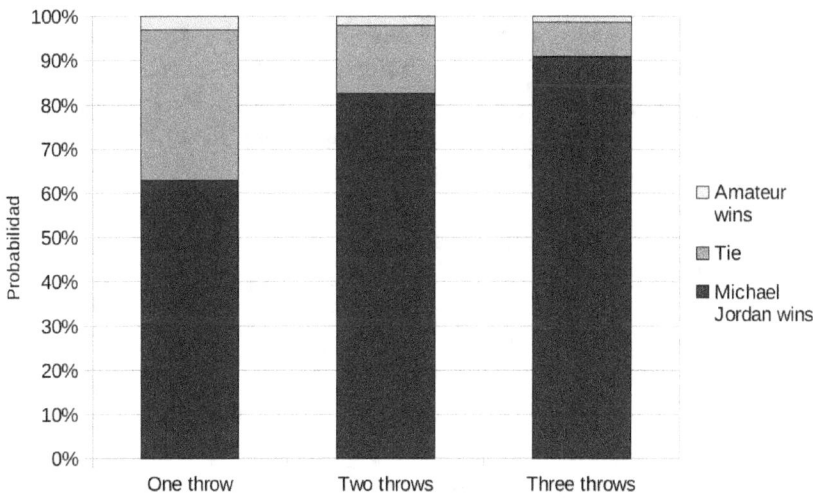

Figure 93. Results from the Table 16, but shown graphically.

The conclusion is: in the short term luck is the predominant factor.

Skill persists, but luck is ephemeral.

— Craig Lazzara, post "Shooting Hoops with Michael Jordan: An Allegory"

2.23.4. Conclusions

There are several conclusions from these SPIVA studies that are striking:

- As a general rule, active mutual funds underperform their benchmarks.
- If you could invest in an index, you would outperform most mutual funds in its category.
- There is a random component in the short term (example: 1 year). However, in the long term (example: 20 years) good luck is offset by bad luck, and it is clear that active managers underperform their benchmarks.
- Persistence: even if a manager outperforms its benchmark one year, it will usually not do so the following year.
- This effect is observed everywhere: in all countries, regions, developed or emerging, size of company capitalization, investment styles, stocks or bonds, etc.
- Active managers underperform their benchmarks in all categories, even in inefficient markets (example: emerging markets, small cap, high yield bonds, etc.). Active managers claim that they can find inefficiencies and profit from them, but this is not what we observe in the data. Therefore, the Efficient Market Hypothesis must be less important than previously thought.

Any retail investor reading these studies has to ask himself to what extent he himself is part of the statistics.

If you invest in the stock market after studying company balance sheets, selecting for dividends, reading the economic news, looking for trends... then you are an active investor and therefore SPIVA conclusions apply to you without mercy. Compare yourself to your benchmark and see how you fare.

2.24. Morningstar Active/Passive Barometer

2.24.1. Report

Title	Morningstar's US Active/Pasive Barometer
Authors	Morningstar staff. In the most recent years: Ryan Jackson, Bryan Armour, and Dimitar Boyadzhiev
Publication	Every 6 months in the Morningstar website.[90]

Figure 94. First lines of the report "Morningstar's US Active/Pasive Barometer Midyear 2023".

2.24.2. Authors

The "Morningstar Barometer" is a series of periodic comparisons between active mutual funds and passive mutual funds, carried out by the company Morningstar.

Morningstar is a multinational financial services company, founded in the USA in 1984, which is widely used for performing research and aggregating information on mutual funds. Therefore these reports use firsthand information.

2.24.3. Content

The first thing that we have to do is to compare these Morningstar reports with the SPIVA reports.

SPIVA reports are famous in the context of passive investors because they show that over the long term active investors underperform their comparable benchmarks.

But SPIVA reports have two problems:

- Standard & Poor's is not just a financial firm. Part of its business is to create and sell indices, both as indicators of the state of the markets and as benchmarks for index mutual funds. This implies a conflict of interest; it is in S&P's own interest to show that the indexes are great products. We advance you the conclusion: yes, they are honest, because the results of both S&P and Morningstar coincide.
- We could say that the SPIVA report compares "apples to oranges". On the one hand there are mutual funds in which an investor can be a unitholder; on the other hand there are indices, ideal representations of the market, in which it is not possible to invest directly. It is necessary to compare "apples to apples", that is: active funds with passive funds. And this is what Morningstar reports do.

The 2023 mid-year Morningstar report contains data on 8218 US-domiciled mutual funds, managing $17 (US) trillion dollars (17 followed by 12 zeros).

In the report, the authors calculate returns for aggregates of passive funds, which are the benchmarks they then use to compare with active funds. These benchmarks are therefore real funds in which one can invest. For example, they implicitly take fees into account.

It also makes a study of the survivorship bias, the fact that poorly performing funds disappear from the statistics, leaving in the long run only the best performing funds, so that when calculating the average returns of the surviving funds they appear to be better than they actually are.

Some conclusions of the report are:

- In the short term, one year, there are categories of active funds that outperform their passive counterparts.

- In the long term, over 10 years, only 1/4 active strategies (small cap, value style, corporate bonds...) outperformed the average of their passive counterparts.

- Cheaper active funds succeeded more often than more expensive ones. Over the 10 years to June 2023, nearly 31% of active funds in the cheapest quintile beat their passive counterpart, versus only 19% of funds in the most expensive quintile.

2.24.3.1. Returns vs. Time

Let us look at the results. The Table 17 shows the percentage of active funds outperforming their passive counterparts, as a function of time. As we have seen in the SPIVA report (see Section 2.23), in the short term (1 year) active funds may outperform passive funds, but in the long term (20 years) it is passive funds that overwhelmingly outperform active funds.

Table 17. Percentage of US-domiciled active funds outperforming comparable passive funds. Based on duration invested. Part of Table 1 of "Morningstar's US Active/Pasive Barometer Midyear 2023".

Category	Percentage of Active Funds Outperforming Passive Funds		
	1 Year	5 Years	20 Years
Large-cap mixed	50%	30%	9.1%
Small-cap mixed	75%	43%	23%

Note: here the **Morningstar** report shows the percentage of active funds that **outperform** their benchmark, the average of comparable passive funds. On the other hand, the **SPIVA** report (Section 2.23) shows the opposite, the percentage of funds that **underperform** their benchmarks. Both reports measure somewhat the same thing, but in opposite ways.

The next Table 18 shows the percentage of active funds outperforming their passive counterparts, comparing cheap funds vs expensive funds. The methodology is to sort the active mutual funds in each category by their fees, and select the first quintile (of all funds, the one-fifth of them that are cheapest), and the last quintile (of all funds, the one-fifth of them that are most expensive).

Table 18. Percentage of US-domiciled active funds outperforming comparable passive funds after 10 years. Comparing the cheapest quintile of funds to the most expensive quintile. It is part of Table 1 of "Morningstar's US Active/Pasive Barometer Midyear 2023".

Category	Cheap Quintile	Expensive Quintile
Large-cap mixed	16%	5.6%
Small-cap mixed	46%	28%

Comparing them shows that the more expensive the active funds are, the less likely they are to outperform their equivalent passive funds. This is exactly what Jack Bogle found, that cost matters a lot, as we have already seen in the Section 2.16 about "An Index Fund Fundamentalist".

Of the large-cap, mixed-style funds, only 16% of the cheap funds outperformed their passive equivalents. Moreover, only 5.6% of the expensive funds did so. So, with respect to mutual funds, the lower their fees the better for the unitholder.

2.24.3.2. Distribution of Active Fund Returns

The Figure 95 shows how active funds have performed compared to their passive equivalent (10-year, annualized returns, US-domiciled funds, investing in US companies, large-cap and mixed style). There are many other similar figures in the Morningstar report, we choose because it is relatively general.

A brief description of the Figure 95:

- The taller the column, the more funds there are in that group.
- The column "0.0" (**A**) indicates the active funds that have earned the same return as the passive funds.
- On the right area (excess return >0%) there are the active funds that have outperformed the passive funds (by up to "+1.5%" annualized).
- On the left area (excess return <0%) there are active funds that have outperformed passive funds (by up to "-7.6%" annualized).

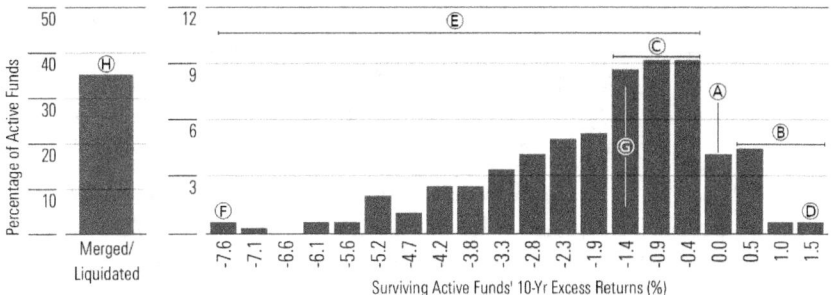

Figure 95. Distribution of the annualized (over 10 years) return of active funds compared to the return of passive funds. These are US large-cap mixed-style funds. Source: Figure 7 from "Morningstar's US Active/Pasive Barometer Midyear 2023" report.

Let us look at the conclusions that can be extracted from Figure 95:

- The number of active funds that have outperformed equivalent passive funds is small. That is, in the area on the right side (**B**), the columns "0.5%", "1.0%", and "1.5%" are relatively small. Active funds in those three groups only represent 5.6% of the total funds.

- Most active funds earn annualized returns of "-1.4%", "-0.9%", and "-0.4%" worse than passive funds (**C**). This is partly because many of them are what is known as Closet Indexing. It refers to mutual funds that claim to be active, but actually track an index. These funds earn the return of the index minus their TER (and these TERs are typically 1.4%-0.4% higher than the TERs of comparable passive funds, which is what we see in the figure). The interesting thing is that Closet Indexing allows managers to charge (expensive) active management fees for a (cheap) passive management service, and pocket the difference without having taken any risk (which is exactly the Holy Grail of finance).

- Note that the best return that a retail investor can aspire to is an annualized return 1.5% higher than comparable passive funds (**D**). Contrary to what one might expect, there are no active managers that achieve better returns. There might be some exceptions: some author funds (with very few unitholders and limited Assets Under Management), or closed-end funds (not accessible to any investor), or managers who declare to invest in large-cap but then invest in another category such as small-cap (because small companies have higher expected returns than large companies, as we know from the Fama-French Three-Factor Model).

205

- The area of the negative columns (**E**, from "-7.6%" to "0.0%") is much larger and more spread out than the positive area (**B**, from "0.0%" to "1.5%"). That is, if you invest in active funds hoping to outperform, you are likely to underperform. Notice that the proportion of funds with worse returns than passive funds after 10 years (zone **E**, roughly 80%-90% of surviving funds) is directly comparable to the Table 12 (and similar) from the SPIVA report (Section 2.23). It is the same information but shown in a different way.

- Watch out for extreme values. Do you want to try to get the 1.5% annual extra return of the best active funds (**D**)? Then be careful because you may end up getting -7.6% (**F**, annualized for 10 consecutive years!). The worst possible damage is much greater than the best possible benefit.

- The average return of active funds is about -1.4% less than comparable passive funds (the vertical line **G** leaves the same area in the left columns as in the right columns). Why invest in an active fund if the expected return is that of the passive fund minus 1.4%? Better to invest directly in a passive fund and receive the market return minus negligible fees (the one in the "0.0" column).

- And look at the left column which is separated from the rest (**H**). So far we only have taken into account active funds that have survived 10 years, but other funds that have been merged with other funds or have been liquidated must also be taken into account. And surely the reason why these funds have disappeared is, for many of them, that they have obtained very poor returns (and nobody wishes to be a unitholder of such a fund). The fund managers hide the bad and only present the good. That is: The situation is worse than what we have seen. There are 35% of merged or liquidated funds that would most probably be in the left zone of the distribution (in the negative returns zone), but that are not being shown. If we were to take them into account, there would surely be active funds with annual returns (relative to passive funds) even worse than the -7.6% of the surviving funds shown here.

The Figure 95 is staggering. It indicates that a passive investor neither "scores low", nor has "low expectations", nor "accepts mediocrity". On the contrary, a passive investor is more realistic and has better return expectations than active investors.

2.24.4. Conclusions

The biannual studies by Morningstar confirm the results of SPIVA independently. They are also better studies than those of SPIVA, as they compare assets in which a retail investor can invest (active vs passive funds). SPIVA, by comparing active vs. index funds, is a less realistic approach.

As we have seen, in the short term chance is predominant, but in the long term passive funds obtain better returns than active funds.

Wanting to get exceptional returns, active fund participants overwhelmingly get worse returns than passive funds, and sometimes even disastrous returns (in the example of the Figure 95, -7.6% per year, relative to their passive equivalents, during 10 consecutive years).

2.25. Mind the Gap

2.25.1. Report

Title   Mind the Gap

Authors   Morningstar Staff, in particular Jeffrey Ptak and Amy C. Arnott

Publication   Annual on the Morningstar website.[90]

Figure 96. First lines of the report "Mind the Gap 2023".

2.25.2. Authors

The authors are:

- Jeffrey Ptak[91], currently Chief Ratings Officer at Morningstar. Bachelor's degree in accounting from the University of Wisconsin, CFA, and having a long career in finance.

- Amy C. Arnott[92], portfolio strategist. Bachelor's degree in English and French from the University of Wisconsin, Madison, holder of a CFA, and also having a long professional career in the world of finance.

In addition, other Morningstar colleagues also contributed to this report. The company Morningstar has been already presented in the Section 2.24.

2.25.3. Content

This report is very similar to the "Trading Is Hazardous for Your Wealth" from the Section 2.15. But in this case it goes further because it is a periodic report (repeated every 6 months), analyzing funds for a longer time (10 years instead of 6 years), and studying mutual funds in general instead of just individual investors.

The "Mind the Gap" report is a series of annual studies, based on US data, comparing two returns:

- the returns of mutual funds, and.
- the returns that investors actually obtain by investing in those mutual funds.

This may seem paradoxical. Is it possible that investors' returns are different from the returns advertised by the mutual funds?

First of all, we confirm that the difference exists. According to the paper, and considering all US-domiciled funds, investors earned a 6.0% annual return over the 10 years ending December 31, 2022 (this data is shown in the Table 19).

Over the same period, mutual funds earned a 7.7% annual return. That is, the unitholders earned a return 1.7% lower than that of the mutual funds in which they invested. In other words, the loss to investors is about 1/5 of the return they could be aiming for (because 1.7% is almost one fifth of 7.7%).

This difference in return is due to buying and selling at times that are negative for the investor, trying to do market timing. This is what gives this effect its name: the "Behavior Gap".

The paper points out other minor factors that also contribute to widening the gap, such as commissions and taxes.

Note the irony: investors actively look for the best time to buy and sell in order to maximize their returns. But when we analyze their results, investors lose money trying to do so.

This return gap is calculated as the difference in two different ways to compute rates of return, each one with a slightly different meaning:[93]

- Money-weighted returns, and
- Time-weighted returns.

The Money-Weighted Rate of Return (MWRR) is a measure of how good or bad an investment strategy has been.

It is calculated using the Internal Rate of Return (IRR). It is the annualized effective compounded return rate, the rate of return that sets the net present value of all cash flows from the investment equal to zero.

To calculate it, the MWRR requires knowledge of the contributions and withdrawals (all inflows and outflows).

This is the best way for the investor to know the performance of his portfolio. But it is not appropriate for the fund manager, because the manager has no control over those contributions and withdrawals. Fund managers need another rate of return.

On the other hand, there is the Time-Weighted Rate of Return (TWRR). What it does is to divide the time period into segments, taking into account contributions and withdrawals, and calculate the return for each of these time segments. In practice, mutual funds calculate this by multiplying their daily returns.

This is the return that a participant would have obtained in the exceptional situation of investing at the beginning and neither contributing nor withdrawing capital.

This is the rate of return used to compare multiple mutual funds with each other.

Therefore, in this report authors calculate the difference (the gap) between these two rates of return:

- The Money Weighted Return, calculated considering the inflows and outflows of the funds. This is the return actually earned by unitholders.
- The Time Weighted Return, which is the return made public by mutual funds, for comparison with other funds. It is equivalent to investing in one go, at the beginning of the period, and just holding it.

Table 19. Behavior Gap for various US fund categories. Over the 10 years ending in 2022. Annualized returns. Source: part of Table 1 of the report.

	Investor return [%]	Total return [%]	Gap (diff.) [%]
US equity	10.99	11.77	-0.78
Sector equity	6.42	10.80	-4.38
All US domiciled funds	6.04	7.71	-1.68

The Table 19 shows the return gap for various fund categories (there are more categories in the original paper, however these are sufficiently representative).

Over this 10-year period, it is normal for unitholders to have a negative return gap. This is, they are doing worse than just buy&hold their mutual funds.

In the case of diversified US stocks, the effect is relatively small. Unitholders "only" lose -0.78% per year relative to the return they could earn. But, in the case of sector funds the Performance Gap is dramatic, in aggregate they lose -4.38% per year. This is explained by the fact that investors in this category tend to be very active, chasing past returns or following economic news.

In addition, the authors find that the higher the volatility of a category, the greater the return gap, and the worse for investors. They argue that this higher volatility is a signal that attracts investors to try to buy low and sell high, even though they actually achieve the opposite.

The paper provides several suggestions for retail investors to minimize their return gap:

- Hold relatively few mutual funds, and have them relatively highly diversified.
- Automate tasks such as rebalancing.
- Avoid funds with high volatilities, which tend to be those with more concentrated assets and niche themes.
- Favor simple, realistic strategies, rather than strategies that are theoretically better but difficult to implement in practice.

But this is not just a behavioral problem, for choosing bad times to buy or sell. Simply by making a monthly purchase we will already find a difference between the return of the fund and the one obtained by the investor. Let us look at it in the next section.

2.25.3.1. Dollar Cost Average

The paper also makes an interesting comparison between the return obtained by the unitholders that just buy&hold, and the return obtained by investors that purchase funds periodically (buying the same number of euros or dollars each time, for example every month).

This procedure for periodic purchases is called DCA, Dollar-Cost Averaging), and was popularized by Benjamin Graham in this book The Intelligent Investor.

Let us compare the returns obtained by these two types of investors, see the Table 20.

Table 20. Return gap for various fund categories compared to periodic purchases. Over the 10 years ending in 2022. Annualized returns. Source: This is a portion of Table 10 in the paper.

	Gap [%]	DCA Gap [%]	Difference [%]
Sector equity	-4.38	-4.94	-0.56
US equity	-0.78	-4.56	-3.78

The Table 20 is staggering: doing DCA would have led to even greater return losses than the return gap.

The authors indicate that averaging cost in principle provides worse results than simply buying at the beginning and holding.

This is explained by the fact that since market returns are usually positive, this cost averaging usually results in lower returns. This is normal, if we assume that by investing everything at the beginning we are taking advantage of the bull market right from the start. Unlike spreading the investment in small monthly purchases, where each time you buy assets that are more expensive, and that have less time available until the end of the period to increase their price.

Conversely, if the stock market were in a bearish period, the opposite would happen. Doing DCA would be advantageous because you would be buying assets towards the end of the period, when they are cheaper and when they are going to spend less time going down. Although all this is only known *a posteriori*, of course.

We should not think that this is an argument against doing DCA. It is simply due to the market performance during that period. The two compared scenarios are very different. In one of the scenarios we are fully invested from the beginning, and in the other we are investing month by month until we have the same total assets. Of course, there is a difference, because in the second case we have been relatively uninvested.

In any case, we can draw the conclusion that doing DCA in a bull market (as the stock markets are during most of the time) implies losing a little return.

If we already have a lump sum, from the numerical point of view it makes sense to invest right from the beginning, not to delay it with small monthly purchases (with DCA). Having said that, it may make sense to do DCA to "diversify over time" as much as it does to diversify by asset class. For a retail investor it may be preferable the peace of mind although the portfolio may generate a little less return.

2.25.4. Conclusions

All this is related to stock picking. It is common for active managers to select stocks in the hope that their returns will be superior to others.

The same is common today, but picking mutual funds, and especially ETFs. Selecting economic sectors, countries, themes, which are expected to outperform others. Jumping from fund to fund looking for returns, chasing new trends.

ETFs have the advantages of mutual funds (diversification, low cost, simplicity, etc.), and they also have a feature that can become a defect: it is very easy to trade them.

In principle, this is a positive idea: being easy to operate removes entry barriers so that anyone can invest. But at the same time it encourages activity on the part of the investor, buying and selling chasing returns. And in the long run, this over-trading is negative because it causes the return drag.

This is the cost the average investor must pay for his own behavior. Making inappropriate decisions, both in terms of the type of funds and the timing of contributions and withdrawals, costs him much more than management fees. And yet most investors focus more on fees and past returns, and less on being aware of how they make investment decisions.

In short: it is preferable not to chase trends and stay invested for the long term.

[1] A great source of ideas for writing the following sections has been the Bogleheads© wiki: https://www.bogleheads.org/wiki/Outline_of_academics

[2] You can find the paper *Théorie de la Spéculation* by Louis Bachelier, original in French, at http://archive.numdam.org/article/ASENS_1900_3_17__21_0.pdf , or an English translation by D. May (University of Western Australia) in 2011, at: https://docs.google.com/viewer?a=v&pid=explorer&chrome=true&srcid=0B5LLDy7-d3SKNGI0M2E0NGItYzFlMS00NGU2LWE2ZDAtODc3MDY3MzdiNmY0

[3] The original paper (*Théorie de la Spéculation*, by Bachelier) states: ... *il est possible d'etudier mathématiquement l'etat statique du marché à un instant donné, c'est-à-dire d'etablir la loi de probabilité des variations de cours qu'admet à cet instant le marché. La recherche d'une formule qui l'exprime ne paraît pas jusqu'à ce jour avoir été publiée; elle sera l'objet de ce travail.*

[4] You can read Einstein's original paper on Brownian Motion, in German, at https://onlinelibrary.wiley.com/doi/10.1002/andp.19053220806 and a translation into English at https://einsteinpapers.press.princeton.edu/vol2-trans/137

[5] The book "The Random Character of Stock Market Prices" by Paul Harold Cootner can be found online at: https://archive.org/details/randomcharacter00coot/page/n7/mode/2up

[6] The paper *Portfolio Selection* by Harry Markowitz can be downloaded from the web: https://www.math.hkust.edu.hk/~maykwok/courses/ma362/07F/markowitz_JF.pdf

[7] See the Nobel Prize web page on the one awarded to Tjalling Koopmans: https://www.nobelprize.org/nobel_prizes/economic-sciences/laureates/1975/index.html

[8] See the Nobel Prize web page on the one awarded to Milton Friedman: https://www.nobelprize.org/nobel_prizes/economic-sciences/laureates/1976/index.html

[9] The anecdote is found in Harry Markowitz's dissertation on receiving the Nobel Prize: https://www.nobelprize.org/uploads/2018/06/markowitz-lecture.pdf

[10] See the Nobel Prize web page on the one awarded to James Tobin (1918-2002): https://www.nobelprize.org/prizes/economic-sciences/1981/summary/

[11] See the Nobel Prize web page on the one awarded to Paul Samuelson: https://www.nobelprize.org/prizes/economic-sciences/1970/summary/

[12] See the Nobel Prize web page on the one awarded to Robert Cox Merton (1944-): https://www.nobelprize.org/prizes/economic-sciences/1997/summary/

[13] See the Nobel Prize web page on the one awarded to Harry Markowitz: https://www.nobelprize.org/prizes/economic-sciences/1990/summary/

[14] See the text of Harry Markowitz's autobiography on the Nobel Prize website: https://www.nobelprize.org/prizes/economic-sciences/1990/markowitz/biographical/

[15] For example the Indexa Capital's website. Their portfolio with the highest proportion of stocks is not 100% stocks, but 90% stocks and 10% bonds: https://indexacapital.com/es/esp/model#model-fund-selection

[16] The paper "Brownian Motion in the Stock Market" by M.F.M. Osborne can be found at http://m.e-m-h.org/Osbo59.pdf

[17] The paper "The Variation of Certain Speculative Prices" by Benoît Mandelbrot can be found at this link: https://web.williams.edu/Mathematics/sjmiller/public_html/341Fa09/econ/Mandelbroit_VariationCertainSpeculativePrices.pdf

[18] Source of figure: M.W. Toews, based on concept by Jeremy Kemp, via Wikipedia, https://en.wikipedia.org/wiki/Normal_distribution

[19] As a curiosity, the resonance of a forced pendulum is also a Cauchy Distribution

[20] Eric W. Weisstein, in his article "Normal Distribution" in the Wolfram MathWorld mathematical encyclopedia, https://mathworld.wolfram.com/NormalDistribution.html

[21] For more information about the Black-Scholes-Merton model you could have a look to Wikipedia: https://en.wikipedia.org/wiki/Black%E2%80%93Scholes_model

[22] "Capital Asset Prices: A Theory of Market Equilibrium Under Conditions of Risk", by

William F. Sharpe, can be found in: https://onlinelibrary.wiley.com/doi/10.1111/j.1540-6261.1964.tb02865.x

[23] For more details about the origin of CAPM you can read "The Capital Asset Pricing Model: Theory and Evidence", for Eugene F. Fama and Kenneth R. French, published in 2004, https://www.aeaweb.org/articles?id=10.1257/0895330042162430

[24] The paper "The Behavior of Stock-Market Prices" by Eugene Fama is available at: http://www.jstor.org/stable/2350752

[25] See the Nobel Prize website about the one given to Eugene Fama: https://www.nobelprize.org/prizes/economic-sciences/2013/summary/

[26] About the Deutsche Bank Prize in Financial Economics given to Eugene Fama, see the web: https://gfk-cfs.de/en/about-us/deutsche-bank-prize-in-financial-economics/

[27] See the Nobel Prize web page on the one awarded to Merton Miller: https://www.nobelprize.org/prizes/economic-sciences/1990/summary/

[28] See the detailed metaphor in the post "The Twenty Dollar Bill", by Larry Swedroe, in the blog "The Evidence-Based Investor": https://www.evidenceinvestor.com/the-twenty-dollar-bill/

[29] You can find the paper "Predictability: Does the Flap of a Butterfly's Wings in Brazil Set off a Tornado in Texas?", written by Edward N. Lorenz, by following the link: https://climate.envsci.rutgers.edu/climdyn2017/LorenzButterfly.pdf

[30] Edward Lorenz's "Deterministic Nonperiodic Flow" paper can be found at https://journals.ametsoc.org/view/journals/atsc/20/2/1520-0469_1963_020_0130_dnf_2_0_co_2.xml

[31] The paper is found in the book "The Collected Scientific Papers of Paul A. Samuelson", volume 4, compiled by Niroaki Nagatani in 1979, available online at Archive.org: https://archive.org/details/trent_0116403027612/mode/2up

[32] See the Nobel Prize website about the one given to Paul Samuelson: https://www.nobelprize.org/prizes/economic-sciences/1970/summary/

[33] According to Bogle's writing "The Professor, the Student, and the Index Fund", on page 2: https://johncbogle.com/wordpress/wp-content/uploads/2011/09/The-Professor-The-Student-and-the-Index-Fund-9-4-11.pdf

[34] The paper "Determinants of Portfolio Performance" can be found online at: https://www.semanticscholar.org/paper/Determinants-of-Portfolio-Performance-Brinson-Hood/ef3a2d1bfbe55685903e538bcf329993eeb958d3

[35] The paper "Does Asset Allocation Policy Explain 40, 90, or 100 Percent of Performance?" by Robert G. Ibbotson and Paul D. Kaplan, can be found here: https://www.researchgate.net/publication/23754375_Does_Asset_Allocation_Policy_Explain_40_90_100_Percent_of_Performance

[36] This diagram is basically the same as the one created by Unai Ansejo and shown at: https://blog.indexacapital.com/2016/02/18/asignacion-estrategica-activos-carteras/

[37] The paper "The Cross-Section of Expected Stock Returns" by Fama and French is found at: https://onlinelibrary.wiley.com/doi/10.1111/j.1540-6261.1992.tb04398.x

[38] Paper "Determining withdrawal rates using historical data" by William P. Bengen is at: https://www.semanticscholar.org/paper/Determining-Withdrawal-Rates-Using-Historical-Data-Bengen/70ede2b84b61da189af9eb2f3fbe6c7baa5435f9

[39] A brief summary of William P. Bengen's life can be found at the following webpage: https://www.fa-mag.com/news/bill-bengen--creator-of-the-4-creator-of-the-4-creator--retirement-rule--sells-firm-and-retires-15499.html

[40] If you are interested in rocket engineering, you can buy his book, it has good reviews: https://www.amazon.com/Topics-Advanced-Model-Rocketry-Press/dp/0262632780

[41] The Trinity Study can be downloaded from: https://www.researchgate.net/profile/Philip-Cooley-2/publication/228707593_Sustainable_withdrawal_rates_from_your_retirement_portfolio/links/

53eb64530cf26f1f689d60b1/Sustainable-withdrawal-rates-from-your-retirement-portfolio.pdf

[42] Early Retirement Now: https://earlyretirementnow.com/safe-withdrawal-rate-series/

[43] Campbell and Shiller's "Valuation Ratios and the Long-Run Stock Market Outlook" is at: http://www.econ.yale.edu/~shiller/online/jpmalt.pdf

[44] See the Nobel Prize web page on the one awarded to Franco Modigliani: https://www.nobelprize.org/prizes/economic-sciences/1985/summary/

[45] On the Deutsche Bank Prize in Financial Economics to Robert Shiller see the website: https://gfk-cfs.de/en/about-us/deutsche-bank-prize-in-financial-economics/

[46] See the personal page of John Y. Campbell at Harvard University: https://scholar.harvard.edu/campbell/home

[47] The famous CAPE figure, from the book "Irrational Exuberance", can be seen here: https://en.wikipedia.org/wiki/Price%E2%80%93earnings_ratio

[48] Robert Shiller's personal website with the data on the CAPE ratio is this: http://www.econ.yale.edu/~shiller/data.htm

[49] You can read the speech by Alan Greenspan in the Federal Reserve webpage: https://www.federalreserve.gov/boarddocs/speeches/1996/19961205.htm

[50] A website with a multitude of information is: https://www.multpl.com/shiller-pe

[51] The paper "Why active fund managers often underperform the S&P 500: The impact of size and skewness" can be downloaded from the internet following this link: https://www.researchgate.net/publication/253217931_Why_Active_Fund_Managers_Often_Underperform_the_SP_500_The_Impact_of_Size_and_Skewness

[52] David L. Ikenberry's personal website: https://davidikenberry.com/

[53] Richard L. Shockley's web page at Indiana University: https://kelley.iu.edu/faculty-research/faculty-directory/profile.html?id=RISHOCKL

[54] Announcement of Kent L. Womack's death by the Rotman School of Management: https://www.rotman.utoronto.ca/Connect/MediaCentre/Announcements/RememberingKentWomack

[55] The paper "A Multifractal Walk Down Wall Street" by Benoît Mandelbrot can be found at: https://www.scientificamerican.com/article/a-multifractal-walk-down-wall-stree/

[56] Benoît Mandelbrot's paper on the length of the coast of Britain can be found at: https://users.math.yale.edu/~bbm3/web_pdfs/howLongIsTheCoastOfBritain.pdf

[57] The image is adapted from the original created by user Avsa available on Wikipedia: https://en.wikipedia.org/wiki/How_Long_Is_the_Coast_of_Britain%3F_Statistical_Self-Similarity_and_Fractional_Dimension

[58] Source of the Mandelbrot Ensemble images: edited from graphics by Dr. Wolfgang Beyer, https://www.wolfgangbeyer.de/

[59] The paper "Trading Is Hazardous to Your Wealth" can be found online at: https://faculty.haas.berkeley.edu/odean/Papers%20current%20versions/Individual_Investor_Performance_Final.pdf

[60] Brad M. Barber's personal website is: https://www.bradmbarber.com/

[61] Jack Bogle's paper "An Index Fund Fundamentalist" can be found at: https://www.bogleheads.org/wiki/List_of_John_C._Bogle_academic_papers_and_articles

[62] See "Jack Bogle is gone, but he's still saving investors 100 billion [dollars] a year [in fees]": https://www.forbes.com/sites/baldwin/2019/01/16/jack-bogle-is-gone-but-hes-still-saving-investors-100-billion-a-year/

[63] You can find the "Bogleheads© local chapters" (groups per country) in: https://www.bogleheads.org/blog/bogleheads-local-chapters/

[64] For more information about the Bogle Fellowship at Princeton, have a look to its page: https://pace.princeton.edu/get-involved/pace-center-programs/john-c-bogle-51-fellows-civic-

service

[65] The Sharpe Ratio is a figure that compares an investment's return according to its risk.

[66] The paper "Disagreement, Tastes, and Asset Prices" by Fama and French can be found at: https://papers.ssrn.com/sol3/papers.cfm?abstract_id=502605

[67] I take this opportunity to thank Indexa Capital for writing about this paper in their blog, thus putting me on their trail. https://blog.indexacapital.com/2023/07/04/eficiencia-mercados-indexacion/

[68] "The Fiduciary Principle: No Man Can Serve Two Masters", by Jack Bogle: https://www.bogleheads.org/wiki/List_of_John_C._Bogle_academic_papers_and_articles

[69] The New York Times: John C. Bogle, Founder of Financial Giant Vanguard, Is Dead at 89: https://www.nytimes.com/2019/01/16/obituaries/john-bogle-vanguard-dead.html

[70] There are many fund managers offering basically the same index funds but with very different fees. See this article about "Why investors park billions in high fee legacy ETFs": https://www.etfstream.com/articles/why-investors-park-billions-in-high-fee-legacy-etfs

[71] This is the link to the MSCI World summary sheet describing this index: https://www.msci.com/www/fact-sheet/msci-world-index/05830501

[72] For a list of UCITS ETFs tracking the MSCI World index you can use the JustETF database: https://www.justetf.com/es/search.html?search=ETFS&index=MSCI%2BWorld

[73] The paper "False Discoveries in Mutual Fund Performance" can be downloaded from: https://papers.ssrn.com/sol3/papers.cfm?abstract_id=869748

[74] Laurent Barras' personal website: https://www.laurentbarras.com/

[75] https://www.unige.ch/gsem/en/research/faculty/all/olivier-scaillet/

[76] The 2010 paper "Is Alpha Just Beta Waiting To Be Discovered?" is available at: https://www.semanticscholar.org/paper/Is-Alpha-Just-Beta-Waiting-To-Be-Discovered-What-of-Kabiller-Principal/7291d86e135ea92cfd8dd4f43397b6bffec7b60f

[77] The Python Pandas library, started at AQR Capital, can be found at: https://pandas.pydata.org/

[78] The paper "The Silent Road to Serfdom: Why Passive Investing is Worse Than Marxism" can be found at: https://www.scribd.com/document/323564709

[79] A biographical note on Inigo Fraser-Jenkins can be found on the web at: https://www.alliancebernstein.com/americas/en/investor/bio.inigo-fraser-jenkins.html

[80] See the Nobel Prize web page on the one awarded to Friedrich Hayek: https://www.nobelprize.org/prizes/economic-sciences/1974/summary/

[81] Bloomberg: "Sanford C. Bernstein compared passive to Marxism and now it has 2 ETFs", https://www.bloomberg.com/news/articles/2017-10-17/sanford-c-bernstein-compared-passive-to-marxism-now-has-2-etfs

[82] Annual Report, 2015, from AllianceBernstein to the SEC: https://www.sec.gov/Archives/edgar/data/825313/000082531316000046/ab-20151231x10k.htm

[83] Article "Bernstein's Passive Investing Assertion Worse Than Marxism" by Allan Roth: https://www.etf.com/sections/index-investor-corner/bernsteins-passive-investing-assertion-worse-marxism

[84] Article from The Wall Street Journal: "Bogle Sounds a Warning on Index Funds", https://www.wsj.com/articles/bogle-sounds-a-warning-on-index-funds-1543504551

[85] The paper "Shooting the Messenger" can be found online at this link: https://www.spglobal.com/spdji/en/research/article/shooting-the-messenger

[86] See the article "In Defense of Active Investing" by Charles D. Ellis at: https://blogs.cfainstitute.org/investor/2015/06/23/in-defense-of-active-investing/

[87] SPIVA's website is: https://www.spglobal.com/spdji/en/research-insights/spiva/

[88] See the SEC "Amendments to Investment Company Advertising Rules": https://www.sec.gov/rule-release/33-8294

[89] The example shown here is a re-elaboration of the post written by Craig Lazzara "Shooting Hoops with Michael Jordan: An Allegory" (Sep/2022), available at Indexology Blog: https://www.indexologyblog.com/2022/09/29/shooting-hoops-with-michael-jordan-an-allegory/

[90] Morningstar's website is: https://www.morningstar.com/lp/active-passive-barometer

[91] See Jeffrey Ptak's website at: https://www.morningstar.com/people/jeffrey-ptak

[92] See Amy C. Arnott website at: https://www.morningstar.com/people/amy-c-arnott

[93] These two ways of calculating the returns are very well explained on the website of Indexa Capital, see their explanation *Diferentes Formas de Medir la Rentabilidad*: https://blog.indexacapital.com/2017/10/10/diferentes-formas-de-medir-la-rentabilidad/

Chapter 3. Conclusions

These have been the papers that we found most relevant for retail investors.

On the one hand we left many topics out, but in this book we focused primarily on papers and reports in the context of passive investing. Texts that contributed to convince us that passive investing is an excellent strategy.

On the other hand, you will certainly have comments on these papers. You may not be convinced by the arguments, or you may find them outdated. It is certainly possible that these papers could be improved. Perhaps Nobel Prize-winning economists could be wrong, maybe, but it is going to be challenging to beat them.

From these papers we can deduce that passive investing is very reasonable for retail investors. Take the ideas that are interesting to you, and adapt them.

3.1. Summary of Papers

The following Table 21 show the ideas we can extract from the papers presented in this book. Ideas valuable for retail investors.

Table 21. List of the papers and reports discussed in this book, and some ideas that could be extracted from them.

Article/Report	Conclusions
Theorie de la Spéculation, L. Bachelier	Using mathematics in finance makes sense. Randomness in stock asset prices. Random walk, Brownian Motion. Normal distribution of asset prices.
Portfolio Selection, Harry Markowitz	The best portfolios to invest in are located in the Efficient Frontier, and are composed of stocks and bonds. The investor has to choose the return/risk ratio that he wants, which corresponds directly to the percentage of stocks and bonds in the portfolio.

Article/Report	Conclusions
Brownian Motion in the Stock Market, M.F.M. Osborne	The normal distribution applies to returns, and not directly to prices. This generates an asymmetry in the distribution of prices, with very high prices being more abundant than very low prices.
The Variation of Certain Speculative Prices, Benoît Mandelbrot	Normal distributions are a first approximation to asset prices. To be more realistic one could consider other distributions that provide "fat tails". There are "wild randomness" processes, which generate events that seemed impossible until they occur.
Capital Asset Prices: A Theory of Market Equilibrium Under Conditions of Risk, William F. Sharpe	It is not worth buying individual stocks, by buying one asset that represents the aggregate market, and another with the risk free asset, we will get the return/risk ratio we want.
The Behavior of Stock-Market Prices, Eugene Fama	Description of the Efficient Market Hypothesis. The three forms of efficiency. Why a market can be efficient even though neither information nor agents are efficient.
Predictability: Does the Flap of a Butterfly's Wings in Brazil Set off a Tornado in Texas?, Edward N. Lorenz	Deterministic chaos, no matter how mathematically predictable a system is, small differences in the initial configuration can lead to totally different final outcomes.

Article/Report	Conclusions
Challenge to Judgment, Paul A. Samuelson	The evidence for the existence of excellent fund managers should be compelling, but the data does not bear this out. Most active managers underperform the market, and those that outperform fail to persist in successive years. The sensible thing to do is to invest in a highly diversified, low-cost mutual fund with minimal asset turnover.
Determinants of Portfolio Performance, Gary P. Brinson, L. Randolph Hood, and Gilbert L. Beebower	The asset class allocation in the portfolio is the most important parameter for the investor to choose. Investors should focus on selecting asset weights in the portfolio (stocks, bonds), rather than choosing assets (individual stocks, or sector ETFs) that they believe will outperform the market.
The Cross-Section of Expected Stock Returns, Eugene Fama and Kenneth French	Small cap and value style stocks have outperformed the market in the past. Fund managers have used this technique to achieve returns above the market. This effect seems to have disappeared in recent years, which justifies the Efficient Market Hypothesis.
Determining withdrawal rates using historical data, William P. Bengen	A practical application of passive investing: the 4% Rule, building your own pension fund for retirement as a do-it-yourself annuity.
Valuation Ratios and the Long-Run Stock Market Outlook, John Y. Campbell and Robert J. Shiller	Can bubbles be predicted with financial ratios? It is a bad idea to invest 100% in stocks, because you never know when the next bubble might burst, it is better to diversify into different asset classes.

Article/Report	Conclusions
Why active fund managers often underperform the S&P 500: The impact of size and skewness, David L. Ikenberry, Richard L. Shockley, and Kent L. Womack	Most active funds, most years, are going to earn returns below their benchmarks. There are at least two reasons for this: lack of portfolio diversification and stock return asymmetry.
A Multifractal Walk Down Wall Street, Benoît Mandelbrot	Fractals and the Stock Market. Critique of Portfolio Theory: risk may be larger than what normal distributions indicate.
Trading Is Hazardous to Your Wealth: The Common Stock Investment Performance of Individual Investors, Brad M. Barber and Terrance Odean	The more you trade in the market, the worse returns you get. This is due to transaction costs and overconfidence.
An Index Fund Fundamentalist, Jack Bogle	The cost of a mutual fund is a good predictor of its return (the higher the cost, the lower the return). Jack Bogle researched passive investing, did outreach about it, and implemented index funds to make them accessible to retail investors.
Disagreement, Tastes, and Asset Prices, Eugene Francis Fama and Kenneth Ronald French	The growth of indexed management does not have to be negative for the market. It can even be positive and increase the efficiency of markets. This happens in the case of less well-informed investors switching from active management to indexed management.
The Fiduciary Principle: No Man Can Serve Two Masters, Jack Bogle	The importance of fund managers' alignment of interests with their unitholders. Fund managers get the management fees, and unitholders get the market return minus the fees.

Article/Report	Conclusions
False Discoveries in Mutual Fund Performance: Measuring Luck in Estimated Alphas, Laurent Barras, Olivier Scaillet, and Russ Wermers	Managers providing positive alpha are rare, perhaps even non-existent. And in addition, the percentage of managers providing positive alpha seems to have declined over the years, until it has virtually disappeared.
Is Alpha Just Beta Waiting To Be Discovered? Adam Berger, David G. Kabiller, and Brian Crowell	The return that was once considered manager alpha is now packaged as market beta. Buying market beta provides the same absolute expected return (before costs) as active managers, but it is virtually cost free. To receive higher returns than market beta, you must take higher risks.
The Silent Road to Serfdom: Why Passive Investing is Worse Than Marxism, report by AllianceBernstein	A society needs capital markets for proper asset allocation and price discovery. If all investments are made in a passive way, then we may have a problem.
Shooting the Messenger, Anu R. Ganti and Craig J. Lazzara	Three reasons why indexing works: the professionalization of investment management, the cost of management, and the asymmetry of stock returns. And there is no need to consider the Efficient Markets Hypothesis.
Standard and Poor's Indices Vs Active (SPIVA), various biannual studies by various authors working for S&P	Active mutual funds underperform their benchmarks, the performance excellence of a good manager does not persist over time, in the short term mutual fund performance is dominated by chance, these results are independent of whether markets are efficient or not.

Article/Report	Conclusions
Morningstar's US Active/Pasive Barometer, biannual study by various authors working for Morningstar.	Active funds get worse returns than comparable passive funds, in the short term mutual fund performance is dominated by chance, there is a lot of closet indexing (fake active funds that are actually indexed), there are many funds that don't show up in the statistics (because they have been merged with others or liquidated) that would make active management performance even worse.
Mind the Gap, annual report from Morningstar	Investors underperform the funds they invest in, in what is called the Behavioral Gap. This is primarily due to trying to do market timing. It is better to stay invested for the long term.

3.2. Passive Investing is Counterintuitive

Passive investment is counterintuitive, like the Prisoner's Dilemma in Game Theory. That is why it has to be explained well.

Let us look at some examples:

- To obtain a high return, the rational thing to do is not to trade, to minimize trading operations, minimize fees. Because the expected return is the return of the market minus our costs.

- To outperform active managers (within the same investing category), the rational thing to do is to buy the entire category. Ideally the entire market. Because this way you are sure to incorporate in your portfolio the few stocks that provide exceptional returns (due to the asymmetry of stock returns).

- Indexing (buying the entire market) provides lower volatility than equivalent active funds, because maximizing diversification eliminates the volatility component from individual stocks, leaving only the volatility from the market as a whole. For

example, if a company in the portfolio goes bankrupt, it is better to have maximized diversification so that its weight in the portfolio is minimal.
- The random component in fund returns means that in the short term any manager can appear to be excellent. In the same way that a basketball amateur may luckily make a free throw, and Michael Jordan's subsequent shot may miss incomprehensibly. But in the long run, after many shots, skill is rewarded.
- It may be the case that the market is more efficient the more investors are indexed. This happens in the case of the mis-informed investors index themselves, since mis-informed investors tend to drive the market away from equilibrium, the fewer mis-informed investors there are, the better for the market as a whole.
- Passive investment makes sense as long as it is not a majority in the market. If most investors were passive, then it may not work (because a few managers would own all the companies in the stock market, because there would be no correct assignation of prices, no incentive to the Creative Destruction by Joseph Schumpeter, etc.)
- Making outreach about passive investment is unusual, because passive fund managers have to minimize their expenses, and therefore they do not have budget for advertisements and explaining the reasons for their success.

3.3. Passive Investing vs. Other Forms of Investing

There may be investors, or investment schools, that get better returns than passive investing. However, a passive investor implies being a "consumer" who makes use of a functioning market, and active strategies are "companies" that seek profits.

There will always be active strategies, just as there will always be companies generating wealth. But for a retail investor it may be better to simply take advantage of the Efficient Market and Adam Smith's Invisible Hand, just as it may be better to go to a professional mechanic to repair one's own car, or to go to a hairdresser instead of getting a haircut oneself.

As active managers are entrepreneurial activities, they work as long as the business niche exists, as long as the inefficiency is not made public. When other active managers discover that this inefficiency provides extra returns, then they will flock to take advantage of it. In the same way that if there is a demand for gyms in a city, new entrepreneurs will open gyms until the need is met. This is why the returns of active managers tend to decline over the long term.

Index investing, however, seeks to get its fair share of the wealth generated by the world's companies. The fair amount of return for the risk taken. In a simple and transparent way.

Getting returns from financial inefficiencies is a "zero sum game", where wealth is not generated, but what one gains another loses. Retail investors want to be on the winning side, but competing with professional investors we will certainly be on the losing side.

Obtaining returns via investing in a business in the stock market implies risks (greater than investing in the whole market, because the business could close) and the doubtful possibility that the business owner will share the wealth he generates with the retail investors who join him (why would he do so? He does not need to share anything, unless he really obtains wealth from his shareholders).

3.4. Final Remarks

Finally, let this book serve as a tribute to so many distinguished thinkers who have dealt with these issues before.

May you take advantage of it and go read the original sources yourself, and then reference them in your investment discussions. In this way we would like to hear arguments such as "I believe that in this crisis we are suffering a fat tail event like Benoît Mandelbrot suggested", "As SPIVA and Morningstar reports show...", "the Efficient Market Hypothesis by Eugene Fama is...", "Are you a newbie and want to set up a portfolio from scratch? Let's start building a portfolio in the Efficient Frontier...", "the enormous voting power of index managers in capitalized companies is...", etc.

If you have not read the papers discussed here, take advantage and enjoy them. I envy those who can read them for the first time.

The objective of this book has been to disseminate the information available at the university, in academic papers, Nobel Prizes, recommendations given by financial advisors, what is studied in professional certifications such as the CFA and similar.

This that has been shown here is science. It is the same for whites, blacks, and yellows; for reds and blues; for Arctic Eskimos and for Argentinians from Ushuaia; for one religion and another.

Notice that this book does not make a call to "do nothing", to be a blind investor, who "jumps into a pool, without looking, in the hope that there will be water and not the hard bottom".

The book demonstrates that once there are agents operating for their own profit in a functioning financial market, the result is such that a retail investor can aspire to buy the whole market and receive his fair return. Receive the proportional share of the wealth generated by the world's listed companies, with simplicity and transparency.

Take note of what interests you, try to refute it when it seems incorrect, enrich your financial knowledge, and try to improve that of your environment.

Good luck.

Acknowledgements

To the Prince of Darkness, landowner in Germany, for igniting the spark that fueled this endeavor.

To the Kantian Funambulist, a true Renaissance man for the 21st century, I am grateful for our conversations over the years. I wish I could write like you.

To our multilingual German neighbors, for treating us so well despite our unconventional ideas.

To Jesús from "Al Fin Libre", for being such an adventurer, breaking new ground and creating community.

To Homo Investor, the phoenix who rises anew each time, mastering new topics with ease. Thank you for sharing your insights and doubts with us.

To Mr 4% Safe, who came to the FIWE meeting in Madrid in 2019, and who has been living life to the fullest and making very accurate comments ever since.

To the Viking ambassador in Spain, for talking together about these things since we met for the first time in Budapest. By coming to the south you changed your life, and the lives of many other people.

To the retail investor community, in particular the Bogleheads© in both the USA and Spain, as well as the organizers of the *Jornadas de Independencia Financiera* in Valencia. What a great outreach you are doing.

To What Life Could Be, Cheese Finance, Econowiser, Mr RIP, Banker on Wheels, and many other bloggers; thanks to their blogs and meetups I realized that investing was possible and made sense in continental Europe.

Thanks to Unai Ansejo, for writing about many of these papers on his website, thus making them accessible to the general public.

I would like to thank James Owen Weatherall, renowned author of "The Physics of Wall Street", that sparked the idea for publishing this book.

And finally my gratitude to the open source software: this book has been written in AsciiDoc[1] format, PDF[2] and EPUB[3] files were generated with Asciidoctor[4], with graphics created with the programming language Python[5], diagrams with LibreOffice[6], images edited with Gimp[7], and all this running on GNU/Linux[8] as operating system.

[1] https://asciidoc.org
[2] https://www.adobe.com/acrobat/about-adobe-pdf.html
[3] https://www.w3.org/publishing/epub3/
[4] https://github.com/asciidoctor/asciidoctor
[5] https://www.python.org
[6] https://www.libreoffice.org
[7] https://www.gimp.org/
[8] https://www.gnu.org/home.en.html

Alphabetical Index

@
4% Rule, 102-107, 110, 223

A
AllianceBernstein, 169, 172-174, 225
American Academy of Arts and Sciences, 96
American Finance Association, 112
Ansejo, Unai, 93, 231
AQR Capital, 97, 162-163
Arbitrage Management, 23
Armour, Bryan, 201
Arnott, Amy C., 208
Asness, Cliff, 97, 163

B
Bachelier, Louis, 12-15, 18-21, 23, 35-37, 48, 60-61, 124, 221
Barber, Brad M., 136, 158, 224
Barnard Medal, 42
Barras, Laurent, 158, 225
Beebower, Gilbert L., 87-88, 223
Behavior Gap, 209, 211
Behavioral Economics, 70, 112, 150
Bengen, William P., 101, 103, 105-106, 108-110, 223
Berger, Adam, 162, 225
Black Swan, 8, 48
Black-Scholes-Merton (model), 21, 23, 49
BlackRock, 97, 155, 175
BMI (Broad Market Index), 192
Bogle, John Clifton, 83, 85-86, 122, 141-143, 145, 148, 154-155, 173-176, 180, 204, 224

Bogleheads©, 7, 58, 64, 102, 142, 231
Booth School of Business, 60, 96
Boyadzhiev, Dimitar, 201
Brinson, Gary P., 87, 92, 223
Brown, Robert, 14
Brownian Motion, 12-16, 40, 221-222

C
Cafeteria Keynesian, 82
Caltech, 88
Campbell, John Young, 111-114, 223
CAPE, 110
Capital Market Line, 53-54
CAPM, 51-52, 54-55, 97, 149-150, 159, 164
Cauchy, Augustin-Louis, 43
CFA (Chartered Financial Analyst), 87, 109, 162-163, 177, 208, 229
CFP (Certified Financial Planner), 101
Closet Indexing, 205
CNRS (*Centre National de la Recherche Scientifique*), 41
Comparative Advantage, 70
Cooley, Philip L., 108
Cootner, Paul Harold, 20, 86
Cowles Foundation, 23
Creative Destruction, 170-171, 227
Crowell, Brian, 162-163, 225

D
Dantzig, George, 23
Dantzig, Tobias, 13, 23

DCA (Dollar-Cost Averaging), 212-213
Deterministic Chaos, 79, 106, 222
Deutsche Bank Prize in Financial Economics, 59, 112
Dimensional Fund Advisors, 96
Doctor Honoris Causa, 51
Dotcom (crisis), 70, 113, 115, 117

E

Efficient Frontier, 23, 25, 29-32, 34, 54-55, 150, 221, 228
Efficient Market Hypothesis, 59-60, 62, 64-65, 67-72, 95, 99, 112-113, 118, 139, 149, 160, 186, 189, 200, 223, 227-228
Einstein, Albert, 13-14
Ellis, Charles D., 178-179
ELO, 190
Elton, E. J., 27

F

Factor Investment, 149
Fama, Eugene Francis, 19, 21, 59-61, 66-67, 71-72, 95-97, 112, 118, 145, 149, 163, 166, 180, 222-224, 228
Father of Modern Finance, 59
Federal Reserve, 117
Ferri, Rick, 102
Fidelity, 155, 175
Fink, Larry, 155
Forbes, 142, 158
Fortune (Magazine), 142
Frank Russell Company, 51
Franklin Medal, 42
Fraser-Jenkins, Inigo, 169
French Revolution, 13
French, Kenneth Ronald, 71, 95-97, 149, 166, 180, 223-224
Friedman, Milton, 22-23, 82

Fundamental Analysis, 33, 67

G

Gait, Paul, 169-170
Game Theory, 226
Ganti, Anu R., 177, 225
Gauss, Carl Friedrich, 42
Geneva Finance Research Institute, 158
Goldman Sachs, 121
Graham, Benjamin, 212
Greenspan, Alan, 117

H

Haas School of Business, 136
Hansen, Lars Peter, 59, 112
Harvard University, 73, 81, 112, 162
Hayek, Friedrich, 170
Hedge Funds, 8, 163, 165-167, 176
Hood, L. Randolph, 87, 223
Hubbard, Carl M., 108

I

Ibbotson, Robert G., 92
IBM, 41, 60
Ideal Market Portfolio, 54
Ikenberry, David L., 121, 224
Indexology Blog, 197
Invisible Hand, 68, 227
IRR (Internal Rate of Return), 210
Irrational Exuberance, 115, 117, 119
iShares, 97

J

Jackson, Ryan, 201
Jensen, Michael, 66
John Hopkins University, 87
John von Neumann Prize, 23
Johnson III, Edward C., 155

Johnson, Lyndon B., 82
Jordan, Michael, 197-199, 227

K
Kabiller, David G., 162-163, 225
Kahneman, Daniel, 137
Kaplan, Paul D., 92
Kelley School of Business, 121
Kellogg School of Management, 121
Kennedy, John F., 82
Keynes, John Maynard, 118
Koopmans, Tjalling, 22
Kyoto Prize, 74

L
Laplace, Pierre-Simon, 42
Lazzara, Craig J., 177, 197, 200, 225
Leeds School of Business, 121
Lehigh University, 95
Lintner, John, 51
Lomonosov Medal, 74
London School of Economics, 112
Lorenz Attractor, 77
Lorenz, Edward Norton, 73-76, 79, 106, 222
Légion d'honneur, 42
Lévy, Paul, 45

M
Malkiel, Burton Gordon, 66, 129
Mandelbrot Set, 131
Mandelbrot, Benoît, 41, 46-47, 49, 60-61, 79, 129, 131-132, 134-135, 222, 224, 228
Markowitz, Harry Max, 22-25, 33, 51, 60, 80, 110, 221
Maxwell, James Clerk, 84
Maxwell's Demon, 84-85
MBA, 60, 64, 87, 95, 136, 162-163, 170
Merrill Lynch, 51
Merton, Robert Cox, 23
Miller, Merton H., 60
MIT, 73, 81, 96, 101, 112
Modigliani, Franco, 112
Morningstar, 72, 119, 122, 143, 201-204, 207-208, 226, 228
MWRR (Money-Weighted Rate of Return), 210

N
National Medal of Science, 82
Navy Research Laboratory, 35
New York Stock Exchange, 39
New York Times, 158
Newsweek, 82
Nobel Prize, 23, 51, 59-60, 82, 112, 137, 229
Northwestern University, 121, 162
NPO (NonProfit Organization), 173
NRL (Naval Reseach Lab), 35

O
Odean, Terrance, 136, 158, 224
Osborne, Matthew Fontaine Maury, 35-40, 48, 60-61, 124, 222
Oxford, 112

P
Pandas (library), 163
Pennsylvania State University, 121
Poincaré, Henri, 13, 23
Post-Modern Portfolio Theory, 33
Princeton University, 112, 141-142
Prisoner's Dilemma, 226

Ptak, Jeffrey, 208

R

RAND Corporation, 23, 50-51
Ricardo, David, 70
Risk Free Asset, 52-55, 58
Risk Premium, 52
Roberts, Harry V., 60

S

S&P 500, 26, 66, 82, 115, 117, 121, 123-125, 182-183, 187, 189
S&P Europe 350, 192
S&P Eurozone BMI, 192
S&P MidCap 400, 189
S&P SmallCap 600, 189
S&P Spain BMI, 192
Sagan, Carl, 84
Samuelson, Paul Anthony, 23, 81-86, 223
Scaillet, Olivier, 158, 225
Schumpeter, Joseph, 170-171, 227
Seattle University, 87
Second Law of Thermodynamics, 84-85
Sharpe Ratio, 51, 145
Sharpe, William Forsyth, 50-51, 180, 222
Sharpe-Russell Research, 51
Shiller, Robert James, 59, 111-115, 117-119, 223
Shockley, Richard L., 121, 224
Smith School of Business, 159
Smith, Adam, 68, 227
Sorbonne, 13
SPIVA, 72, 122, 134-135, 177, 187, 192, 194, 200, 202-203, 206-207, 225, 228
Stanford University, 51
State Street, 175
Swedroe, Larry, 64

Swiss Bank Corporation, 87
Swiss Institute of Finance, 158

T

Taleb, Nassim Nicholas, 8
Technical Analysis, 33, 67, 72
Time (Magazine), 142
Tobin Tax, 23
Tobin, James, 23
Treynor, Jack, 51
Trinity Study, 109
Trinity University, 108
Tufts University, 60
TWRR (Time-Weighted Rate of Return), 210

U

UBS, 87, 163
University at Dartmouth, 73
University of Besançon, 13
University of California
   Berkeley, 50, 136
   Davis, 136
   Irvine, 51
   Los Angeles, 50, 159
   San Diego, 23
University of Chicago, 22-24, 60, 81, 87, 96, 136, 163
University of Colorado
   Boulder, 121
University of Geneva, 158
University of Illinois, 121, 136
University of Luxembourg, 158
University of Maryland, 35, 159
University of Michigan, 112
University of Minnesota, 112
University of Paris-Dauphine, 159
University of Pennsylvania, 112
University of Rochester, 95
University of Toronto, 121
University of Washington, 51

University of Wisconsin, Madison, 208

V

Value-at-Risk (VaR), 33
van Brugge, Robert, 173
Vanguard, 86, 138, 141-142, 154-157, 175

W

Wall Street Journal, The, 112, 174-175
Walz, Daniel T., 108
Washington State University, 87
Weatherall, James Owen, 231
Weisstein, Eric M., 44
Wells Fargo, 51
Wermers, Russ, 158, 225
Wharton Business School, 162
Williams, John Burr, 24
Womack, Kent L., 121, 224

Y

Yale Business School, 96
Yale University, 112

www.ingramcontent.com/pod-product-compliance
Lightning Source LLC
Chambersburg PA
CBHW052146220526
45471CB00004B/1555